World Philosophy

World Philosophy

An East-West Comparative Introduction to Philosophy

H. Gene Blocker

Ohio University

PRENTICE HALL, *Upper Saddle River, New Jersey 07458*

Library of Congress Cataloging-in-Publication Data

Blocker, H. Gene.
   World philosophy : an East-West comparative introduction to
philosophy / H. Gene Blocker.
     p. cm.
   Includes bibliographical references and index.
   ISBN 0-13-862012-1
   1. Philosophy, Comparative. 2. East and West. I. Title.

B799.B57 1999
100—dc21   98-33926
                                          CIP

Acquisitions Editor: Karita France
Editorial Assistant: Jennifer Ackerman
Production Editor: Jean Lapidus
Manufacturing Buyer: Tricia Kenny
Copy Editor: Michele Lansing
Line Art Coordinator: Guy Ruggiero
Artist: Maria Piper
Cover Design: Bruce Kenselaar

This book was set in 10.5/12.5 Baskerville by Pub-Set, Inc.
and was printed and bound by RR Donnelley & Sons Company.
The cover was printed by Phoenix Color Corp.

 © 1999 by Prentice-Hall, Inc.
Simon & Schuster/A Viacom Company
Upper Saddle River, New Jersey 07458

Printed in the United States of America
10 9 8 7 6 5 4 3 2 1

ISBN 0-13-862012-1

PRENTICE-HALL INTERNATIONAL (UK) LIMITED, *London*
PRENTICE-HALL OF AUSTRALIA PTY. LIMITED, *Sydney*
PRENTICE-HALL CANADA INC., *Toronto*
PRENTICE-HALL HISPANOAMERICANA, S.A., *Mexico*
PRENTICE-HALL OF INDIA PRIVATE LIMITED, *New Delhi*
PRENTICE-HALL OF JAPAN, INC., *Tokyo*
SIMON & SCHUSTER ASIA PTE. LTD., *Singapore*
EDITORA PRENTICE-HALL DO BRASIL, LTDA., *Rio de Janeiro*

Contents

Preface

This is a different kind of introduction to a philosophy textbook. Most are limited to Western philosophy, whether they offer a topics, a historical, an anthology-reader, or a single-author approach. The few "East–West" or "world philosophy" textbooks that are available present Western, Chinese, and Indian (and possibly other) philosophies separately, in distinct sections of the book. In the process, they also tend to combine different elements (mixing apples and oranges, as we say), comparing Western *philosophy* with non-Western *mythology*, *folklore*, and *mysticism*. In this book, Chinese, Indian, and Western philosophers of roughly the same sort and of comparable stature are brought together on the same philosophical topics and issues (arranged, for convenience, in traditional clusters—logic in chapter 2, epistemology in chapter 3, metaphysics in chapter 4, ethics in chapter 5, and social and political philosophy in chapter 6).

Why study comparative philosophy, and why this particular approach to comparative philosophy? Non-Western philosophy is important in its own right, and college students want and need to know something about non-Western cultures. Of course, it could be argued that Western students need to learn about their own Western backgrounds and roots before they can attempt to learn about other cultures. And so they need to study Western philosophy as an important part of Western civilization. But are our students Western? Their roots are European, to be sure, but they also are African, Chinese, Mideastern, Native American, and all sorts of mixtures of the aforementioned. Also, as our world becomes increasingly smaller, even students with a predominantly European ancestry belong to a much larger world that they need, and I think want, to know.

But even granted all of that, what is the best way to accomplish this? The most obvious approach is to present the different traditions separately—and there are undoubtedly good reasons for doing it that way. It is admittedly difficult and dangerous to try to separate the philosophy from the culture as a whole, and since Eastern and Western cultures are obviously quite different from one another, it might seem better to present Chinese philosophy as an aspect of and a way to learn Chinese culture, Indian philosophy as an aspect of and a way to learn Indian culture, and so on.

The problem with that approach, however, is that it tends to marginalize non-Western philosophy. Assuming that in almost all cases the bulk of university instruction in philosophy deals with Western philosophy and Western philosophers, the occasional course offered in Asian, Chinese, or Indian philosophy cannot but seem something out of the way, off the beaten track, something that does not easily relate to (and indeed is largely irrelevant to) the rest of philosophy. And since the "rest of philosophy" is for the most part Western philosophy, then, really, for all practical purposes, philosophy *is* just Western philosophy for most undergraduate students.

Later, when more advanced students (viz., undergraduate majors and master of arts students) begin to work on philosophical problems on their own, they are not likely to think of those problems in terms of the one course they may have had in non-Western philosophy, but they are far more likely to think through those problems in terms of a Western philosophy with which they are more familiar and in terms of which most philosophical problems were introduced to them in the first place. Eastern philosophy becomes, then, realistically, an introduction to an alien culture—such as a course in non-Western history or anthropology. This is, of course, valuable in its own right, but it does not contribute much, if anything, to an expansion or enrichment of *philosophy*, bringing non-Western philosophy and philosophers into the discussion of Western philosophy.

If philosophy students do think seriously of Eastern philosophy, it probably will be only as an area of historical specialization for those few who go on to advanced graduate study—learning classical Chinese and specializing in the history of Confucianism, for example, and eventually becoming professors of Chinese studies (and probably not of philosophy). Given the structure of American graduate programs, this will take students *away from* the study of "philosophy" as it exists in universities today. What is not likely to happen, in any of these cases, is any interaction between, and/or mutual enrichment of, Western and non-Western philosophy. For this to happen, I think we must, from the beginning, present to our students Western and non-Western philosophers who are working on similar problems in similar ways.

Since most students are not familiar with philosophy of any kind before they reach the university level, it is my hope and belief that they will not find Indian and Chinese philosophers any more obscure or strange than their Western counterparts. It is only the instructors' greater familiarity with the history of Western philosophy that makes us forget our students' amazement to learn that there were famous Western philosophers, not certifiably insane, who held that physical objects do not exist outside of the mind, that numbers are more real than tables and chairs, or that the entire world is a kind of gigantic world soul! Certainly if we relate "apples to apples" and not "apples to oranges," comparing Western and non-Western philosophers of roughly the same time period, the differences are not as great as might be imagined. There are few Indian or Chinese philosophers of the earliest period (500–200 B.C.E.) whom students will find any stranger than Parmenides (who, after all, claimed that nothing could move!), or Heraclitus (who said one could not step twice in the same river!). Similarly, many Madhyamika and Yogacara Buddhist writers will strike an undergraduate student in his or her first course in philosophy as being no less weird or crazy than almost any other Western metaphysician. More positively, I have no doubt that first-year students will find non-Western philosophers such as Mozi, Ramanuja, Xunzi, Nagarjuna, and Zhuangzi accessible and attractive.

Though this is certainly controversial, it is my view that philosophy, strictly defined (that is, excluding folklore, mythology, prephilosophical religious writings, and so on), is not as culture dependent as are other aspects of culture, and that as a result, non-Western accounts of the self, causality, human nature, virtue, appearance and reality, and sensation and reason are comparable with Western versions. Indeed, it has been my experience that those who are familiar with and trained in philosophy (i.e., Western philosophy) are generally unable to distinguish statements from Western and Eastern philosophers, unless given the philosophers' names, frequently attributing to the early Greek philosopher Zeno, for example, the statement that "The shadow of a flying bird never moves and the wheel of a chariot never touches the ground," which in fact come from sixth-century B.C.E. Chinese logicians; or, wondering where Hobbes said,

> Now let someone try doing away with the authority of the ruler, . . . and then watch and see how the people of the world treat each other. He will find that the powerful impose upon the weak and rob them, the many terrorize the few

and extort from them, and in no time the whole world will be given up to chaos and mutual destruction.

(It was the third-century B.C.E. Chinese philosopher Xunzi.) Or, again, trying to remember where the following statement of Parmenides (or maybe one of his followers, such as Zeno or Melissus) comes from:

> Whatsoever has already arisen will not be able to arise. Whatsoever has not arisen will not arise. Either a phenomenon has already arisen or else it will arise; there is no other possibility beyond these two. . . . If a phenomenon were to exist inherently it should be permanent. If a phenomenon were to exist inherently it would either exist permanently or else undergo complete disintegration: it cannot occur in a way which is different from these two.

(It comes from the second-century Indian philosopher Nagarjuna.) Or perhaps searching for some less well-known Western, perhaps Roman, materialist, who said,

> Only perceptual evidence is authoritative; the elements are earth, water, fire and air; wealth and enjoyment are the objects of human existence. Matter can think. There is no other world. Death is the end of all.

(This comes from the sixth-century B.C.E. Indian Carvacans.) Or, looking for the obscure twentieth-century British or American sense-datum epistemologist, who said,

> When the observer cognizes the tree, what he actually perceives is only its part nearest to himself; and certainly that one part alone is not the 'tree,' so that when the man cognizes the 'tree' as a whole what happens is that there is an inference from the part he sees to the rest of it which he does not see.

(This also comes from the Indian Carvacans.) Or, wondering where exactly Aristotle said,

> What is denoted by the word 'cow' is not the mere individual by itself, without any qualifications, and as apart from the universal to which it belongs, but the individual as qualified by and along with the universal.

(It was the fifth-century B.C.E. Indian Nyaya logicians.) Or, finally, research-ing which Greek or Roman hedonist said,

> While life is yours, live joyously;
> None can escape Death's searching eye:
> When once this frame of ours is gone,
> How shall it ever again return?

(It was, once again, the Indian Carvacans.)

In this book, I treat the strictly philosophical arguments as being roughly similar across cultures, while the larger cultural contexts in which they occur I present as being considerably different. The Indian back-ground of karma, for example, is quite distinct from anything in the West (except, perhaps, Socrates's and Plato's belief in reincarnation), but karma raises serious questions about the nature of causality, and when Indian philosophers tackle the problem of causality, their analyses are very similar and certainly comprehensible to their Western counterparts (who also are interested in causality, but for different reasons). Thus, students will get a chance to learn something about the differences among West-ern and non-Western cultures, while at the same time recognizing some of the philosophical similarities.

By comparing unequals (apples and oranges), a stubborn myth per-sists that all of Western philosophy is hard-edged, analytical, and logically rigorous, while all Eastern thought is fuzzy, mystical, and holistic—in terms of which Westerners who *like* Eastern thought are generally those who do *not like* philosophy! What I have tried to do is compare equals to equals—logicians to logicians, metaphysicians to metaphysicians, ethicists to ethicists (and more specifically, comparing Indian, Chinese, and West-ern empiricists, utilitarians, hedonists, egoists, atheists, theists, monists, pluralists, idealists, materialists, dualists, skeptics, relativists, political real-ists, and so on). Of course, if we wanted to (although I have not done so in this book), we could compare Eastern and Western mystics, poets, romantics, and religiously meditative writing; or Eastern and Western cos-mologies, mythologies, religions, folk wisdom, or popular culture. Only when we compare Western philosophers to Eastern mystics do we get the typical essentialist "them" and "us" stereotypes (they are holistic, we are atomistic; they are synthetic, we are analytic; they are affective, we are cerebral; they are communal, we are individualistic egoists; they are spiri-tual, we are materialistic; and so on).

Finally, speaking more modestly and realistically, one introductory philosophy textbook is not going to change the world. Let's just say that this book offers an alternative, a different take on philosophical thinking around the globe. I invite the student to take a look at it, to see how it works in the classroom, and to make up his or her own mind. Even if the student rejects or ignores the East–West comparisons, the philosophical issues discussed in this book are central by anyone's reckoning, including the types of topics and issues most philosophy instructors feel a one-course introduction to philosophy should include. These issues are discussed at a level accessible to today's incoming first-year North American college students.

H. Gene Blocker

World Philosophy

1

Introduction: What Is Philosophy?

"*E*AST is east and West is west, and never the twain shall meet," so wrote Rudyard Kipling after many years of service in the British colonial government in India. Certainly the cultures of the "East" (primarily India, China, and Japan—which are by no means identical to one another) are, as a group, quite different (or were 100 years ago) from those in the West (primarily Europe and North America—which, again, include many cultures quite different from one another), but that does not mean each culture is incapable of understanding certain features of the other. It does not mean that the two cultures cannot be compared. However different Eastern and Western cultures are, precise points of similarity and difference can be constructively brought out in a comparative study. As the world becomes "smaller" year by year, it is increasingly important to develop an understanding of culture centers around the globe that are different from our own.

One way to equate cultures is to compare and contrast their different religions, art forms, educational systems, family practices, and governmental institutions—assuming that all cultures have *some* form of religion, art, government, education, and so on. But what about *philosophy*? Does every culture have a philosophy, however different from the philosophies of other cultures? It depends on what we mean by the term *philosophy*. There is, in ordinary English, an everyday sense of the word "philosophy" in which we say that each person has his or her own "philosophy" (or "philosophy of life"). As the late nineteenth- and early twentieth-century American philosopher and psychologist William James said in one of his famous public lectures,

> I know that you, ladies and gentlemen, have a philosophy, each and all of you, and
> that the most interesting and important thing about you is the way in which it deter-
> mines the perspective in your several worlds.
>
> (William James, *Pragmatism*, 1907)

The same could be said about whole societies or cultures. Insofar as each society or culture has its own idea of itself, its own conception of what is important in life, and its own notions of what the world is like in general terms,
there is a sense in which each society or culture can be said to have its own
"philosophy" (or worldview). This is one of the things sociologists and anthro-
pologists study when they examine different societies and cultures—what was
(or is) the American Indian "philosophy," or "philosophy of life" (worldview),
and how did (or does) that differ from, say, the ancient Egyptians' "philosophy," or "philosophy of life" (worldview)?

But the word "philosophy" also is used in a more technical sense to indicate a particular methodology—a specialized way of investigating and organizing ideas, one that is critical, logical, analytical, and systematic. This is the
sense in which we might hear someone say that they are "majoring in philosophy," or "reading a new book in philosophy," or that they "hadn't studied philosophy until they got to university," or that while they "think philosophy is
interesting, it is very difficult and not very practical." And in *that* sense, *not*
everyone is a philosopher or has a philosophy. In this second sense, European
philosophy arose at a particular point in Greek history. Greeks before Thales
(around 600 B.C.E.) did *not* have philosophy in this sense. And if the
Greeks before Thales had no philosophy or philosophers, it is possible that
other societies and cultures also did not. Notice how the East African philosopher, D. A. Masolo, distinguishes these two senses of the term *philosophy* in his
new book, *African Philosophy in Search of Identity*.

> There are two senses of the word *philosophy*, but with a good deal of relation to each
> other. The first sense is usually also called the *ordinary* sense, and refers to some
> kinds of opinions and commitments to certain ideas or ways of interpreting things,
> to values and beliefs about the general nature of things. . . . In this sense, philoso-
> phy can be held by individuals and be assumed of groups—communities, societies,
> etc.—as part of the covert culture which is made up of the reasons behind the
> observable cultural practices and expressions.
>
> In the second sense, philosophy is, to use Antony Flew's [twentieth-century
> British philosopher] expression, what appears as the main subject of most of the
> writings of Plato, Aristotle, St. Thomas Aquinas, Descartes, Hegel, Wiredu, Houn-
> tondji, and others. In this sense, philosophy is a commitment to an investigation
> rather than to any specific idea(s) or opinion(s). It is a study of a variety of subjects
> from a specific type of approach—an open, rational analysis and synthesis—and can
> therefore not be expressed in the formula "my philosophy is . . ." Because it is not

merely a body of opinions, and does not aim primarily at formulating workable principles, but rather at *understanding*, philosophy in this sense becomes primarily an academic practice, a study, a systematic investigation of ideas.

(Masolo, 1994)

Just as philosophy in this second sense arose in European culture at a
particular time and place, so it also is possible that philosophy arose at various points in time in other, non-European cultures. In this second sense of
"philosophy," it may turn out that some cultures have philosophy and some
do not, and we cannot dogmatically assert before examining the facts that
either *all* cultures must have philosophy or that *none* do except European cultures. We must more patiently and empirically look at each culture to see
whether it does or does not have a philosophy. And, of course, if it does, then
we will naturally want to study it—either alongside of European philosophy or
perhaps by incorporating of all the different regional philosophies into a
more comprehensive "world philosophy." In the past, when major cultures
were relatively isolated from one another, it seemed appropriate for each to
study its own culture. But in the increasing globalization of all aspects of culture in our world today, this isolationist approach is no longer appropriate.
If there are philosophies, in our second, more technical sense, in other cultures, then we must make an effort to identify and to study them along with
Western philosophy.

In this book we will be concerned with philosophy in this second, more
technical sense, and from now on, that is the sense of philosophy we will be
talking about. What exactly is "philosophy" in this second, more technical
sense? In the narrower, technical sense, philosophy is a critical reflection on
basic and general normative questions with the aim of providing logically
defensible and systematic answers to some very fundamental questions: What
is the best way to live? What is knowledge and what can we really know? What is
the best way to organize society and govern ourselves? Is beauty culturally relative or is it crossculturally universal, and if so, what is beauty? As Kwame
Gyekye says in his recent book *Tradition and Modernity: Philosophical Reflections
on the African Experience*,

A close examination of the nature and purpose of the intellectual activities of
thinkers from various cultures and societies of the world reveals . . . that philosophy
is essentially a critical and systematic inquiry into the fundamental ideas or principles underlying human thought, conduct, and experience. Ideas, which include the
beliefs and presuppositions that we hold and cherish, relate to the various aspects of
human experience: to the origins of the world, the existence of God, the nature
of the good society, the basis of political authority, and so on.

(Gyekye, *Tradition and Modernity: Philosophical Reflections . . .*, 1997)

"Reflective," "normative," "critical," "rational," "systematic"—let us look at each of these crucial terms to see what they mean for philosophy. By "reflective," we mean that philosophy examines the most basic, underlying assumptions of its own cultural traditions. By "normative," we mean that philosophy is always concerned with the value-laden distinction between "correct" and "incorrect" ways of thinking—correct and incorrect notions about what is good, real, true, and so on. Imagine a society that for thousands of years has educated its children by having them memorize mythological stories of the gods and goddesses. A philosopher might raise the normative question of whether this was "really education": Are we really educating our children by having them memorize these stories? Are these stories of warring gods and goddesses really true? Is this what the world is really like? And is this knowledge really useful to us? Does it really explain why we sometimes experience periods of drought and famine, for example? What evidence is there for thinking that these stories are true—or that they are any more true than the myths of our neighbors? Is there a better way to learn what is true, real, and important in life? How *should* we be investigating what is real, true, and good? How *should* we be educating our children? In short, what *is* education, really?

Philosophy therefore tries to discover universal standards or criteria for logically correct ways of thinking (as opposed to incorrect or fallacious ways of thinking), for what is real (as opposed to what merely seems or appears to be real but is not), for what is true (as opposed to what people think or believe is true but may not be true), for what is good (as opposed to what people have become "comfortable" with and traditionally say is good but perhaps is not), and for what can be rationally defended and justified (as opposed to what people say and believe simply on the basis of traditional authority).

Philosophy is "critical" in the sense that it does not take for granted but challenges long-accepted traditional beliefs. Philosophy is "rational" in the sense that it demands and tries to supply reasons why we should believe one theory over another. And finally, philosophy is "systematic" in the sense that it tries to see how everything hangs together, how all of the pieces fit into one larger picture, aiming for a synthesis of all of our theories on art, religion, politics, morality, education, work, love, and warfare.

In its move toward systematic theory, philosophy also generally relies on a long tradition of accumulated concepts, distinctions, argument strategies, and a repertoire of the most commonly held philosophical positions. Once philosophy has begun, there is a written backlog of previous philosophy available for use, and even if one disagrees with everything that has previously been said, one nonetheless has access to the terminology, the strong and weak points of previous theories—the tools of the trade, we might say, and a clearer sense, therefore, of how to continue in philosophy—whether, for example, to reject both of two extreme theories and to try to work out a compromise between the two, or to strengthen an existing theory by buttressing what has already been shown to be its weak points (and perhaps also constructing new and better arguments against its opponents). In this sense, people who "study philosophy" build on the past, studying the works of previous philosophers such as Plato, Nagarjuna, and Mozi and discussing contemporary issues in terms originally used by these ancient philosophers, although often drawing quite different conclusions.

This is what makes communication in philosophy possible; if every generation had to "reinvent the wheel" each time someone wanted to rationally reflect on and critique the traditional presuppositions of one's society, it would take a lifetime to explain what one was talking about—what is an "argument," "evidence," "concept," "verification," "idea," "fact," "theory," "presupposition," and so on. Even philosophers in the early stages of philosophy, such as Aristotle, Ramanuja, and Dong Zhongshu, discussed their ideas by critiquing previous philosophers, using an already established common philosophical vocabulary and methodology. This is why in the absence of a written language it is extremely difficult to provide a sufficient backlog of philosophical material, and even the possession of a written language does not guarantee the development of a philosophical tradition of philosophers, theories, arguments, concepts, and so on, sufficient to sustain a philosophical tradition beyond a generation or two.

Of course, there are oral traditions, but it is difficult to maintain in an oral tradition the wealth of concepts, arguments, distinctions, and theories necessary to maintain a viable philosophical tradition. An oral tradition is capable of sustaining traditional cosmologies or mythologies for hundreds of years, but hardly the entire catalog of generations of many different theories, arguments, counterarguments, defenses, definitions, distinctions, and reformulations. Once a philosophical tradition exists, however, it can be used to reflect on the oral traditions of preliterate peoples. When Native Americans, Africans, and others from preliterate cultures began, in the 1950s, to philosophically reflect on their own cultural traditions and to articulate that in an established philosophical language, they began to create new areas of philosophy, including "Native American Philosophy" and "African Philosophy," for example, Ghanaian philosopher Kwame Gyekye's recent book *Tradition and Modernity: Philosophical Reflections on the African Experience.* The use of writing has made possible the retention of a much greater storehouse of material than could be possible in an oral tradition, as we can see from walking through any major library (where the history of Western philosophy is just sitting there on one or two aisles). Today we see an even greater explosion of information through the Internet.

To summarize, philosophy is a critical reflection on basic and general normative questions, with the goal of providing logically defensible and systematic answers to fundamental questions—along with the accumulated history of previous efforts to practice philosophy in this sense. This is the sense of "philosophy" we are talking about when we talk about "studying philosophy," "majoring in philosophy," or "taking a course in philosophy."

We can see from this that philosophy in the narrow, technical sense is more of a practice than a theory, that is, it is more concerned with a way of thinking than it is with a particular view of reality (which is precisely what philosophy in the broad, popular sense is mainly concerned with). Indeed, philosophy in the broad, popular sense is really nothing more than the worldview of a particular group of people, so there will be as many worldviews (philosophies in the popular sense) as there are and have been different social groups of people in the world. But the rational critique of those traditional worldviews (philosophy in the narrow, technical sense) will not be so numerous. Therefore, as we will see throughout this book, there is a much greater variety of philosophies around the world in the broad, popular sense of the word than there is in the narrow, technical sense of the word. Taking "philosophy" as a worldview we would expect to find vast differences between the way Asian Indians, Africans, Chinese, Native Americans, and Europeans look at things. But if we consider "philosophy" a reflective, logical, and critical tool of thought (in our more narrow and technical sense), then it turns out, as we will see, that Indian, Chinese, and Western philosophical critiques of their own quite different worldviews are much more similar to one another than we might at first suspect.

At any rate, it is this second, more technical sense of philosophy that we have in mind when we define the philosophy with which we in the West are more familiar, that is, Western philosophy, and it is therefore in this sense that we ask whether other (non-European) cultures also have or had philosophy. That is, we are looking to see, not whether different groups of people had their own worldviews (which of course they all did), but whether and how they philosophically critiqued and systematically organized these worldviews.

At this point you are probably wondering (doing a little philosophy of your own) if this way of putting the question is terribly "ethnocentric" or "Eurocentric," that is, biased in favor of our own culture being naturally superior to all others. Are we not, in effect, judging other cultures by our own particular culture's definition of "philosophy"? Just as philosophy is "normative," distinguishing what *is* the case from what *ought* to be the case, so the very *word* "philosophy" is also normative, that is, value laden. To say that a culture did not develop a philosophy sounds belittling or demeaning, and to say that it had a philosophy sounds like a compliment. As each region of our planet tries to define itself in as positive a manner as possible, each becomes highly sensitive to pejorative or belittling assessments of its own culture—especially those made by outsiders. But the question of whether there is any non-

European philosophy is generally a question raised by European philosophers about some other, non-European group, and whenever one group attempts to describe some other group there is always a possibility of cultural bias.

At first, the solution might seem fairly obvious. Since it is clearly unfair to describe *their* thought systems in *our* terms, why not describe *their* thought systems in *their* terms? To avoid the errors of ethnocentrism, why not describe the alien society from within its own perspective and point of view? But, unfortunately, this will prove to be impossible for a number of related reasons. First is the obvious problem of coming to understand another culture. Initially, that is, there is the problem of simply acquiring enough information about this other culture. But even if one *could* amass all of this information, there is the additional problem of coming to share the beliefs, attitudes, and points of view of another culture. To truly be an insider, one must not only *know* what he or she believes, but must actually *believe* it—and believe it as something given, unquestioned, and simply taken for granted. But how is that possible when the outsider has been brought up in a different culture, with different values and belief sets?

And finally, even if we *could* describe their world from their point of view, it would make no sense and would be of no interest to those of us on the outside to whom the description is addressed, supposing the description is offered in our language. Whether right or wrong, the entire enterprise of such a crosscultural description is to answer questions and concerns that *we* have in *our* culture, and it is only in terms of these concerns of *ours* that the description can have any meaning or interest for *us*. When we borrow beliefs, attitudes, or values from other cultures, which we often do, these beliefs are always, and must be, transformed into our own conceptual framework. California Zen is not the same as Japanese Zen (which is not the same as Chinese *Ch'an na*, which is not the same as Indian Madhyamika *dhyana*).

The conclusion, then, is inevitable—a crosscultural comparison is unavoidable in any crosscultural description; the concepts must be ours while the beliefs are theirs. But how can that possibly be fair? Only if the concepts by which we describe their beliefs and the concepts by which they describe the same beliefs in their society are synonymous or at least similar in meaning.

So, in the present case, whose conception or definition of philosophy are we using when we ask of the thought systems of other cultures whether they count as "philosophy"? If we are writing or talking in English or some other European language, then we are obviously thinking of the *European* conception of philosophy (the narrow, technical sense just defined)—not because that is the best of many conceptions or definitions of the word "philosophy" available to us, but simply because that is all we have! "Philosophy" is an English word that arose within, and whose meaning was determined by, Western, European thought. The word "philosophy" (with slightly different spellings in other European languages ("philosophie," or "filosofia," for example) comes from the sixth century B.C.E. Greek word the Greeks coined from two words—"philos," meaning love, as in "philanthropy" (love of people) and Philadelphia (city of brotherly love), and "sophy," meaning wisdom or learning, as in "sophisticated" and "sophomore." Philosophy originally meant, then, love of wisdom and learning (a philosopher being a friend or a lover of learning and wisdom).

At first (beginning in the sixth century B.C.E.), the term was used to refer to a new group of individuals who specialized in critical and systematic learning. Later (from the time of Plato in the fourth century B.C.E. until the rise of modern science around 1500), the word "philosophy" was extended to all areas of systematic, thoroughly grounded scientific knowledge, and in the modern period (since 1500), to what remains of this rational, systematic knowledge after the individual sciences (chemistry, physics, zoology, etc.) split off from the main body, each going its separate way. As such, the word has come to designate a group of specific individuals, universally recognized in Western culture as "philosophers," including pre-Socratic Greeks such as Thales, Anaximander, Anaximines, Parmenides, and Heraclitus; post-Socratic Greeks such as Plato, Aristotle, and Epicurus; Roman philosophers such as Lucretius and Marcus Aurelius; medieval Christian philosophers such as Augustine, Aquinas, and Ockham; modern philosophers such as Descartes, Spinoza, Leibniz, Locke, Berkeley, Hume, and Kant; and contemporary philosophers such as Jean-Paul Sartre, Bertrand Russell, A. J. Ayer, William James, Edmund Husserl, Martin Heidegger, and Ludwig Wittgenstein.

This is what the word "philosophy" means. When we talk about non-Western philosophy, we are applying a Western concept to non-Western thought systems. We are comparing their thought systems to our own literature, judging their literature by our standards. For better or for worse, no matter how "tolerant," or "fair-minded" we may try to be, any description of another culture's thought systems must be *comparative* in nature, at least at the beginning, comparing their thought systems to our own.

If Europeans, or European-trained scholars are the speakers or writers, then, at least at the beginning, they must use their language (with the standard meanings of their words, terms, and concepts) to talk about (and judge) non-European thought systems. If Indian or Chinese intellectuals had begun the discussion, talking and writing about European thought traditions, the exact same principle would apply—the Indians and Chinese would use their own language, with their words and concepts, into which they would try as best they could to fit European concepts. That is, they would compare the European concepts to their own, using their own notions as models and standards in terms of which to judge European notions.

Perhaps when Alexander the Great (who had studied a little philosophy with early Greek philosopher Aristotle) conquered northern India in the fourth century B.C.E., Hindu scholars might have asked Alexander's generals whether there were any "rishis" among the Greeks ("rishi" is an Indian word referring to the highly revered religious hermits who retreat into the forests toward the end of their lives seeking mystical wisdom). What could these Greek army officers say? There was no comparable tradition in Greece of such forest hermits. But if they say they have no rishis, it makes them look bad.

We also can imagine Marco Polo trying to satisfy the curiosity of Yuan dynasty (1280–1367) Confucian administrators concerning the presence or absence in Europe of "zi" ("zi" is a Chinese word, sometimes spelled "tzu," meaning "master" as in "Lao Zi," "Master Lao," the man who wrote the Taoist classic *Tao De Jing*.) "We have a long tradition," they might say, "of important thinkers we call zi—Kongzi, Mengzi, Laozi, Zhuangzi, Mozi, Xunzi, Han Feizi, and many others, who have made our culture great. What about you? Do you have any zi among your people?" We can imagine Marco Polo's dilemma—it is hard for him to say yes, and it is hard for him to say no. It is hard to say yes, since there really is no tradition in Europe identical or even similar to the Chinese zi. There were European saints and university professors, for example, but these are not the same as zi. On the other hand, if he admits that there are no European zi, he seems to belittle his own culture—admitting, in effect, that his people could claim none of those intellectual giants who make a culture great. Of course, Marco Polo and Alexander's generals could say, "No, but we have 'philosophers',," but then the Chinese and Indians could only wonder, "What is a 'philosopher'?"

Part of the problem of comparative philosophy is simply the problem of linguistic translation. In India, the word we translate as "philosophy" is "darshana" (written in Sanskrit script, of course, not in the letters of the Roman alphabet), a word whose roots mean "to see," as in insight or viewpoint. As written texts, the darshanas were originally (from the sixth century B.C.E.) commentaries on the "sutras," which were highly abbreviated written outlines of memorized oral traditions—so truncated and abbreviated, in fact, that by themselves (without the commentaries) they are virtually unintelligible (like your own class notes may seem to you ten years from now!). And yet within these darshanas sophisticated debates are developed on topics we know in the West as "philosophy."

It seems clear that in trying to translate the Sanskrit word "darshana," we are searching among words in English for the one that is closest in meaning to "darshana." When English-speaking scholars who can read Sanskrit read the "darshanas," they must ask themselves what these texts are all about, what they are like. Are they like what we call "poetry," or are they more like what we call "history," or a "prayer," or a "diary," or a "shopping list"? English-speaking scholars working in Sanskrit agree that the darshanas most closely resemble what we call, in English, "philosophy." But is it exactly like what professors of philosophy teach in British and American universities today? No, writes Gavin Flood, a well-known scholar of Hinduism, in his *An Introduction to Hinduism.*

> While there are undoubted similarities between traditional Hindu thinking and modern Western philosophy, what traditional Hindu thinkers do would only be partially recognized in contemporary departments of philosophy in Western universities.
>
> (from *An Introduction to Hinduism*)

A similar problem of translation occurs in the study of Chinese texts. The first reference to any Chinese writing as "philosophy" was in 1687, in a book written in Latin by Roman Catholic Jesuit missionaries, under Matteo Ricci, who were trying to understand the Chinese whom they were trying to convert to Christianity. Kongzi, Latinized for the first time as "Confucius," was said to be a "philosopher" (as that word appears in Latin). Shortly thereafter, Mengzi, Latinized as Mencius, was similarly designated by the Jesuits as a "philosopher." But what is the word in Chinese these Jesuits translated as "philosopher"? As already indicated, Confucius and Mencius are called, in Chinese, Kongzi and Mengzi (written, of course, in Chinese characters, not in letters of the Roman alphabet), in which the Chinese word "zi" means something like "master," so Kongzi is "Master Kong" and Mengzi is "Master Meng." By the first century C.E., Chinese also used the word "jia," which literally means "house," to refer to different "schools" of thought—thus there was the "Ru Jia" (the Confucianists), the "Mo Jia" (the Mohists, followers of Mo Ti, or Mozi), the "Dao Jia" (the Daoist, or Taoist, thinkers), the "Ming Jia" (literally "the school of names," often referred to in English as the "logicians"), and so on.

English-speaking scholars who can read Chinese and who read these texts of the Mohists, the Ming Jia, and so on, say that while they are not *exactly* like *anything* in the West, they most closely resemble what Westerners call "philosophy." And indeed, when those of us who do not read Chinese read these texts, we feel we can relate to them as philosophical texts. In fact, translated and taken out of context, whole paragraphs of Indian and Chinese writing can be so successfully smuggled into a discussion of Western philosophy that even trained Western philosophers think the writing is from some obscure Western philosopher. And we imagine that these writers from India, China, and Greece could have argued with one another—if they could have met and been accompanied with good translators (or, better, learned one another's languages—as they may actually have done, in the case of Alexander's generals and Marco Polo).

So, initially, there is no alternative but for the culture initiating the investigation to use its own concepts to judge the culture under investigation. Because of European military, economic, scientific, and technological dominance during the eighteenth and nineteenth centuries, it was the Europeans who judged the Chinese and Indian cultures by comparing them to their own European standards. Later, as Europeans learn enough about Chinese or Indian culture to recognize significant similarities between their own thought systems and those of China and India, and begin to consider them together, it is likely that European concepts will be influenced by Chinese and Indian concepts and vice versa, and that all of these will undergo a gradual modification and mutual accommodation toward the others.

Because of the military dominance of Europeans in the modern period, the Indians and Chinese also were faced with the problem of how to understand these aggressive foreigners—not to colonize them or convert them to Hinduism, Buddhism, or Confucianism, but to avoid being conquered and colonized and converted by them, or in the case of India, which was already colonized, to try to understand how this had happened and how it might have been overcome. If Western culture had become powerful enough to conquer and colonize almost the whole world (from Africa to India to Malaysia to Vietnam to North and South America to Indonesia to the Philippines—and knocking at the door of China and Japan), then non-Western peoples needed to know what had made the Europeans so strong and how they could learn and incorporate some of these scientific and technological techniques— "fighting fire with fire," we might say, "If you can't beat 'em, join 'em."

In the 1850s, Europeans, mainly the British and French, began to control China, though never (except in the case of Macau and Hong Kong) completely reducing China to a European colony, and also in the 1850s, the American Commodore Perry forced Japan, against its will (by threat of sheer military superiority), to open its doors to Western trade and influence. The Japanese responded (in the Meiji period beginning in 1868) to "fight fire with fire," that is, to learn as much as they could about Western science and technology to avoid being colonized as India had been and as China seemed on the verge of becoming. As the Japanese set up Western-style universities, at first hiring American and European professors but gradually training their own Japanese professors, they had to first find a way to translate into their own Japanese language the names of all of the Western sciences—physics, chemistry, engineering, philosophy, zoology, and so on. And so they needed a word for "philosophy."

Since the Japanese use about 2,000 Chinese characters (kanji) as part of their own written script, they used pairs of kanji (Chinese words, or characters) to translate these European sciences or disciplines, and they accordingly selected a pair of Chinese characters to refer to "philosophy." Since the Chinese used the same characters, though the Chinese and Japanese pronounced them quite differently, the Chinese adopted the Japanese convention for translating "philosophy," and so, around 1900, the Japanese and

Chinese used the same written words to translate "philosophy," pronounced "tetsugaku" in Japanese and "zhushway" in Chinese. But then, interestingly, around 1920, the Chinese decided that some of their own traditional writing (Confucianism, Taoism, Mohism, and Ming Jia) also should be called "zhushway" (philosophy), as well as some Indian texts, so that by 1923 the Chinese said there were three major philosophical traditions—Chinese, Indian, and Western. To some extent, the Chinese were influenced in this regard by two Western philosophers—Englishman Bertrand Russell and American John Dewey—who visited China just after the First World War (i.e., around 1920). Russell told Chinese scholars that philosophy was *not* one of the sciences, as they and the Japanese had supposed, because it was speculative rather than empirical, and normative (i.e., evaluative) rather than factual and objective (i.e., value neutral). As such, Russell and Dewey said, it is more similar to ancient Chinese thought systems of the Confucianists, Taoists, Mohists, and others than it is to Western sciences like physics and chemistry. The Japanese, however, did not accept this reasoning and went in the opposite direction, saying that "tetsugaku" should only be used to refer to Western philosophy, not to any non-Western writings, that there was only one "tetsugaku," only one philosophy—Western philosophy (though the Japanese now say that a Western-inspired Japanese philosophy began just after the Second World War, that is, around 1950, and continues today).

And what did Indian scholars have to say about this? Around the same time, 1920, British-trained Indian scholars such as Sarvepalli Radhakrishnan argued that the Indian darshanas should be included within what Indian scholars had come to recognize from the British as "philosophy," and should include as well the Chinese "zi" or "jia," agreeing with the Chinese (against the Japanese) that there were three major traditions of philosophy—Indian, Western, and Chinese.

There are significant differences, of course, not only between but also *within* each of these philosophical systems, in each case ranging from the more "tender-hearted" mystical to the more "tough-minded" logical perspectives (to use the distinction introduced by early twentieth-century American philosopher and psychologist William James). And while it may be true that on the whole Eastern philosophy is more "tender-hearted" and Western philosophy is more "tough-minded," Eastern philosophy nonetheless has its more "tough-minded" side and Western philosophy its more "tender-hearted" side. Interestingly, Eastern philosophers have tended to ignore their own more tough-minded philosophers, just as Western philosophers have tended to ignore their own more tender-hearted philosophers, creating the illusion that *all* Eastern philosophy is tender-hearted and *all* Western philosophy is tough-minded. But this is not true, as we will see throughout this book. Nonetheless, given these stereotypes, comparing Chinese or Indian thought with

Western philosophy might shift the European sense of philosophy away from the more rigorous, scientific, and analytic (i.e., "tough-minded") regions of Western philosophy (Aristotle, Descartes, or Kant) to the more mystical, practical, and wisdom-oriented (i.e., "tender-hearted") Western philosophers (Epicurus, Plotinus, Spinoza, Kierkegaard, or Nietzsche), who more closely resemble stereotypical Indian and Chinese thinkers. And, by the same token, as Indian and Chinese scholars compare their traditional thinkers to Western philosophers, they may begin to think more highly of those traditionally marginalized Indian and Chinese thinkers who resemble rigorous analytic Western philosophers, that is, Indian and Chinese materialists, skeptics, egoists, and logicians.

Unconsciously, by studying each other's philosophies, Western philosophers will gradually come to practice philosophy more like their colleagues in China and India; and vice versa, Indian and Chinese philosophers, as they study Western philosophy, will gradually begin to do their own philosophy more and more like their Western counterparts. But initially, if Europeans begin the investigation, then they must begin with their own language and their own cultural baggage, with all of the admitted dangers of bias and misunderstanding that this approach inevitably involves. To understand another culture is necessarily to misunderstand it, at least at the beginning, to a certain extent.

This also is true more generally, even in the case of art and religion. We generally assume that every culture has its own art and religion, but even when we ask about "Indian religion," for example, we have to realize that "religion" is an English word that we are trying to impose on an alien culture. Perhaps they do not have a word in their own language that translates exactly as our word "religion." "Hinduism," for example, is a word that refers to a 5,000-year tradition of various religious practices and beliefs on the Indian subcontinent, but as a word designating what Europeans call a "religion," comparable to Christianity, Judaism, Islam, or Buddhism, it has only recently been coined (during the last hundred years or so). One hundred fifty years ago it would not have occurred to anyone to ask what "the religion" is of all those Indians who are not Buddhists, Muslims, Sikhs, Jains, or Christians. At first, no one assumed, in other words, that the ancient, traditional practices of Asian Indians constituted "a religion." But just as early Jesuit missionaries to China found it natural to think of Confucianism as a competing "Chinese religion," so Europeans found it natural to describe all of the different ancient Indian ritual and ceremonial practices as "a religion," which the Europeans named "Hinduism," after the "Indus" River, from which the word "India" comes (India itself sometimes referred to in the nineteenth and early twentieth centuries as "Hindustan"). As a "religion," however, Hinduism seems quite confusing to the outsider. What is Hinduism (as a "religion")?

This question, which would be fairly easy to answer, at least in broad outlines, in the case of other religions such as Judaism, Christianity, or Islam, is almost impossible to answer in regard to Hinduism. Some "Hindus" believe in many gods, some believe in no gods; among those who believe in many gods, some favor the god Vishnu, others favor the god Shiva; and among those who favor Vishnu, some follow one avatar (reincarnation) of Vishnu, while others follow other avatars (reincarnations) of Vishnu; for some Hindus ritual sacrifice is central, while for others, it is bhakti devotion to a particular avatar of one of the gods (such as the Hare Krishna cult). Now, rather than reject this European "invention" or "construction" of a "Hindu religion," many contemporary Indians embrace the concept as a way of unifying the many ethnic, linguistic, and religious traditions on the Indian subcontinent into one country (nation-state), that is, beginning in 1947 the country we now call India.

Similarly, in the case of "African art" or "American Indian art," the very question "What kind of art did the American Indians have?" presupposes something that may well be false—namely, that the American Indians not only made things that we see as fitting *our* concept (in English) of "art," but that *they* too had a similar concept, that is, a word reasonably, accurately translated as "art"—a word that they understood to mean something very much like what we understand the word "art" to mean. But this may be a mistaken assumption. Other cultures may simply not *have* words or concepts similar in meaning to our "art" and "religion." In fact, there are good reasons for thinking that they probably do *not* have such concepts.

One reason is that these concepts in English and other European languages presuppose a division of society and culture into distinct functional regions in which art is more or less separated from religion, which is more or less separated from agricultural, military, political, and scientific concerns, as in European culture. In many world cultures, no such separation ever took place, and in cultures where what we call artistic activities are mixed with what we call religious, agricultural, military, and political activities, concepts like our art and religion simply do not arise.

In such cultures it makes no sense (even if you speak their language and they yours) to ask "What is your religion, what is your art?" Until Buddhism arose in India, what we call "Hinduism" was not perceived as a separate "religion" but was simply a part of the everyday life of people. Similarly, in China and Japan—until Buddhism was introduced—what we know today as Chinese religious "Taoism" and Japanese "Shinto" was not recognized by the indigenous peoples as a separate "religion," and so for African and Native American religious practices before the introduction of Christianity and, in Africa, Islam. Before that, what we call "religious" practices were simply a normal, routine part of every person's life, part of the common culture shared by all.

Similar was "art." Africans and Native Americans two or three hundred years ago made wooden statues for ancestor spirits to temporarily "occupy," to which they made offerings of food and drink and of which they asked (that is, "prayed") for help for a successful harvest, battle, or marriage; but they had no sense of which part of this complex ritual practice was their "art," which part "religion," which part "agriculture" or "military," and so on. These questions would have made no sense to them, though they will, of course, make sense to us. *We* are the ones interested in *their* "art" and "religion." From the time of the first Christian missionaries like Ricci in the seventeenth century until today, it is a serious question whether Confucianism, Taoism, and Hinduism are competing "religions" in the sense in which Christianity, Judaism, Buddhism, or Islam are said to be "religions."

So even in the case of "art" and "religion," where it is widely believed that *all* cultures and societies have some art and some religion, the possibility of bias and misunderstanding arising from crosscultural comparison presents a serious problem—not only for the scientific investigations of the anthropologist and sociologist, but in adequately taking account of the cultural sensitivities of the groups we are describing.

All cultural descriptions are therefore *comparative*—inevitably, culture A must use A's words and concepts to describe culture B (what else do they have?) In some cases, it is true, translating from one language to another is not terribly difficult—we simply find the words in each language that have the same meaning ("rouge," "rot," and "hong," for example, all have pretty much the same meaning—"red"). But sometimes we face the far more serious problem that there is simply no word in our language that has the same meaning as the word in their language, or vice versa, there is no word in their language for the word in our language.

The Temne of Sierra Leone, West Africa, pay respects to their immediately dead ancestors (that is, their parents and grandparents, but not their great-great grandparents), which they call their "mboda." They offer the mboda food and drink and often ask their advice on important family matters. What if a Temne speaker were to ask why you do not show the proper respect to your mboda? Why are you so disrespectful toward your mboda? What would you say? You are not really showing your mboda disrespect since you never heard of them; you have no idea or concept of mboda. Of course, you remember your deceased grandmother or grandfather, and you may occasionally place flowers on their graves, and you may believe that their souls are now in Heaven—but you have no concept of the "living-dead" ancestor who still needs food and drink from you and who is available to give you advice on family matters. The question of your disrespectful behavior to your mboda does not make any sense. In your world as you conceive it, there are no mboda! But when the Temne try to describe us, they will naturally do so in their own terms, saying that we do not seem to show much respect for our mboda, just as we will describe them using our concepts and frames of reference. So, inevitably, at least in the beginning, we (whoever "we" are) must use our own words with their common meanings when we try to understand the cultures of other people.

Suppose we now take the word "philosophy" as defined in our second, more technical sense (where philosophy is understood as a critical, reflective, rational, and systematic approach, involving, as we said, a traditional backlog of "tools of the trade," to normative questions of very general interest) and apply that definition to different thought systems around the world. Are any of these non-Western thought systems "philosophy" in this sense, and if so, which ones? Even if we accept this second sense of philosophy as being the most appropriate for our purposes, it will not be easy to apply our new standard to different thought systems, for we must still decide exactly what we *mean* by "critical," "rational," and so on, and how and to what extent this thought system must count as philosophy. And so there continues to be a great deal of debate among philosophers on this question.

Nonetheless, many philosophers today hold (and have held since around 1920) that there are three great original centers of philosophy in the world—Greek (or Western philosophy), Indian, and Chinese. All three originated at approximately the same time (roughly 500 B.C.E.), though, as far as we know, quite independently of one another. All three arose as critical reflections on their own cultural traditions. From these centers of origin, philosophy then spread to other cultures—Greek philosophy adopted and modified by the Romans and later by the Arabs (for a time), the Europeans, the Americans (North and South), Australians, South Africans, and so on; Chinese philosophy adopted and modified by the Koreans, Japanese, and Vietnamese; and Indian philosophy adopted and modified by the Tibetans, Burmese, Cambodians, and Balinese.

Cultures that are not philosophical in this sense are those that tend to accept their own religious, mythological worldview simply on the authority of tradition: "We believe this because it is our ancient belief; our people have always believed this." (Or, if isolated individuals occasionally raise skeptical questions about their own culture, which they must have done from time to time, they do not have the resources to sustain that discussion into the future and so it dies out with the death of these occasional, eccentric individuals.) Philosophy, in contrast, arises precisely at that point in the history of a culture when, for various reasons, that traditional outlook is called into question (the breakdown of the Zhou dynasty in China, the challenge of Buddhism and Jainism in India, and the collapse of the Greek "city state" culture): "We have always been taught to see the world in this way, but how can we be sure that this is really correct, especially now that our traditions no longer seem to be working for us?" (And, as we have said, this spirit of critical reflection must then take root, becoming a permanent part of the culture, developing a tradition of its own.)

Philosophy, we are saying, arises out of reflection on traditional ritualistic, religious, and mythological culture. But this does not happen all at once, "out of the blue," for no apparent reason. Nor does it occur out of idle curiosity, and not simply because highly intelligent people like to do this sort of thing. It arises when a cultural crisis has occurred that is widely recognized and feared as something undermining the foundations of the traditional culture. As Kwame Gyekye, in *Tradition and Modernity: Philosophical Reflections on the African Experience*, puts it,

> In times of wonder, confusion, instability, and uncertainty, in times when the definition and articulation of values and goals become most urgent, in times when the search for fundamental principles of human activity becomes most pressing and is seen as the way to dispel confusions and unclarities as well as the way to draw attention to new or alternative modes of thought and action—in such times, the services of the intellectual enterprise called philosophy become indispensable. For philosophy . . . is a conceptual response to the problems posed in any given epoch for a given society or culture.
>
> *(Tradition and Modernity: Philosophical Reflections on the African Experience)*

As Gyekye points out, this can occur at any point in time, and Gyekye is particularly concerned with the development of African philosophy as a response to the crisis of culture occurring in Africa since the end of colonialism (around 1960). But in literate cultures, this crisis of culture occurs with the collapse of traditional culture in the sixth century B.C.E.

In China, it comes with the breakdown of the "feudal" aristocracy—the Shang and the long-decaying Zhou dynasties. This feudal system was completely and forever replaced from the third century B.C.E. until 1911 by an alternating cycle of military imperial dynasties (beginning with the Qin and Han, and continuing in the Tang, Song, Ming, and Ching dynasties), interspersed with periods of disunity and "warring states" (and/or foreign invasions) in between. In the feudal period, the traditional culture seemed to be working, and there was no need for philosophers to try to fix it; only when their traditions seemed to be crumbling did the need for philosophy arise.

This feudal order broke down through the rise of militarist rulers—not hereditary nobility of an elite class or caste (as in Europe in the Middle Ages), but simply the strongest military general, often a commoner, who could defeat other armies and thereby conquer more and more territory. In China, the era 700–200 B.C.E. is known as the Warring States period in which the military leaders of a dozen small feudal kingdoms fought for military supremacy until Ying Cheng of the Chin state (from which the word "China" comes) emerged as the overall winner and ruler (calling himself Shih Huang Di, "the first emperor") of all of what is now known as China.

So, from 700 B.C.E., it became increasingly clear that the Chinese feudal system was crumbling. It could no longer be taken for granted that Heaven had appointed the king who was able, through ritual ceremonies, to ensure continued good harvests, immunity from outside attack, and peaceful and harmonious relations among various hierarchically arranged classes of people: If this ancient system is coming undone, what will happen to us? Will the four seasons continue as they have in the past? Will our crops continue to grow as before? Can we count on the continued procreation of ourselves and our livestock?

Of more particular interest to philosophy, what will happen to the scholars, no longer employed by hereditary rulers in feudal castes as interpreters and advisors on state ceremonial rituals? Out of work, these are the people we think became the first Chinese philosophers—establishing schools for the first time, as private citizens, teaching, writing books, attracting students, and charging tuition (sometimes a bundle of dried fish!), each absolutely convinced that they have figured out the problem of the collapsing culture and have a (the only) solution, each trying to get their ideas accepted by the military rulers of the day—all in a private capacity, and of course in competition with other private scholars/teachers. Of course, if this were to continue, these early philosophy teachers had to be successful in establishing a new tradition of competing schools of philosophy, each with its famous philosophers with their books and students and ideas, and so on. And so emerges in India and China and Greece at about the same time dozens of competing schools of thought, all vying for attention, all arguing for their views and against all of the others, each in competition with every other.

The first signs of such a critical, questioning, and reforming reflection come from what we might call the "precursors" of philosophy—not quite philosophy per se, not yet philosophy in the full-blown, fully developed sense, but in the early beginning, transitional stages, in an intermediary zone somewhere between religious mythology and philosophy proper. Often the first philosophers are those who have been recently ousted socially and politically by revolutions affecting the "crisis of culture." The twentieth-century Chinese philosopher Fung Yulan argues that the Ru (the literati, or Confucianists) developed out of the disbanded masters of ritual ceremonies (those few literate individuals employed by the feudal lords to direct the elaborate ceremonies of state) as they were literally thrown out of a job and had to fend for themselves (the Mohists, according to Fung Yulan, similarly arose out of the military class as they were cut off from their feudal attachment to the hereditary aristocratic rulers).

In this sense, the *Upanishads* are examples of precursors to Indian philosophy, and the *I Jing* and *Spring and Autumn Annals* are precursors to Chinese philosophy. Even in the ancient Hindu *Rig Veda* (roughly 2000 to 1000 B.C.E.), there are signs of the beginnings of speculative wonder about the origin of all things and the tentative search for answers:

> *[In the beginning] neither Being nor Not-being was,*
> *Nor atmosphere, nor firmament, nor what is beyond.*
> *What did it encompass? Where? In whose protection?*
> *What was the water, the deep, the unfathomable?*
>
> *Neither death nor immortality was there then,*
> *No sign of night or day.*
> *That One breathed, windless, by its own energy:*
> *Nought else existed then.*
>
> *In the beginning was darkness swathed in darkness;*
> *All this was but unmanifested water.*
> *Whatever was, that One coming into being,*
> *Hidden by the Void,*
> *Was generated by the power of heat.*
>
> *In the beginning this [One] evolved,*
> *Became desire, first seed of mind.*
> *Wise seers, searching within their hearts,*
> *Found the bond of Being in Not-being.*
>
> *Whence this emanation hath arisen,*
> *Whether [God] disposed it, or whether he did not,*
> *Only He who is its overseer in highest heaven knows.*
> *[He only knows,] or perhaps He does not know!*
>
> (*Rig Veda*)

To us, this mixture of religious, psychological, physical, and philosophical concepts seems strange, but this is quite common to the "precursors" of philosophy. In the *Chandogya Upanishad*, just before the appearance of philosophy proper, there is an extended discussion of the essential identity of all things as the impersonal Brahman which, though still mixing philosophical, physical, psychological and religious concepts, comes very close to an ontology, or a metaphysical monism, later to appear in philosophy in the narrow, technical sense:

> What is called Brahman, that is what this space outside a man is; and what that space outside a man is, that is what this space within a man is; and what that space within a man is, that is what this space within the heart is. . . . This whole universe is Brahman. . . . All works, all desires, all scents, all tastes belong to it: it encompasses all this universe, does not speak and has no care. This my Self within the heart is that Brahman.
>
> *(Chandogya Upanishad)*

Also in that same (Chandogya) Upanishad we find the first beginnings in Indian thought of an attempt to explain logically and rationally the more mysterious sayings of the earlier *Rig Veda*. In the passage previously quoted from the *Rig Veda*, for example, what sense does it make to say that in the beginning there was neither Being nor Not-being? Of course, if we are looking for the absolute beginnings of everything, then it might at first seem to make sense to say that there must have been something even before being and non-being, something even more primordial than either, out of which both being and non-being came. And that sort of reasoning also appears in the Chinese precursor to philosophy, the *Dao De Jing*. But when we stop to think about it, how could something be neither being nor not-being? How can we think of something (or talk about something) that is neither of these? Surely whatever this original entity was, it must have been one or the other; and how could Being come from Not-being? (You know the song, "Nothing from nothing . . .") Logically, it can only make sense to say that in the beginning there was Being. As stated in the *Chandogya Upanishad*,

> In the beginning, . . . this [universe] was Being only—one only—without a second. True, some say that in the beginning this [universe] was Not-being only—one only—without a second, and that from that Not-being Being was born. But, . . . whence could this be? . . . How could Being be born from Not-being? No, it was Being alone that was this [universe] in the beginning—one only, without a second." [Being] had this thought: "Would that I were many; fain would I procreate! [And so from the One came the Many.]
>
> *(Chandogya Upanishad)*

There also were precursors to Greek philosophy. In the seventh century B.C.E., Greek city states began to move dramatically away from aristocratic forms of government by family elites to a commercial "middle class," broader-based "democracy," presenting a similar challenge to traditional culture ("crisis of culture") as we saw in India and China. Just as in China, the "new" rulers began to create new traditions, inviting to their courts famous "wise men," in most cases probably those out-of-work former advisors to the aristocrats. From this developed new attitudes—not so much in philosophy per se, still in its immature or adolescent phase, but in new kinds of poetry and other forms of literature. A new satirical poetry arose, for example, which stressed individual criticism and judgments of society. A new poetry also sprang up, trying to find a new foundation for morality (if the gods are called into question, why should we follow the traditional morality we used to think they demanded of us? And if we no longer have confidence in the old religiously inspired morality, where can we now turn for moral guidance?).

In Hesiod's *Theogony* (eighth century B.C.E.), we find a passage much like the one quoted earlier from the Indian *Rig Veda*, similarly speculating about the beginning of everything, where everything came from (and, like the *Rig Veda*, similarly confusing us with its mixture of psychological, religious, physical, and philosophical notions:

> Tell me this, you Muses who have your home on Olympus, from the beginning, tell me what first came into being. First of all came the Chasm; and then wide-bosomed Earth, the eternal safe seat of all the immortals who hold the heights of snowy Olympus, and murky Tartarus in the recesses of the wide-pathed land, and Love, who is fairest among the immortal gods, loosener of limbs, by whom all gods and all men find their thoughts and wise counsels overcome in their breasts. From Chasm came black Darkness and Night; and from Night came Ether and Day whom she conceived and bore after mingling in love with Darkness.
>
> *(Rig Veda)*

And, much like the passage from the *Chandogya Upanishad*, quoted earlier, we also can see the first critical reflection by Greek thinkers on the problem of the absolute origin of things.

As Sextus Empiricus, in *Against the Mathematicians*, says

> The poet who writes, First of all came the Chasm; and then wide-bosomed Earth, the eternal seat of all . . . refutes himself. For if someone asks him what the Chasm came from, he will not be able to answer.
>
> (from Sextus Empiricus, *Against the Mathematicians*)

As in China and India, these "precursors" to philosophy fall into two broad groups—the revolutionaries and the conservatives. The revolutionaries are happy to tear down what is to them the oppressive old order and replace it with a "brave new world," while the conservatives, fearful of such radical change, try to find a new and different foundation for the (best of) the old order (religion, morality, and politics). We should not be surprised to find that these different precursors represent different political groups, the children of the old elite being more conservative than the children of the new commercial classes. Interestingly, in India, China, and among the Greeks, it is always the conservatives who win out in the long run. Thus, Kongzi (Confucius), Plato, and the six orthodox (i.e., Hindu) schools of Indian philosophy not only win out over but almost totally obliterate their more revolutionary and radical critics (the Ming Jia of China, the Carvacans of India, and the Sophists of Greece, all of whom will be discussed later in this book).

So, for example, the radical revolutionaries among the Greeks, known as the Sophists, argued among other things, that all moral, political, religious, and aesthetic ideals are relative to particular cultures and that there are therefore no universal, crosscultural eternal norms or standards. This view was opposed by the more conservative thinkers, who feared that this would simply create cultural chaos and anarchy, and who therefore sought a new, more rational universal base for the old standards—gradually leading up to the full-blown philosophy we find in Plato and Aristotle (fourth century B.C.E.). G. C. Field writes, in *Plato and His Contemporaries,*

> Plato grew up in a period when the established order and accepted standards seemed on the verge of dissolution under the pressure of political events and theoretical criticism. . . . He turned to philosophical speculation as the only direction from which help might come. From one point of view, indeed, the chief aim of Plato's philosophy may be regarded as the attempt to re-establish standards of thought and conduct for a civilization that seemed on the verge of dissolution.
>
> (G. C. Field, *Plato and His Contemporaries*)

Even before Plato, Greek poets had begun to reflect on existing social norms and explore ways to establish moral standards on a new basis. In Windeband's *History of Ancient Philosophy,*

> Any extended reflection upon maxims of moral judgment shows immediately that the validity of morality has been questioned in some way, that social consciousness has become unsettled, and that the individual in his growing independence has transcended the bounds authoritatively drawn by the universal [traditional] consciousness. Therefore it was entirely characteristic of this Gnomic poetry to recommend moderation; to show how universal standards of life had been endangered by the unbridled careers of single persons [the dictators], and how in the presence of threatening or present anarchy the individual must try to reestablish these rules through independent reflection.
>
> (Windeband's *History of Ancient Philosophy,* Cushman, trans.)

This is what led in Greece to the transitional "precursors" to philosophy known as the "Seven Wise Men."

It was an age of reflection. The simple devotion to the conventions of the previous age had ceased, and social consciousness was profoundly disturbed. Individuals began to go their own ways. Notable men appeared, and earnestly exhorted society to come back to its senses. Rules of life were established. In riddle, in anecdote, in epigram, the moralizing sermon was made palatable, and "winged words" passed from mouth to mouth. But, let it be remembered, these homilies are possible only when the individual opposes the vagaries of the mob, and with independent judgement brings to consciousness the maxims of right conduct.

(Windeband *ibid.*)

The fact that Thales (generally referred to as the first Western or Greek philosopher) also is sometimes mentioned as one of the "Seven Wise Men" indicates the transitory nature of the "precursors" to the philosophers proper.

The transition from Greek tradition to philosophy also can be seen in the new cosmologies—based on traditional mythology (somewhat like Indian cosmologies), but attempting to more rationally, but still religiously, speculate on the origin of the world (e.g., "in the beginning," it might be said, for example, "was a dark, undifferentiated mass out of which, through the forces of Heat and Love, more organized forms of matter and life evolved," or in the Indian cosmology quoted earlier, the One Being at the beginning of the universe says, "I'd like to multiply, procreate and so become many"). These transitional cosmologies (halfway between religion and philosophy) evolved from the moralizing and rationalizing of traditional religion, moving, for example, from polytheism (a chaotic group of many gods and goddesses) toward monotheism (a more systematic ordering of the many gods into some sort of hierarchy, or leadership structure, headed by one main god or goddess, for example, Zeus, like the Indian Indra, as the chief of many lesser gods, ruling the universe from a set of rational moral laws for all to follow—an idea leading eventually to the idea of a universe "governed" by eternal, immutable, logical, and scientific "laws" of nature).

Similar changes were occurring within Indian society—specifically the rise of urbanism and the decline of small village agricultural life, a rising commercial class that strengthened individualism (and weakened traditional, religious authority). This individualism encouraged the idea of each person finding his or her own way, working it out for himself or herself. This, in turn, encouraged a search for a universal basis within all human beings, not tied to caste, race, or specific dogmatic texts, but based simply on the fact that each one of us is equally a human being—the idea, for example, in Buddhism and Jainism (beginning around 500 B.C.E.), that *all* human beings, simply by virtue of being human beings, suffer for roughly similar reasons, the solution or cure for which is therefore the same and something each person must seek for themselves.

The older Hinduism was more socially contexted, a hierarchy in which the high Brahman caste control the orthodox ritual within a highly structured society, while the new Buddhist, Jain, and Upanishadic traditions (from 500 B.C.E.) are based on the efforts of individuals outside of this highly structured society to escape all this seemingly arbitrary, traditional dogmatism in order to get down to the essentials, the basics: What is the root cause of human suffering? How can an individual person on his or her own, regardless of caste or access to ritual liturgy, with the help of an individual teacher (guru) figure this out and through one's own knowledge overcome it? This is the meditation, knowledge-orientation of the new Buddhism, Jainism, and late Upanishadic traditions.

The transition to philosophy also can be seen (again in China, India, and Greece) in the move away from small, esoteric, secret literate societies, in which knowledge is guarded and kept from the general public, to attempts to popularize for a much broader audience, in ever-expanding educational circles, all that was known at the time in history, astronomy, medicine, mathematics—not quite *universal* education, but education for all the sons of the rising merchant class, young men who (like most young men today) did not plan to devote their whole lives to scholarly or scientific research but who wanted the maximum practical benefit from what was known at the time—at the very least to appear knowledgeable, literate, and argumentatively persuasive in the courts of law and more generally in the political arena.

In Greece, the Sophists moved from town to town offering "short courses" of instruction. This was opposed by Plato and then Aristotle, who favored a system of education more like our current university system of professional scholars and scientists to whom students came for years of concentrated study in permanent sites, such as Plato's "Academy" and Aristotle's "Lyceum," before branching out into other careers—occasionally becoming university instructors themselves, but more often entering politics, business, or law. In much the same way, Kongzi (Confucius) became China's first professional educator, as well as its first philosopher. And similar "schools" developed in India. It is through these first "universities" that the stable tradition of philosophical discipline was established and maintained (Plato's Academy lasting some 800 years, from the fourth century B.C.E. until the fourth century C.E., and Confucianism becoming the officially recognized center of scholarly study in China for nearly 2,000 years), and the six orthodox (i.e., Hindu) and unorthodox (i.e., Buddhist, Jain, and Carvacan) schools evolved over several thousand years.

It is important to realize the different role learning and writing played in ancient cultures. In the Chinese feudal system (2000–700 B.C.E.), writing was invented and evolved, but almost all in the service of the kings. In this feudal period, no private books were written nor privately taught or read as we find today in our society where books are written to be bought and read and taught in an individual capacity. Instead, attached to the king's court was the need for a few scholars who could read the ancient texts in order to advise the government on precisely how to perform the religious ceremonial duties of the king (the Spring and Fall sacrifices, for example). Similarly, in India, what we know today as the ancient *Rig Veda* was not originally written down, much less read by ordinary persons, but was memorized to be recited on special ritual occasions by a privileged "Brahman" elite. In both India and China, this educated elite in the service of the ritual state ceremonies formed a small hereditary class or caste. Others outside of that small hereditary group were not allowed to read or recite, or in general to know or even own the sacred, ritual texts. This was one reason Indian Brahmans did not want the Vedas written down, even after the invention of writing, for fear that non-Brahmans would learn how to read and invade their privileged domain.

The beginning of philosophy, whether in China, India, or Greece, is marked by the appearance of individual philosophers (whom we can identify by name) who come forward with the boldness and audacity, and we might even say the conceit, to claim to have figured it all out by themselves—that is, beginning at the very beginning, asking the most basic, fundamental questions, confident that they could (in a single lifetime) come up with the right answers! As we will see, these early philosophers thought that they could help their societies find a way out of the debilitating and destabilizing "crisis of culture," and Confucius, Plato, Mencius, and Aristotle actually tried to train and advise the rulers of their day (though without much success).

The beginning of philosophy is therefore the beginning of individual thinking. No longer do we say, "This is how our people see the world," but rather, (among Western philosophers), "Parmenides said that change and motion were impossible; Heraclitus disagreed, arguing that everything was constantly changing and in motion and that nothing was permanent, while Plato disagreed with both and with his theory of Forms sought a middle ground between Parmenides and Heraclitus." And (among Chinese philosophers), "Gaozi argued that there was no common human nature; Mengzi held that there was a human nature and that it is basically good; Xunzi agreed with Mengzi that there was a common human nature but disagreed that it was good, arguing instead that human beings are by nature selfish and aggressive, while Dong Zhongshu tried to combine the two." Finally (among Indian philosophers), "Carvacans were materialistic atheists, denying the existence of gods or souls, or indeed anything but matter; Shankara argued that everything in the world was part of a spiritual Brahman, but that Brahman was not a personal god, while Madhva and Ramanuja believed in the existence of a plurality of physical and spiritual objects and gods." The beginning of philosophy is therefore characterized by a proliferation of very different, competing theories, each held by a named individual and his or her followers.

As early as the fourth century B.C.E., the Chinese Confucian philosopher Mengzi (known in Europe as Mencius) writes about his mission to combat the dominant philosophies of his day: at one extreme, Yang Zhu, an egoist who would not sacrifice a single hair of his body to gain (or in some translations, to save) the whole world and Mozi, at the other extreme, who argued that people should love everyone equally. As the Chinese *Huai-nanzi* says,

> The orchestra, drum, and dance for the performance of music; obeisances and bowing for the cultivation of good manners; generous expenditure in funerals and protracted mourning for the obsequies of the dead: these were what Confucius established and were condemned by Mozi. Universal love, exaltation of the worthy, assistance to the spirits and anti-fatalism: these were what Mozi established, and were condemned by Yangzi [Yang Zhu]. Completeness of living, preservation of what is genuine, and not allowing outside things to entangle one's person: these were what Yangzi [Yang Zhu] established, and were condemned by Mencius.
>
> (*Huai-nanzi*, in Fung Yulan, *A History of Chinese Philosophy*)

One of the earliest Indian Buddhist texts, *Digha Nikaya*, contains a passage in which King Ajatasatru describes the wide range of teachers and teachings he encountered before meeting Siddhartha (the historical Buddha) in the sixth century B.C.E. Each of these schools of thought was critical of the traditional India (Hindu) theory of "karma," the idea that all of our actions have consequences in a future life (that good people will be reborn in a better state and evil people in a worse state).

The first teacher was Purana Kassapa, who denied any causal connection between human action and its good or bad consequences in a future life ("karma").

> He who performs an act or causes an act to be performed, he who destroys life, the thief, the housebreaker, the plunderer, . . . the adulterer and the liar . . . commits no sin. Even if with a razor-sharp blade a man were to reduce all the life on earth to a single heap of flesh he would commit no sin. . . . From liberality, self-control, abstinence, and honesty is derived neither merit nor the approach of merit.
>
> (*Digha Nikaya*, in Embree, *Sources of Indian Tradition*)

The second teacher was Makkhali Gosala, a complete determinist, who argued that nothing can alter one's destiny; whatever one does, one's fate is already sealed and unavoidable; there is nothing anyone can do to alter or change one's allotted fate.

There is no deed performed either by oneself or by others [that can affect one's future births], no human action, no strength, no courage, no human endurance or human prowess [that can affect one's destiny in this life]. All beings, all that have breath, all that are born, all that have life, are without power, strength, or virtue, but are determined by destiny, chance, and nature.

(ibid.)

The third teacher the king met in his pursuit of enlightenment was Ajita Kesa-kambala, a materialist (perhaps a forerunner of the Carvacans, whom we will discuss later), who denied the existence of anything immaterial, whether gods, spirits, karmic consequences, or an afterlife.

There is no [merit in] almsgiving, sacrifice, or offering, no result or ripening of good or evil deeds. There is no passing from this world to the next. . . . There is no afterlife. . . . Man is formed of the four elements; when he dies earth returns to the aggregate of earth, water to water, fire to fire, and air to air, while the senses vanish into space. . . . They are fools who preach almsgiving, and those who maintain the existence of immaterial categories speak vain and lying nonsense. When the body dies, both fool and wise alike are cut off and perish. They do not survive after death.

(ibid.)

The fourth teacher King Ajatasatru met before turning to the Buddha was Pakudha Kacchayana, an atomist, who argued that nothing can alter the atoms in any way, and since these atoms are the only true reality, nothing any-one does to anything can in the least affect the underlying reality of that thing. Even if you kill someone, you have not in any way harmed, altered, or destroyed the reality, that is, the atoms.

The seven elementary categories [the atoms] are neither made nor ordered, neither caused nor constructed; they are barren, as firm as mountains, as stable as pillars. They neither change nor develop; they do not injure one another, and one has no effect on the joy or the sorrow . . . of another. What are the seven? The [micro-scopic] bodies of earth, water, fire, air, joy, and sorrow, with life as the seventh. . . . No man slays or causes to slay, hears or causes to hear, knows or causes to know. Even if a man cleave another's head with a sharp sword, he does not take life, for the sword-cut passes between the seven elements [atoms].

(ibid.)

The fifth teacher, Nigantha Nataputta, was probably Mahavira, the founder of the Jain religion, which still exists in India today, who taught the king that there are millions of souls (jiva), including the king's own soul, entrapped in matter, and who promised salvation as a means of releasing the jiva from its material prison. The sixth and last teacher with whom the king studied before seeking out Siddhartha (the Buddha) was Sanjaya Belatthiputa, a skeptic who denied the possibility of any genuine knowledge, denying that we can know whether there is or is not a soul, whether it can or cannot be freed, and so on.

> If you asked me "Is there another world?" and I believed that there was, I should tell you so. But that is not what I say. I do not say that it is so; I do not say that it is otherwise; I do not say that it is not so; nor do I say that is not not so.
>
> (ibid.)

Far from a traditional uniformity of opinion, the onset of philosophy, as we can see from the aforementioned, is generally marked by the rise of many different, competing views, whose proponents engage in endless debates for their favorite doctrines and against all of the others.

But why should we believe *any* of these philosophers with their new and radically different ideas? Certainly not from any traditional authority (which they all reject), but only from the weight of rational evidence that they adduce. In this sense, early Greek, Indian, and Chinese thinkers tried to prove their individual theories by carefully defining their terms, drawing distinctions, and constructing arguments for their positions and counterarguments against the positions of their opponents. Notice how the early twentieth-century Indian philosopher Sarvepalli Radhakrishnan, in *Indian Philosophy*, characterizes the beginnings of Indian philosophy:

> The age of Buddha (596–483 B.C.E.) represents the great springtide of philosophic spirit in India. The progress of philosophy is generally due to a powerful attack on a historical tradition when men feel themselves compelled to go back on their steps and raise once more the fundamental questions which their fathers had disposed of by the older schemes. The revolt of Buddhism and Jainism . . . forms an era in the history of Indian thought, since it finally exploded the method of dogmatism and helped to bring about a critical point of view. For the great Buddhist thinkers, logic was the main arsenal where were forged the weapons of universal destructive criticism. . . . The conservative schools were compelled to codify their views and set forth logical defenses of them.
>
> (Sarvepalli Radhakrishnan, *Indian Philosophy*)

To be fair, we should add that this characterization of philosophy as the critical chazllenge to traditional dogmatism most accurately represents only the *beginning* stages of philosophy, when it *first* arose in Greece, China, and

India. Later, its criticism of tradition itself becomes traditional. At first this is merely the necessary development of its own philosophical backlog or storehouse of basic ideas, concepts, logical and analytic tools that we spoke of earlier when defining philosophy. But this also can degenerate into a philosophical tradition of dogmatically accepted beliefs which is why later Greek and Roman philosophy, as well as later Chinese and Indian philosophy, tend to become orthodox and conservative.

When alien cultures borrow these original philosophies, they generally receive them in their well-established, conservative late phase. To the Romans, and later the Medieval Europeans, Greek philosophy was a highly revered, virtually completed system of thought. Similarly, Chinese philosophy was introduced into Japan with much the same aura of an established tradition of sanctified doctrine. Nonetheless, there still occur from time to time within well-defined philosophical traditions, whether Indian, Chinese, or Western, new philosophical movements (Romantic, Positivist, Existentialist, etc.) that philosophically challenge older schools of philosophy and even philosophy itself as traditionally understood, calling into question even the privileged role of reason as the final arbitrator of Truth and Goodness.

Like many cultural products, therefore, the history of philosophy tends to go through a predictable cycle of different stages—first a period of exciting innovation, followed by a period of more sober consolidation, and coming finally to a period of decline in which philosophy becomes momentarily exhausted, only to be reawakened once more by a return to the original phase of the cycle, a new period of exciting innovation, and so the cycle begins again. Thus, there is always a tension in any cultural product, such as philosophy or art, between innovation and tradition. To understand one another we must rely on a common vocabulary and a common tradition, but in order to speak to new issues we must also be constantly prepared to speak in new ways. One of the ways we can achieve this is to broaden our horizons by comparing philosophical traditions with artistic, religious, or scientific traditions, and also by comparing the philosophical traditions of our own culture with those of other cultures. Thus Greek philosophy stimulated Christian theology, modern science and mathematics sparked the growth of modern philosophy, Buddhism awakened the development of Hindu philosophy, and later Chinese philosophy, Western philosophy encouraged the reconstruction of Indian and Chinese philosophy around the turn of the twentieth century, and now Indian and Chinese philosophy are having a positive impact on Western philosophy.

It also follows from this scenario that the most interesting periods of philosophy may not always be the ones the orthodox defenders of that philosophical tradition think are best. From the twelfth century, Chinese philosophers have tended to regard their own neo-Confucianism as the culmination of the whole of Chinese philosophy, whereas philosophers today regard the earlier period (500 B.C.E.–400 C.E.) in which many different schools of philosophy flourished, actively vying with one another, as being far more important and interesting philosophically, though largely ignored by mainstream neo-Confucianism. Similarly, Indian philosophers at the turn of the twentieth century tended to think of the monistic Vedanta Hindu philosophy of Shankara as the peak and perfection of Indian philosophical development, virtually ignoring all of the earlier competing schools of Indian philosophy, while philosophers today tend to see the earlier period (500 B.C.E.–400 C.E.) as a much more lively and fruitful period of Indian philosophy.

Although philosophy arises out of an earlier religious and mythological orientation to the world, it does not replace religion, which continues to exist alongside philosophy, influencing and being influenced by it. Later, with the rise of modern science in the sixteenth century, we find religion, philosophy, and science all existing side by side, mutually influencing and being influenced by one another. Because philosophy arose gradually out of an earlier religious, mythological age, another problem we face in defining what philosophy is is in trying to differentiate philosophical from religious writing. Much of what we would probably want to include as Indian or Chinese philosophy is also classified as "religion," that is, as "religious" writing, especially Hinduism and Buddhism, but also Taoism and Confucianism.

But this is a problem that arises in the study of all of the philosophical traditions. Most Western philosophy during the medieval period in Europe (500–1500) is Christian philosophy, just as much, though by no means all, Indian and Chinese philosophy is Hindu, Buddhist, and Taoist. And here we must acknowledge that there is no firm consensus among scholars. Some Chinese experts exclude Buddhist writings from the catalogue of Chinese philosophy, while others, such as Fung Yulan and Hu Shih, include some (but not all) Buddhist texts within Chinese philosophy. Similarly, Indian scholars cannot agree about whether some parts of Hinduism, Buddhism, and Jainism qualify as philosophy or whether all such writing should be considered religion.

In this book we will argue on the side of those who *support* a *distinction* between religious and philosophical writings within Hinduism, Jainism, Buddhism, Taoism, and Christianity. But within Christianity, Hinduism, and Buddhism, how do we separate the religion from the philosophy? This is a large and difficult question, but let us begin by saying that religion is primarily a combination of personal faith (felt inner experience) and communal ritual activity, while the philosophy associated with religion is the attempt to intellectually explain, criticize, justify, and systematize religious beliefs, to resolve problems that arise in interpreting and defending religious texts, and to systematize many apparently different and even conflicting doctrines within a single all-embracing intelligible whole.

Religious texts speak, for example, of the difference between body and soul, but they do not bother to explain exactly what that distinction is or how the two are related; or we find scattered throughout religious texts statements which, taken together, appear contradictory. The "problem of evil," for example, is the problem of how to reconcile the religious beliefs that God is all powerful, and all good, and that evil, nonetheless, exists. If God is good and all-powerful, how could God allow evil to exist in our world? Any two of these three beliefs are logically consistent, but the three together seem contradictory. Perhaps God is good and all-powerful and there really is no evil (only the illusion of it). Or, maybe God is good but not all powerful (or all powerful and not completely good), and so there is no problem explaining how evil is possible. But how can evil exist if God is good and all powerful?

Similarly, there is the problem of intellectually reconciling in Buddhism how the soul can be born into a different body after death when, according to Buddhism, the soul does not exist. Or, within Christian religious doctrine, how God can be said to be eternal, supreme, and perfect and still be worried and concerned about human beings. (If God is absolutely perfect, needing and wanting nothing, wouldn't He be serenely indifferent? Or, on the other hand, if God worries about us, doesn't this indicate that He wants something He doesn't have and so is not absolutely perfect and self-contained?) Indian Hindu, Jain, and Buddhist schools all accepted the doctrine of karmic causality (what you do in this life affects what you will be in your next life), but this opened up the philosophical debate concerning precisely what is meant by causality, and in particular, whether causality produces something new, or whether the effect already exists in some sense in the cause. Finally, there is the intellectual problem of the meaning of religious language. If God is so completely different from us, how can we apply to God words like "love," "caring," "knowing," "making," and so on (which are normally applied to ordinary creatures, like ourselves)? And if we do not use words of ordinary language, how can we talk about God at all?

These are not *religious* problems, not problems for religious belief. But they can become problems for intellectuals, creating a stumbling block to religious belief. They are intellectual problems that must be resolved before these intellectuals can continue their religious progress. And of course it is precisely these intellectual (philosophical) problems associated with religious texts and religious beliefs that the critics of any religion will focus on in attacking that religion. So defenders of a particular religion will have to be prepared to answer such attacks, not those from the inside, so to speak, but attacks from the outside seeking to undermine the religion and supplant it with another. So the early Christian philosophers, such as Augustine, used philosophy (already 1,000 years old at the time) to refute other competing religions, such as Manicheanism (which Augustine himself followed for a time), to support some interpretations of Christian belief (that Jesus was both God and man, for example) and to argue against competing Christian interpretations (that Jesus was merely a man or that he was God merely pretending to be a man), and finally to defend Christianity against its critics (the followers of Mithric and Manichean religions, for example, or traditional Roman religion, or various well-established philosophical alternatives to religion, such as Stoicism and Epicurianism).

Of course, in order to use philosophy, Christian thinkers had to weed out of ancient pre-Christian Greek philosophy all of those ideas that directly contradicted the Bible. Greek philosophers held, for example, that the material world was eternal, that is, infinitely old, which was in direct conflict with the biblical doctrine that God had created the material world at some point in time. Nonetheless, reconciling the two did not prove terribly difficult. By rejecting the Greek idea that matter is eternal, they were able to utilize the rest of the Greek conception of matter, such as the atomic theory of matter developed by some of the Greek philosophers. By saying that God had created the atoms and the laws governing atoms, Christian philosophers and scientists could go on to describe scientifically how atoms behave after they had been created by God. And since some of the Greek philosophers (Socrates and Plato) had argued that the soul is immaterial and eternal, there was little difficulty in blending the Greek notion of a person as a combination of an immaterial soul in a material body with the Christian doctrine that God creates the immortal soul of each person (though, again, the Christian philosophers had to reject the Socratic doctrine that the soul existed eternally both before and after birth—like matter, God creates each soul at a particular point in time, more or less around the time of birth, plus or minus nine months, and so the soul is eternal not before but only after birth or quickening or conception).

Buddhists and Jains similarly developed philosophy to attack and refute traditional Hinduism (and to demonstrate the truth of Buddhism and Jainism), and Hindus were forced, in response, to develop their own philosophical weapons to defend themselves and to attack the rival Buddhists and Jains. Sometimes in the midst of defending their own religion against competing ones, a religion will absorb elements of the alien religion. (In general, the best way to defeat your opponent is to claim that his or her position is no different from your own!) Thus, for example (as we will see later), in defending Hinduism against Buddhism, Shankara developed the notion of God (Brahman) as an impersonal totality encompassing and absorbing into itself everything in the world. According to Shankara's interpretation of the ancient Hindu texts, there is only one real thing in the world, and that is God, or Brahman; everything else, like you and I, and all of the plants and animals and mountains and rivers and so on, do not exist as separate, individual entities, but are really just parts of God, or Brahman. This undermined the Buddhist argument against the mainstream Hindu conception of independently existing things in the world by claiming that this Buddhist conception was really Hindu! And by coopting a large part of Buddhism, Shankara was able to halt the spread of Buddhism, that is, the conversion by Hindus to Buddhism. But other Hindu philosophers, such as Ramanuja and Madhva, thought that Shankara had conceded too much to Buddhism. They argued instead for the more traditional and popular Hindu view, that God and individual selves, like you and I, and everything in the physical world, are individual entities separately existing in their own right.

For many religious thinkers, these intellectual problems and philosophical solutions are a decidedly nonreligious distraction to be tolerated, at best, if at all, only temporarily, as one might need to clear a roadblock before getting on with the really important task of continuing the journey. The early Christian church father, Tertullian, and the original Shakyamuni Buddha were quite concerned that philosophical questions not replace or become a substitute for religious concerns. However much philosophy may be able to reconcile apparent contradictions within religious belief or construct arguments for one religion and against another or rationally integrate different ideas within one logical system, there is still a great deal of any religion that can never be known by philosophy alone or expressed philosophically—the individual's experience of God, for example, or the details of a particular religion, like the Christian idea of the Trinity, which are revealed only in sacred scriptures.

As we will see in subsequent chapters, religious thinkers often want to say things that cannot be said within the logical limitations of philosophy. That does not mean those things are not true or meaningful, just that they cannot be part of philosophy. Reason and philosophy can only take us so far along the religious path; at some point the religious person must go beyond philosophy into a uniquely religious quest. As Tertullian said of distinctively religious beliefs, "I believe because it is absurd." The most famous medieval philosopher, Thomas Aquinas (who successfully, though not within his lifetime, introduced Aristotelianism into Christian theology), abandoned philosophy altogether toward the end of his life for a uniquely religious experience of strictly spiritual matters. And the nineteenth-century Danish Christian thinker, Soren Kierkegaard, said that in order to reach strictly religious beliefs, we must make a "leap of faith."

After approximately a century and a half of Islamic philosophy, Islamic religious leaders decided that it was not a good idea to try to mix religion with Greek philosophy, but that it was better to keep the religion pure and free of philosophical theorizing. But Islam is exceptional among the world religions in that regard. Christianity, Buddhism, and Hinduism made an early decision that however different philosophy and religion were, and however much more important, from their point of view, religion was than philosophy, nonetheless philosophy was necessary to remove intellectual obstacles to religious progress, to justify faith to skeptics, to defend the religion against attack, and to systematize and unify religious belief. In that sense, Nagarjuna, Seng Zhau, Hui Neng, Kukai are Buddhist philosophers, Shankara, Ramanuja, and Madhva are Hindu philosophers, and Augustine and Aquinas are Christian philosophers.

Religion is certainly one of the ways in which Chinese, Indian, and Western cultures are different. While they are generally *similar* in their *philosophical* analyses, they often are quite *different* from one another in the *religious* problem that the philosophical analysis is supposed to solve or clarify. As we noted earlier, while the worldviews of various cultures are different, the philosophical analysis, critique, and justification of those worldviews are much more similar. And, of course, religion is a large part of the worldview of a people, much more widely known than its philosophy. While the philosophical clarification of the concept of causality, for example, is basically the same in all three major traditions, Western philosophers (with the notable exceptions of Socrates and Plato) were not concerned with the Indian *religious* worry about karma and reincarnation. And while Indian, Western, and Chinese philosophers have all been interested in roughly similar ways of how to define Being, Non-being, and the Self, the *religious* motivation behind these analyses was quite different.

As we will see in subsequent chapters, the idea of self or mind in Western thought is quite different, for example, from the idea of the self or mind in Indian thought. Westerners tend to include within the self (mind) much more of our everyday consciousness and experience than Indians, who tend to lump together much of our everyday consciousness with the body and its five senses and emotions, reserving for the self (mind) something most of us do not ordinarily experience and are not familiar with in everyday life. So while analyses of mind (e.g., the relation of sensation to cognition and memory and prediction) are roughly the same in Western and non-Western philosophies, the religious notions of the "self" as something that survives or does not survive death (depending on the religion) are very different. In Western cultures, but not in India, the self that survives death is the self one knows from everyday experience. Since in Indian popular religious orientations elements of personality and self-identity (e.g., memory) are thought of as parts of the body and not of the self, they are not considered to be reincarnated from body to body, whereas in Western popular religious orientations, the self or soul includes the conscious mind (thinking, planning, remembering, knowing who we are, and so on), and this is what is thought to live on after death, whether in other bodies (Socrates and Plato) or in Heaven/Hell (later Christian thinkers).

In this sense, we can understand religious philosophy as a critique and analysis of a preexisting religion and therefore generally arising long after the religion has become established. Hindu religion existed in India thousands of years before Hindu philosophy arose around 500 B.C.E., as Radhakrishnan points out in his earlier quotation. This means that the important Hindu writings, known as the *Upanishads*, most of which appeared *before* 500 B.C.E., will *not* be considered part of Indian "philosophy," however awe inspiring and profound they are in other respects. They represent, as we said earlier, the *precursors* of Indian philosophy, in the same way the cosmological writing of Hesiod in the eighth century B.C.E. is a precursor to Greek philosophy and the *Spring and Autumn Annals* (tenth century B.C.E.) and the *I Jing* (eighth century B.C.E.) may be considered precursors of Chinese philosophy.

As well-known Ghanian philosopher Kwasi Wiredu has insisted, in any cultural comparison we must compare "equals with equals." That is, if we are going to include the Upanishads as part of Indian philosophy, then we must include Hesiod; and if we follow Western philosophical tradition in excluding Hesiod from Western philosophy, then by the same token, we must exclude the early Upanishads. These "precursors" of philosophy, we may say, are what philosophers were talking and writing *about*—that is, what they were trying to clarify, systematize, justify, and criticize. Thus, Confucian and Taoist philosophers wrote *about* the *I Jing*, and Shankara, Ramanuja, and Madhva wrote *about* the *Upanishads*.

If we compare Western *philosophy*, as we have defined it, with Indian religion and Chinese *cosmology*, then, of course, comparing unequals ("apples and oranges"), we will find great differences between East and West, just as we would find great differences if we compared *Western* philosophy to *Western* religion or ancient cosmologies. But if we compare equals to equals ("apples with apples"), then we need to compare Western philosophy, as distinguished from Western religion and cosmologies, to non-Western philosophy, also distinguished from non-Western religion and cosmologies, and then East–West differences will not be so great, as we will see throughout this book.

Putting the point more generally, we need to distinguish the philosophy of a culture from that culture in general. We cannot assume that because Aristotle discussed problems of knowledge in ways we still find useful today that the entire culture of Aristotle's Greece in the fourth century B.C.E. is identical or even similar to our own. Our ideas of education, industrial production, science, religion, political equality, and the nation-state are all fundamentally alien to those with which Aristotle was familiar. As we said earlier in discussing the role of philosophy in religion, problems of knowledge may arise in very different ways in different cultures—one culture being interested in knowledge as a means of mastering "nature," another as a means of achieving religious "salvation," another as a way to establish objective criteria for rational debate, and yet another to understand and assimilate one's own cultural heritage. Nonetheless, once knowledge has been recognized as a fundamental problem to be solved for any of these various cultural reasons, the analysis of knowledge generally proceeds in quite similar ways.

Similarly, the problem of the relation of mind and body may arise in different ways in different cultures—one culture being concerned with the separation of the mind from the body after death; another culture being more interested in the problem of "free will," that is, how the mind can cause the body to move and act; and still another culture being obsessed with the problem of how the body relays knowledge to the mind through the five bodily sense organs. Nonetheless, once mind has been isolated as a problem to be solved, the analysis of mind is generally the same. In a like way, alchemy (out of which modern chemistry evolved) developed in China and Europe in similar ways, though for very different reasons—in China as a way to achieve immortality and in Europe as a way to master nature (turning base metals into gold, for example).

Consider the philosophy of language. The cultural background for the problem of linguistic analysis is distinctly different in Chinese, Indian, and Western cultures. In India, for example, there is an ancient tradition (long before philosophy) in which the sacred scriptures, the Vedas, are said to be eternal. That is, the ancient Hindu religious belief is that these sacred words existed even before they were written down, first spoken by human beings, and first thought of by the gods. Rather, the idea is, they have *always* existed —before the gods, before human beings, before oral or written language—indeed, before the universe itself emerged. But of course that raises the question, how is that possible? How can there be language without human or other creatures speaking or writing that language? And that gets us into the question of what language is. But once Indian intellectuals take on this question the answers they provide are similar to those in the Chinese and Greek philosophy of language. How much of language is conventional, and how much of it is based on reality? What is the relation between nouns and verbs, proper and common nouns, and so on?

To take another example, the traditional Indian problem of "consciousness" is quite different from that in the West. In the West we think of consciousness as what human beings do when they think (as we know this from our own experience) and then transfer that more or less to God when we think of God (or gods) as thinking about what they want to do and how to go about doing it. But in India there is an ancient Hindu religious tradition (much older than the beginning of Indian philosophy) in which consciousness is identified with the underlying reality of the universe (which in turn is identified with Brahman—and with the self, Atman). But that raises all sorts of problems about what sort of consciousness the universe itself could have.

What would it be conscious *of?* There is nothing else besides itself that it *could* be conscious of, and does it make any sense to speak of a consciousness that is not conscious *of* something? In that case, what are we talking about? And does this kind of talk really make sense? We know from the sacred Vedic texts that it is not the usual sort of consciousness we are familiar with in our own everyday conscious lives (desiring this or that, planning how to get it, going after it, and later either enjoying it or feeling bad we missed it, and so on). But if it is not this ordinary sort of consciousness, what else can it be?

This then led Indian philosophers to a deeper reflection and analysis of mind and thought and consciousness. Perhaps, as Shankara later said (see chapter 3), there are different levels of consciousness—a middle of the day, "two cups of coffee" type of consciousness, for example, but also an "automatic pilot" kind of consciousness that we employ when we are doing something familiar, such as driving a car; and maybe also the type of reverie we experience just before we fall asleep; there also is dream consciousness; and finally, maybe even the kind of consciousness of deep, dreamless sleep (but does that count as consciousness? (On the one hand, we would say that we were "unconscious," but on the other hand, the fact that we are able to report the next morning that "we slept well" during the night does seem to suggest—maybe—some degree of consciousness.) Perhaps it is this last sort of consciousness that the universe (Atman, Brahman) experiences.

But other Indian Hindu Vedanta philosophers, Ramanuja and Madhva, believed that Brahman was a personal God which was distinct both from the physical world and also from individual selves. They therefore opposed Shankara's attempt to merge the individual self into Brahman in which the individuality of the self would be lost, as the individuality of a drop of rain water is lost when it falls into the ocean. And so they vigorously argued against Shankara. They doubted whether this cosmic unconsciousness could really be considered a form of consciousness. If Brahman is conscious, then Brahman must be conscious of things other than Brahman. And so, rejecting Shankara's monistic One, Ramanuja and Madhva would return us to the familiar common sense plurality of many different physical objects, along with many different minds, and possibly one or more gods.

And, if Shankara is right, then this deepest unconscious sort of consciousness is the consciousness of our "real" selves and so the key to religious salvation is to learn how to move from the ordinary sorts of consciousness we experience in daily life to this mysterious but basic sort of consciousness—that of dreamless sleep (without actually going to sleep, of course)—a wildly counterintuitive notion that Ramanuja and Madhva strongly opposed. So, even though the religious problem to be solved, the background cultural situation or context, is quite different from what we are familiar with in the West, Indian philosophers in trying to solve that problem nonetheless developed some extremely interesting theories about human consciousness that are very similar to Western (the Freudian unconscious, for example) and Chinese theories.

In this way we may be able to distinguish the relatively more universal from the relatively more specific aspects of a culture. While all cultural products, including philosophy, are integrated into the broader culture, some are relatively more independent and therefore more crossculturally universal—art and philosophy, for example, being relatively more universal than specific forms of government or marriage customs. As contemporary Ghanaian philosopher Kwame Gyekye, in *Tradition and Modernity: Philosophical Reflections on the African Experience*, puts it,

> The universality of philosophical ideas may be put down to the fact that human beings, irrespective of their cultures and histories, share certain basic values; our common humanity grounds the adoption and acceptance of some ideas, values, and perceptions, as well as the appreciation of the significance of events taking place beyond specific cultural borders. This being so, problems dealt with by philosophers may be seen as human problems—rather than as African, European, or Asian—and hence, as universal. . . . The main point, however, . . . is that human problems can invariably be contextualized, for they arise in, or out of, certain historical or cultural situations. This being so, the approach to solving them need not be the same; different ideas and therapies may be required, even though one need not deny that the required ideas and therapies may in fact be adopted from the experiences of other peoples and cultures.

(Gyekye, *Tradition and Modernity: Philosophical Reflections on the African Experience*)

But even in those relatively more specific aspects of culture, we need to be careful not to accept too readily simplistic stereotypes of divergent Western and Asian cultural "values." We are often told, for example, that Asian people are more communal than Westerners (and that Westerners are, in contrast, more individualistic than Asians). That is, Asians are said to see themselves in terms of the group, and are therefore more willing to sacrifice for and serve the group interests, even when these may conflict with their own individual preferences or interests, whereas Westerners tend to see themselves as being more isolated, self-interested, and self-sufficient individuals in competition with others, more willing to "step over" other people in order to successfully compete, and, more important, more willing to sacrifice the good of the group for their own individual good.

This is a compelling and in many ways appealing picture of broad cultural differences, one that is fairly straightforward and easy to grasp. It might seem useful to turn to philosophy as a way of explaining these fundamental cultural differences. Indeed, one reason Indian and Chinese intellectuals around 1920 explored the idea of three different original world philosophies, Indian, Chinese, and Western, was to develop the idea that these philosophies represent three distinct worldviews, that the Indian people have always looked at the world in a unique way that is fundamentally different from that of the Chinese, who have always seen things completely differently from Indians or Westerners. Just as the Chinese are racially different from the Indians who are racially different from the Europeans, so the idea was there are absolutely fundamental, unalterable, biological differences in the world outlooks of these different peoples. And philosophy, they thought, is an excellent way to understand these distinct human perspectives on the world. If one wants to understand the Indian people, read their philosophy; if one wants to know more about the Chinese and how they view things, study their philosophy; and if one wonders how Europeans got to be so technologically and militarily aggressive, read Western philosophy.

At the same time, however, this simple picture is challenged by several conflicting factors. First is the obvious fact that these opposed paradigms at best represent only *part* of the total picture. One of the main ideas underlying the notion that Chinese thought is communal is the perception that Chinese thought is Confucian and Confucianism is generally thought to be communal. But, as we will see in later chapters, not *all* Chinese theory and practice is Confucian; there also is Taoism, Buddhism, and other schools of philosophy that argue directly against Confucianism, especially Taoism, which has vigorously opposed for several thousand years the Confucian human-centered communal ideal in favor of an extreme individualism in which the individual identifies with nature, rather than with society. There also are considerable differences, as we will see, *within* Confucianism. Most notable in this regard is Xunzi's theory of human nature as being selfish and aggressive (in need of the modifying influences of social acculturation), and therefore highly individualistic.

Nor is Western thought and practice any more uniformly individualistic, as we will see in subsequent chapters. For every influential individualist, such as Thomas Hobbes (English, seventeenth century) or John Stuart Mill (English, nineteenth century), one can find plenty of Western communitarians, for example, Plato (Greek, fourth century B.C.E.), Rousseau (Swiss, eighteenth century), Hegel (German, nineteenth century) and Marx (German Jew, nineteenth century). At most, we could only say that the Western ideal tends to be more individualistic, and that the Asian ideal tends to be relatively more communal.

This relatively simple and straightforward contrast of Western and Asian cultures is further complicated when we notice that many non-Western groups outside of Asia are also said to be communal. So, for example, African society is said to be communal, thus resembling the Confucian ideal. Notice how Nigerian philosopher Ifeanyi Menkiti puts it: "As far as Africans are concerned, the reality of the communal world takes precedence over the reality of the individual life histories; . . . it is the community which defines the person as person" (in *African Philosophy*, 3d ed., edited by Richard A. Wright, ed.) Similarly, Native American, American Hispanic, and indeed virtually every non-Western society is said to be communal. Even more confusing is the fact that in the gender debates over women's liberation, women (even Western women) are said to be more communal in their outlook than men. So it begins to look as though everyone in the world is this way, except Western males. But when we look back in history, we see that even they were communal in outlook until fairly recently, that is, until the seventeenth century or so. If we look at Plato's *The Republic*, for example, we see a clear example of communalism.

Adding to the confusion, we learn that the most traditionally communal societies are now becoming *less* so (as judged by standard measures of communalism, such as family size and integrity). Japan is perhaps the most communal society in the world, yet even here we find each year an increase in the number and percentage of older Japanese (with living family members) living out their lives alone in nursing homes, as well as an increase in the number and percentage of single young people (male and female) moving out of their parent's home after they have finished school and begun work, but before they marry. Similarly, in Africa, the size of households decreases yearly from large "extended families" of twenty or more to small "nuclear families" of less than ten. The same seems to be true if we look at other empirical criteria of "communalism." Of course, by any empirical measures, Japanese and African societies are still more communal than most Western societies, but the point is that they are becoming *less* so, year by year.

At the same time, and this too is confusing, Chinese, Japanese, and African countries (among many others) *bemoan* these changes that are occurring within their own societies. In other words, these societies do not *behave* as they say they *believe*. For this reason it often is unclear what is meant when it is said that Asian societies are communal—whether it means that they were traditionally and historically communal in the past, or that communalism is highly valued, praised, and admired today by Asian people who no longer "practice what they preach," or that Asian social practices are in fact still communal. Misunderstanding occurs when empirical claims are confused with nostalgic evaluative claims regarding ancient traditional values, such as when outsiders are led to believe that Asian societies continue to be highly communal (which may in fact be false), because the speaker *wishes* Asian societies could continue to uphold communal values.

Putting all of this confusing data together, what sense can we make of the East–West distinction as one of communalism versus individualism? It begins to look more and more like a distinction between different stages of historical and technological development, and less and less like an eternal, "essentialist" or racial distinction between cultures or peoples. What we find when we have sifted through this maze of confusing data is that all traditional societies tend to be more or less communal, while all modern societies tend to be more or less individualistic. It does not matter whether the societies in question are European, African, Asian, or Native American. Less modern (more traditional) European societies such as Portugal, Albania, or Romania are more communal and less individualistic than those of Germany, Britain, or France, while more modern Asian societies such as South Korea, Singapore, Hong Kong, and Taiwan are less communal and more individualistic than more traditional Asian societies such as mainland China, Vietnam, Cambodia, or Laos. So-called Asian, African, and Islamic values seem to diminish with the rise of a viable middle class.

We need to be cautious, therefore, and "take with a grain of salt" the claim that Asians are communal in outlook whereas Westerners are individualistic. At the very most, this claim amounts to little more than the generalization that societies tend, on the whole, to become more individualistic as they modernize and that more modern, developed societies therefore tend, on the whole, to be more individualistic than less modern, developing societies, which, by contrast, tend, on the whole, to be more communal.

We also need to be sensitive to the reasons people may have for *making* these claims. Some Westerners might be unhappy with what they perceive to be the materialistic, aggressive, egoistic side of their own culture and therefore might be tempted to look to Asia to provide a more spiritual, holistic, and communal antidote. By the same token, some developing societies may be tempted to overcome colonially induced feelings of inferiority by describing their own underdeveloped society as being superior in spiritual and communal values, though poor economically and technologically backward. And here a paradoxical meeting of minds results, reinforcing these essentialist, racialist stereotypes between a Western stereotype of the Asian "other" and an Asian stereotype of itself. Some governments of developing countries may be tempted to excuse problems of rising crime and corruption in their countries as the result of introducing too many Western (materialistic, individualistic) values too quickly, thereby undermining "Asian (spiritual, communal) values." And the rulers of some developing countries may be tempted to excuse their own suppression of human rights by saying that they embrace "Asian values" of hierarchical authoritarianism and reject "Western values" of individual rights and freedoms. And, by the same token, some Western countries and corporations may excuse corrupt business practices and human rights abuses in developing countries in which they are operating by assuming the posture of a "tolerant respect for Asian values which are very different from our own."

Nonetheless, when all is said and done, important cultural differences remain—whether due to historical, developmental, or more essential factors—though we will find there are fewer differences in philosophy than in other aspects of culture. In this book we will look at both the *differences* in Indian, Chinese, and European *cultures* and the *similarities* in their *philosophies*.

2

Logic and Language

HILOSOPHY, we have said, is a critique of commonsense, traditional views. But how can philosophers convince others? Philosophers criticize the authority of tradition as well as unusual mystical experiences as proper sources of belief. Why? Because these sources of belief are not crossculturally universal. But do philosophers have a *better* way to discover the truth? If so, what is it, and *why* is it better? How can they answer these questions in a way that will be convincing to everyone from every culture or time period or geographical area? But this just raises the more general question, what *is* (real or genuine) knowledge, truth, evidence, and justified belief? This is why philosophers have always been centrally concerned with logic (which we will examine in this chapter) and epistemology, or the theory of knowledge (which we will discuss in the next chapter).

Before we can criticize traditional knowledge claims and before we try to advance our own knowledge claims in opposition to the claims of other philosophers, we need to become clear about what exactly knowledge is, how it can be attained, and why some knowledge claims have a better right to be believed than others. Before we can hope to convince others that God exists or does not exist, that pleasure is or is not the only good thing in life, or that democracy is or is not the best form of government, we must first answer the questions: How do you *know*? What is good evidence? What counts as proof or justification?

One thing we know is that philosophical evidence is not empirical or factual, as is true in the natural sciences. In chapter 1 we defined philosophy as a critical, rational, and normative reflection of what we already know in an intuitive way. Philosophy is not, therefore, a science; it cannot discover any new facts or give us any new information. Philosophical disputes generally begin after all of the empirical facts have been agreed upon. In the abortion debate, for example, everyone agrees about what a human embryo is like at five or six weeks, and what it can and cannot do at that stage. The philosophical question is whether the embryo is a human being or not. Like most philosophical questions, this is a conceptual, not a factual, question. What does it *mean* for something to be a human being? What does this word or concept of "human being" entail?

How *do* we define "human being"? Ordinarily we think of a human being as something that is able to walk and talk, for example, which the embryo cannot do; but on the other hand, we think of a human being as the offspring of other human beings and as something having the genetic coding (DNA) of a human being, which the embryo certainly does have. So, while it is clear that my roommate is a human being (though a rather gross one) and my study lamp is not, it is not so clear in the case of a human embryo at one month. According to part of the ordinary meaning of the concept of a human being, the fetus *is* a human being, and according to another part of the ordinary meaning, it is *not*—and that is precisely why abortion, like other philosophical problems, is such a difficult issue. Philosophical questions, then, are conceptual, not factual or empirical.

Philosophy, we are saying, is a "reflection" on our ordinary ways of seeing, talking, and thinking about (that is, our ordinary concepts of) the world. Philosophy can therefore be defined (as it is defined by contemporary American philosopher Arthur Danto) as the relationship between words and objects (concepts and reality). This is one way in which philosophy is different from our ordinary way of looking at things. Ordinarily we do not concentrate on the words we use to describe objects, but simply on the objects themselves that those words refer to. When I am looking over the menu in my favorite restaurant (especially if I am hungry), I am not thinking about the printing fonts of the words, but of the food those words refer to. Words, as ways of thinking and talking, we might say, are normally "transparent" to us.

That is, words normally seem like "natural" labels for things. Indeed, words are normally so intimately associated with the objects they refer to that we generally do not really distinguish between the two. A West African proverb says that "a skunk has no nose"; that is, a skunk is so used to the smell of other skunks that it no longer notices it (much less is offended by it!). The ancient Chinese Taoists have an expression: "When you point to the moon, don't mistake the finger for the moon." The Chinese word for finger ("zhi") is also the word for concept, so the expression also means, "When you describe something or think about it, don't confuse your description or thought for the thing you are describing and thinking about." Who would ever make such a mistake, you might wonder. But, of course, the Taoists would only advise us *not* to do this if they thought that that is precisely what we ordinarily *do*, that is, confuse words with the objects they refer to.

But when we do begin to concentrate and reflect on the ways in which we describe and think about the world (rather than the world itself) and to think about the relationship between words and objects, strange things begin to happen—words appear *more* permanent, while physical objects seem *less* permanent than we had imagined before—and this leads to all sorts of interesting problems. Words (or concepts, that is, the *meaning* of words) considered in isolation from particular physical objects are unchanging, while the physical objects that these words name are constantly changing, never remaining the same from one moment to the next. Cats change from kittens to fat, lazy cats, but the meaning of the word "c-a-t" is the same today as it was thousands of years ago when the Egyptians worshipped them.

You are different than you were fifteen years ago, but your mother still recognizes you, calling you by the same name and regarding you as the same person. In everyday life, before philosophical reflection, we *combine* word and object and act as though you are the *same* person you were fifteen years ago. In reality, of course, you are very different, both physically and mentally and in terms of your interests, tastes, and abilities, but since the same words apply to you ("person," and your name), we act as though you are the same. A tree also is changing all of the time (losing its leaves in the fall, growing new leaves and branches in the spring, gradually getting taller and more hollow inside, and so on); but during many years of change, it still remains a tree, though *some* changes will cause the tree to stop being a tree. When does a tree *stop* being a tree? When it is cut down and made into lumber or firewood or newsprint—that is, when it no longer fits our definition of the word "tree" and begins to fit our definition of words like "lumber" or "firewood." Ironically, then, it is words that give objects their longevity!

How do you classify and identify yourself (that is, into what category or concept do you put yourself)? As a "human being" you exist from birth till death. But suppose you identify yourself, not with your body, but with your soul, which you believe exists eternally (through reincarnation) both in the past and also into the future. Then you are no long twenty-something years old but well over a million years old! Or suppose you join a religious cult in which you are "reborn" as a "born-again" entity, which you now think of as your real self. In that case you are only one year old!

In everyday life, word and object are unconsciously joined together. We see things *in terms of* our words; growing up in a particular society we automatically see this thing as a cat and that thing as a butterfly. Only when we begin to philosophically reflect on the relation of word and object do the two begin to split apart—the word on one side and the object on the other side. As we have just seen, when we reflect on words apart from the objects they refer to, the words seem more permanent than ordinary objects. And by separating word and object, the objects seem far less permanent than usual.

Out of this separation of word and object arises logical paradoxes, that is, statements that seem to be logically correct but that obviously are false to common sense—and this is where philosophy begins. The sixth-century B.C.E. Greek philosopher, Heraclitus said, "You can't step twice into the same river," to which Cratylus replied, "You can't step even *once* into the same river." Why not? Because the river is constantly changing—the river you step into the second time is a different river; indeed, the river you first stick your toe into is different from the river a split second later when your foot has reached the bottom of the riverbed. Chinese Neo-Taoist philosophers (third to sixth century C.E.) argued similarly that the finger ("zhi") could not reach the table, and if it did, it could not be removed.

> The Minister Yueh was asked by a visitor about the statement, "A zhi (finger) does not reach." Yueh did not analyze the sentence but immediately touched the table with the handle of a deer's-tail fly-whisk, saying, "Does it reach or not?" The visitor answered, "It does." Yueh then raised the fly-whisk and asked, "If there was a reaching, how can it be removed?"
>
> (Chinese Neo-Taoist philosopher, *Contemporary Records*, in Chan, *A Sourcebook in Chinese Philosophy*)

But this directly contradicts common sense, which firmly believes that this is the same river we have been crossing and recrossing for hundreds of years, just as it is perfectly obvious that I can easily touch the table with my finger (or fly-whisk) and then just as easily lift it from the table. Another logical puzzle is Chinese philosopher Gong-Sun Lung's (fourth century B.C.E.) famous paradox, "a white horse is not a horse." But of course, a white horse *is* a horse, just as we certainly *can* step once, twice, and indeed many times into the same river, and touch the table and remove our finger as often as we like. Because these claims of reason directly contradict common sense, they are ultimately unacceptable, though it is not clear why they are wrong, where and how, exactly, they are mistaken—and this is what makes them so puzzling. And it is precisely to solve these puzzles that logic (and philosophy) is born.

As we saw in chapter 1, besides factual, empirical questions, there also are normative and definitional questions: Is a five-week embryo a "human being"? Is a urinal taken from a men's room (Duchamp's "The Fountain") a "work of art"? Is Scientology a "religion"? These normative and definitional questions are generally the ones left for the philosophers (especially after the scientists have taken over all of the strictly empirical questions). How do philosophers deal with these nonempirical (definitional and normative) questions? Through reasoning, that is, through logic.

In our earlier example concerning the debate over abortion, all parties to the dispute agree on all of the facts—how the fetus has developed and what it looks like at two months or three months, what will happen to it if it is removed, what will probably happen to it if it is left in the woman's womb, and so on. The philosophical question is whether or not the fetus is a human being, that is, if "human being" is the right expression or concept to use when describing the fetus.

Consider a brain-dead person. Is he or she a human being? Is he or she dead or alive? It depends on how one defines the words "dead" and "alive," that is, what one *means* by these expressions. The heart is still beating; he or she continues breathing and digesting food; he or she is still warm—and yet he or she also seems more like a vegetable than a living human being. Of course, you already know what the words "dead" and "alive" mean, but in these puzzling, borderline cases we realize that our ordinary, intuitive notions are not quite clear, so we begin to philosophically reflect on and try to clarify these concepts.

Also consider the debate over distributive justice, that is, the question of what is the most fair and just way to divide the economic pie. Should we distribute things according to merit and talent (giving more to some and less to others), or should we simply divide the economic pie into equal shares, as we do a late-night pizza, giving each person the same amount, regardless of merit or contribution? In debates like this, everyone agrees on the facts—that the distribution of wealth by merit and ability leads eventually to inequality of wealth (the smarter and more talented people getting more); that inequality of wealth leads to inequality of educational opportunities for the next generation (because wealthy families will try to give their children every advantage over other children); that competition leads to greater national wealth (the success of capitalism over communism), while lack of competition tends to stifle motivation, and so on. Of course, each side in the debate will tend to emphasize those facts that best support its case and to play down those more damaging facts, but nonetheless, all sides in the debate agree basically on what the facts are. It is only after all of the empirical facts are agreed upon that the philosophical debate begins: Is abortion right or wrong? Is equal pay for equal ability (and unequal pay for unequal ability) fair and just?

In these kinds of debates, we must turn from empirical verification to logical analysis. Philosophers have therefore always concentrated on logic. Logic may be defined as the science of correct reasoning. (Notice that the term *correct* indicates, again, the normative nature of philosophical inquiry, differentiating logic, for example, from psychology, which investigates, among other things, *not correct* reasoning but how people *actually do* reason—sometimes, as in times of great stress, quite *incorrectly.*)

A great deal of logic is concerned with the relations words have to one another. Just from the meaning of the words "horse," "unicorn," and "grass eating," quite apart from any physical objects in the real world these words may or may not refer to, we know that if there are any unicorns they probably eat grass (because unicorns are just like horses, except for the horn, and horses eat grass, so unicorns must also eat grass). If I tell you that I plan to carry Judy, my pet guppy, into town tonight in my shirt pocket, you will probably fear for Judy's life. Why? You've never even met Judy! But you know that Judy is a guppy and, even if you have never seen a guppy, you know that the meaning of the word is related to the word "fish" and that that word is related to the word "aquatic." So without knowing anything about Judy, except that she is a guppy, you know that she is a fish and therefore cannot live out of water, so she will surely die in my shirt pocket on the way into town this evening.

The meaning of the word guppy is completely contained within the meaning of the word fish, and the meaning of the word fish is completely contained within the meaning of the word aquatic (meaning "must live in water, cannot live out of water"). Since the word "all" captures this sense of the meaning of one word being completely contained within the meaning of another word, we can express the relations among these words in the following logical argument: "Judy is a guppy; all guppies are fish; all fish require water; therefore, Judy requires water." Putting the point another way, the meaning of the word fish completely excludes the meaning of "air breathing"—so we can say, "No fish is air breathing," and then reconstruct the aforementioned argument as follows: "Judy is a guppy; all guppies are fish; no fish is air breathing; therefore, Judy is not air breathing." Or we can express these relations of words to one another using the hypothetical language of "if . . . then": "If anything is a fish, then it cannot live outside of water; Judy is a fish; therefore, Judy cannot live outside of water." Logic, therefore, turns attention away from the things in the world to the words we use to describe those things, concentrating on the logical relationships words have to one another.

In our earlier example, if we decide that the fetus is a human being, then abortion is murder. Why? Because of the meaning of the word "murder." Can a cat murder a mouse? Can a tiger murder a human being? Can a human being murder a cockroach? No. A cat can *kill* a mouse; a tiger can *kill* a human being; and a human being can *kill* a cockroach, but none of these are acts of murder. Why not? Because the word "murder" means the deliberate killing by one human being of another human being—unless *both* are human beings (and the action was deliberate), it is not murder. But in the case of abortion, the doctor is certainly a human being and she or he certainly kills the fetus deliberately, so by the ordinary English meaning of the word "murder," if the fetus is also a human being, then it follows that abortion is murder—all of this follows from the meanings of words. But *is* a fetus a human being? That depends, as we saw earlier, on what we *mean* by the words "human being."

But, of course, if we are not to wind up wasting our time building conceptual castles in the sky (or corrals for unicorns), we must have some assurance that our words are also correctly (there is that normative word again!) related to things in the world that those words are supposed to refer to, represent, classify, or designate. We have said that philosophy is a "reflection" of ordinary ways of seeing, talking, and thinking about the world—in other words, thinking about how our ordinary ways of thinking connect (or do not connect) with reality. This is part of the concern of philosophers with the relationship between words and objects (that is, thought and language on one side and reality and the world on the other).

Another way to put this is to say that philosophy is concerned with the way language "represents" the world. As we saw earlier, we do not see objects as mere things, but only as things of a certain meaningful kind—we see this as a cat and that as a butterfly—we see objects *through* the words we use to describe them. As the Indian Nyaya philosophers put it, "What is denoted by the word 'cow' is not the mere individual by itself, without any qualifications, and as apart from the universal [cows in general] to which it belongs, but the individual as qualified by and along with the universal [cows in general]." We cannot grasp the world directly, just as it is in itself; we can only represent the world to ourselves through the medium of signs and symbols, that is, through language. The question is, *how well* does language represent the world? Are our linguistic representations of the world accurate or inaccurate, realistic or illusory, true or false? And how do we *know* that? If we never see the world itself, how can we compare it with our representations of it? How can we *compare* the two? How can we even *see the distinction* between the two?

Contemporary French "deconstructionist" philosophers like Jacques Derrida argue that since there is ultimately no way to tell which linguistic description is more accurate than another, linguistic descriptions cease to be representations, that is, they are not about the world at all, but exist in their own sphere as visible marks on paper or as an audible sound. This would be like an archer shooting arrows but without any target. Without a target it would make no sense to say that the archer was shooting at anything, accurately or inaccurately.

Similarly, the contemporary American philosopher Willard V. O. Quine has argued that it is impossible to ever know for sure what a foreign language speaker is referring to or how he thinks of whatever it is he is referring to. In his famous argument for the "indeterminacy of translation," Quine imagines that we are observing a native speaker who shouts, pointing to a rabbit running across the field, "Gavagai!" At first we think "Gavagai" means what "rabbit" means in English, but as Quine points out, how can we be sure "Gavagai" does not refer to a part of the rabbit's body (the tail, for example, and not the rabbit as a whole) or to an event which the rabbit is engaged in (not "rabbit" but "running fast across an open space"). At first we might think we can settle these doubts, correct any inaccuracies, and improve our translation by further observation of the native speaker's behavior and accompanying speech, but, as Quine points out, each new observation runs into exactly the same problem all over again. Like double-checking measurements with a faulty tape measure, we just keep repeating and multiplying our mistakes. Double-checking our translation of "event," for example, or "tail," it is still unclear whether the native speaker is referring to an "event" or to the "surrounding physical environment," to the "tail," or to "white," or perhaps "bobbing," thus getting us no closer to an answer after all!

It is possible, therefore, for two equally competent translators to come up with different translations of the language of the native speaker, and there is no way to ever tell which translation is better. (You can imagine what Quine would think of the attempt described in chapter 1 to determine whether "philosophy" is a good translation of "zi," "jia," and "darshana"!) Thus, by observing the native speaker's speech patterns and accompanying behavior, we can never know what he means or how he sees things. Without the assurance that our language accurately refers to things in the world that can be understood by others, we seem to live, each of us, in his or her private, insulated world, closed off from all contact with other human beings. (If this example seems far fetched—remember it is only a thought experiment—there are plenty of actual examples to consider, as, for example, when the Portuguese, in teaching Japanese a few words of Portuguese in the sixteenth century, pointed to a cake in a castle-shaped box, saying "cake" (in Portuguese); the Japanese thought the word "cake" (in Portuguese) referred to castles, and the word stuck—"We'd like to invite you to tour our tenth-century cake.")

Every normative question in philosophy (How can we get it right?) has a possible *skeptical* answer: "You can never get it right; it is impossible!" Deconstruction and Quinian indeterminacy are twentieth-century skeptical answers to the question: How can we make sure our words accurately correspond to reality? But such skeptical responses are as old as philosophy itself, and there are many examples of ancient Greek, Indian, and Chinese skeptics questioning the possibility of language correctly representing reality. Recall the sixth-century B.C.E. Indian skeptic Sanjaya Belatthiputa, mentioned in chapter 1, who denied the possibility of our knowing anything. As the fourth-century B.C.E. Chinese Taoist philosopher Zhuangzi points out, everyone has a different opinion about everything, and each person, whether he is a fool or a sage, thinks his representation of the world is better than everyone else's. But since there is no way to tell which opinions are better representations than others, then in the end can we honestly say that any of them are really representations? And in that case, isn't all of this talk just a lot of noise and hot air?

> If men are to be guided by opinions, who will not have such a guide? Not only those who know . . . have opinions; the fools have theirs too. But if we cannot adjudicate among these opinions, which is right and which is wrong, we are driven to absurdities, as inconceivable as that one goes to Yueh today, but arrived there yesterday. That is to make what is not what is. How to make what is not what is even the sage Yu could not know. So, how can I do it? Speech is not merely the blowing of wind. It is intending to say something. But what it has succeeded in saying is not absolutely established. If so, then is there really such a thing as speech? Is there really no such thing as speech? We normally consider speech as different from the chirping of young birds. But is there any distinction between them, or is there no distinction?
>
> (Zhuangzi, 1994)

We should not imagine that the philosophers who raise these paradoxes are always frustrated, bewildered, perplexed, or frightened by them, or indeed take them too seriously. Often, as with Zhuangzi, they are engaged in playfully, as we can see in the following humorous exchange between Zhuangzi and Hui Shih:

> Zhuangzi and Hui Shih were once strolling along a path which led across a small stream, when Zhuangzi turned to Hui Shih and said, "Look how the fish are jumping; it seems to give them pleasure." Hui Shih answered, "You are not a fish, so how do you know what gives them pleasure?" Zhuangzi said, "You are not I, so how do you know that I do not know what gives pleasure to the fish?" Hui Shih replied, "I am not you, and therefore do not know what you know and what you do not know. But one thing I do know for sure is that you are not a fish, and therefore it has to be proved that you know what gives pleasure to the fish." Zhuangzi said, "Let us return to the first question. You were asking me, 'How do you know what gives pleasure to the fish?' But this very question presupposes that I do know; otherwise you would never have asked how I knew it!"
>
> (Zhuangzi 1994)

There also were many such skeptics in the same period of ancient Greek philosophy. The fifth-century B.C.E. Greek Sophist, Gorgias, for example, argued

> first that nothing exists, secondly that even if anything existed it could not be known by men, and thirdly that even if anything could be known by anyone it could not be communicated to anyone else.
>
> (Gorgias, in Windeband, *History*)

His argument for the first proposition, that nothing exists, is based on the difficulties presented by Parmenides and Heraclitus, which we will examine later (chapter 4), that if something is, it cannot change, but things do change, therefore they cannot truly exist. His argument for the second proposition, that what exists cannot be known, is based on the difference between things and our ideas (concepts) of things. My romantic idea of the moon, for example, is a very different thing from the moon itself—the one is in my mind, the other is out there in the world. And his argument for the third proposition, that what is known cannot be communicated, is based on the difference between words and ideas. If I tell you about the moon I saw last night, the idea you form of the moon in your mind is not exactly the same as the idea in my mind.

Obviously, many of our ways of representing the world to ourselves are biased, subjective, culturally relative, and anthrocentric. Returning to our earlier discussion about the meaning of the word "murder," it is obvious that this is a very anthropomorphic, anthrocentric (human-centered) way of representing things, singling out, from all of the creatures in the world, the killing of and by human beings as "murder," therefore something specially horrible and reprehensible. What if the cockroach could speak; what would it say? "You guys have been systematically murdering us in huge numbers for thousands of years; and you act like there is absolutely nothing wrong in this deliberate policy of genocide!" As the first-century Chinese philosopher Wang Chung writes,

> Suppose insects had intelligence, they would scold man saying: "You eat the produce of Heaven, and we eat it as well. You regard us as a plague, but are unaware that you yourself are a calamity to us."
>
> (Wang Chung, in Fung Yulan, *A History of Chinese Philosophy*)

"Plague," "disease," "pest," "weed"—can you think of other anthrocentric words?

Philosophy, then, is quite different from ordinary ways of thinking in that philosophy concentrates on the distinction between words and objects, focusing on the words themselves and how they (how *well* they) relate to objects. Ordinarily we do not focus on words but on objects. As we noted earlier, words (ways of thinking, talking) seem "transparent" to us. We normally see the world *through* our words, just as those of us who wear glasses see the world through our glasses. But as we get used to wearing them, we do not notice them—the glasses have become "transparent." Of course, if our glasses become very dirty, then we do notice them—they are no longer "transparent" but "opaque" to us. And so we clean them. In the same way, philosophers become aware of distortions in our ordinary ways of seeing, describing, and thinking about things, and then our symbolic representation of the world (our language) becomes visible ("opaque") to us and we can examine, criticize, and perhaps modify it—and then we are "doing" philosophy.

Out of this separation of word and object arise logical paradoxes that mark the beginning stages of philosophy, whether in India, Greece, or China. As Zhuangzi (fourth century B.C.E., Chinese) points out, unless we can get the representational function of language right, so that our words correctly and accurately discriminate what is really different and identify what is really the same, then words lead us into a strange, confusing and, at least for Zhuangzi, playfully weird world of their own.

> Now I have something to say. I do not know whether or not what I shall say is the same as what others say or not. Nonetheless, let me try to explain myself. There is beginning; there is no beginning. There is no no-beginning. There is being; there is nonbeing. There is no nonbeing. There is no no-nonbeing. Suddenly there is a distinction of being and nonbeing. Still, between being and nonbeing, I do not know which is really being and which is really nonbeing. I have just said something; but I do not know whether what I have said is really something said or not.
>
> (Zhuangzi 1994)

When we take words out of their everyday context, they can backfire on us! Suppose we say that there was a beginning to the world. Well, when was that exactly? What was happening a few moments before that? How long was it before the world began? But obviously whatever "date" we give, we can always ask the same question about what was happening before *that* time. But how can there be a time before the beginning of everything? And so, it seems there cannot be a beginning. "There is a beginning and there is no beginning." But that does not make any sense! As the fourth-century B.C.E. Greek philosopher Aristotle said, if we contradict ourselves, have we really said anything? Even before we can consider whether an assertion is true or not, we must first decide whether someone has actually asserted anything—that is, whether he or she has represented in speech a possible state of affairs, something that might or might not actually exist. If I say that up is down, what have I really succeeded in asserting? As Aristotle points out, the person who utters such a contradiction is like a cauliflower—that is, a vegetable that cannot say anything!

Or suppose I say that while horses exist (being), unicorns do not exist (nonbeing). But as the early Greek philosopher Parmenides said, how can we even talk about something that does not exist; what sense does it make to even speak about nonbeing. What are you talking about? There is nothing for you to say anything about. So maybe we should say there is no nonbeing. But we just said something about it! What is going on here? We feel frustrated and confused. (Not just for you, the beginning student, now suddenly really happy to be majoring in physical therapy, but deeply frustrating for philosophers like Zhuangzi and Parmenides.) This is a natural state of philosophy, especially in its beginning phases. The twentieth-century Austrian–British philosopher Ludwig Wittgenstein said that in the everyday context of ordinary language, language functions normally in a nonparadoxical way. But when we begin to reflect on the relation of names to things, we focus on names and words and concepts apart from particular things, taking words out of their ordinary language context, and then paradoxes inevitably result.

These paradoxes almost always have to do with the fact that most words of a natural language refer ambiguously both to particular objects and to general classes or kinds of things. Suppose someone asks you, "What's that you're holding?" And you answer, "A pen." But the expression "a pen" refers to both a particular physical object of which there is only one (the one you are holding), and also an abstract, general class of things of which there are many (pens in general, as when we say "A pen is usually more expensive than a pencil"). The first is an object existing in the world, and the second is a concept or idea that can be defined and understood. The one refers to things in the world and the other refers to our words, concepts, and thoughts (which we use to talk and think about things in the world)—the one exists in the external world and the other in the world of ideas.

As the Indian Nyaya philosophers say, the word "cow" refers to a particular cow, Bossy, but also to the class of all cows, that is, cows in general (the "universal," cow), as well as to those distinctive marks and features of Bossy, its "form" or shape, which tells us that this is indeed a cow.

There is doubt as to what a word (noun) really means, as it invariably presents to us an individual, a form, and a genus. Some say that the word (noun) denotes only an individual, because it is only in respect of individuals that we can use [the demonstrative pronoun] "that." . . . [But] a word (noun) does not denote an individual alone, because it is not restricted to the latter. What is denoted by the word 'cow' is not the mere individual by itself, without any qualifications, and as apart from the universal (to which it belongs), but the individual as qualified by (and along with) the universal. . . . [Nor] is it the genus [universal] alone that is meant by a word (noun), because the manifestation of genus depends on the form and individual. The meaning of a word (noun) is, according to us, the genus, the form and the individual. An individual is that which has a definite form and is the abode of particular qualities. The form is that which [indicates or] is called the token of the genus. The 'universal' is the cause (or basis) of comprehension and cognition.

(Nyaya Sutra, in Radhakrishnan & Moore, *A Sourcebook of Indian Philosophy*)

The writer of this passage is distinguishing three different things—the individual object (Bossy), the genus (or concept or class of cows as a whole), and the visible form of a cow (the visible marks and features that distinguish a cow from a horse or a dog and which we must all learn as young children in order to be able to correctly apply the word "cow" to cows and not to horses or dogs).

Think for a moment about the word we use in English to refer, not to cows in the field chewing their cud, but to the word or concept of cow. The name for cows is "cow"; fine, but what is the word for the *word* we use to *refer* to cow? Of course, there is no such word; all we can do is use the word "cow" again, but this time we do not mean the actual cows but the concept or universal "cow." You can see how confusing this can be—a cow eats grass but cow has three letters (c, o, and w); the individual cow is born and will die but not the concept cow. In the twentieth century, some philosophers adopted the convention of putting quotation marks around the word when it refers to the word, concept, or universal to distinguish that from the same word used to refer to actual objects in the world—so a cow eats grass and "cow" has three letters.

Puzzles and paradoxes are created through lack of clarity concerning the relationships between universals and particulars, and among the universals themselves. In everyday life (ordinary language context) particulars are not separated from universals and so such paradoxes do not arise ("it's a pen; what's your problem!"). By naively combining (confusing) word and object, as we just saw, we create the sense in which the thing we call a "tree" seems to remain more or less the same for fifty or one hundred years—although in fact it is constantly changing year by year, day by day, hour by hour. Of course, it is useful and even necessary to us in everyday life to be able to create this appearance of relative permanence—otherwise we could not talk or think about things at all.

Suppose you were a different entity every day (or every hour, every minute, every second)—different name, different object—how could your philosophy instructor call the roll every day, and how could you get a grade for work done over a period of ten to fifteen weeks? Did *you* do all of this work, or was it a hundred, a thousand, a million, a billion different individuals? As the eighteenth-century German philosopher Immanuel Kant said, and as empirically supported more recently by modern cognitive psychologists, this seems to be the only way the human brain can function, that is, by classifying things into broad categories. Hence, it is perfectly natural for us as human beings to see individual things as belonging to this or that category. In fact, we never see things as mere things; we see this as a dog, that as a tree, and so on. We see the individual through our general classifications and the individual things therefore "last" as long as they can fit the category into which we place them—as long as that thing fits our definition of "tree," it remains a tree; as soon as it ceases to fit that definition, it ceases to be a "tree" (and becomes instead a "log," "lumber," or "firewood.") As long as that body of water flow-ing between those banks is called the Wabash River, then we can step into the same river as many times as we like (though you can save your shoes by using the bridge). It all depends on the definition of the word "river."

When does a person start being a person? And when does a person stop being a person? We often think a person starts being a person when he or she is born—from that moment on that thing is what we call a person, a human being (and before that it was an embryo or a fetus, but not a human being). When a baby is born there is one more human being on the planet, and when someone dies there is one less. If you are the official census taker in a small town, then as soon as a baby is born you have to go out and change the sign leading into the town, "Hell Hole, pop. 326" to "Hell Hole, pop. 327." And when someone dies, then by the same token, you have to change the number back to 326! But some religious groups think that this person started being a person earlier, when it was still in its mother's womb—at exactly what point is not clear, and different religious groups have different opinions, some saying that it is a person from the moment of conception, oth-ers that it starts being a person at "quickening" (that is, several months after conception when the fetus's movements within the womb become noticeable to the mother). It obviously is an important question, when the fetus becomes a human being, since deliberately killing the fetus (abortion) would be mur-der if the entity we kill turns out to be a human being! And when does a per-son stop being a person? Well, we say, when he or she dies, but when exactly does that occur? In Japan there were no heart transplants prior to 1997. Why? (The Japanese medical profession certainly had the skill and technology.) Because to get a viable heart, you have to remove it from someone who is still alive in every respect, except that he or she is "brain dead." Removing the heart from a living person will obviously kill the person, and that means you have murdered that person—contrary to morality, law, and religion. Why do we in America (and now in Japan as well) remove beating hearts from "brain-dead" people who are still breathing, whose other organs are still functioning, who are still warm, and so on? Because we have decided that a brain-dead per-son is "dead," and so removing their heart is not considered murder.

In everyday life, we think of individual things in terms of the categories in which we place them—and individual things will then last as long as they can fulfill the definition of that particular category in which we place them. Since there are no individuals apart from the categories in which we place them, we can say, however strange it may sound, that without general concepts and categories there are no individual things—nothing (literally no things) to look at, think, or talk about! But by classifying things as we normally do (bring-ing things within concepts, combining (confusing) word and object), we live in a familiar world of semipermanent objects we at least partially know and understand (what they are and how they are likely to behave). But in philosophical reflection, we separate particulars from universals and, as noted earlier, the particulars then begin to appear so impermanent and changeable that they scarcely can be said to exist as distinct objects at all (the river does not last long enough for you to take one step into it), while the universals are so eternally unchanging that they seem utterly isolated from the world and irrelevant to human discourse.

Everything is constantly in flux, according to the sixth-century B.C.E. Greek philosopher Heraclitus, who once said, "It is one and the same thing to be living and dead, awake or asleep, young or old." Similarly, Hui Shih (a friend of Zhuangzi, fourth century B.C.E.) said, "The sun at noon is the sun declining; the creature born is the creature dying." If things are constantly changing, then what do we say about ordinary physical objects that we normally think remain the same over a period of time? We could go in one of two ways, both of which are going to be very strange! If we say a thing is different from second to second, we at first seem to be dividing one thing into many different things—so, as we said earlier, you become a million or a billion people during the academic quarter or semester. But of course this same thing (you, for example) is also changing *within* that second, from split second to split second, and within minute fractions of those split seconds until— what? Until there is nothing left! Suppose you divide a finite quantity into infinitely many units. How big is each unit? Infinitely small, and how big is that? Zero; zip; nothing. That alternative is scary!

But the other alternative is equally strange and wonderful. If you are different than you were a moment ago, then you are not the same person you were a moment ago; you have not changed from the past into the present, but the past you remains in the past and is different from the present you. In the famous Leopold–Loeb Chicago murder trial of the 1920s, Loeb, after serving thirty years in prison (a long time to brush up on his philosophy!), argued at one of his parole hearings that he was not the person who had committed the murder thirty years earlier; he was a different person; the 1920s' Loeb is a different person from the 1950s' Loeb ("you got the wrong guy"). Did it work? (What do you think?)

Taking this second alternative, Zhuangzi says (talking about Hui Shih and the other "Ming Jia," or "School of Names" philosophers) if a thing is constantly changing, then it is a different thing from one moment to another and therefore not the same thing that changes from one moment to another and therefore there is nothing that changes from one moment to the next! "The shadow of a flying bird never moves and the wheel of a chariot never touches the ground." An equally strange alternative! In the first alternative, the individual dissolves into nothing; but in the second alternative, we have an infinite number of distinct individuals, each of which remains constant, not changing at all—the you two minutes ago, the you an hour ago, the you a day and a half ago, and so on and so on. Each is different and none of these "yous" moves through time—there is no sixteen-year-old you who is now sweating it out in a college philosophy class. The old you is a thing of the past, not today's new and improved you. During a school holiday you arrive at your parents' door, "Ma, here's my dirty laundry; where's the lasagna?" But your mother, having been reading Zhuangzi, says, "Who are you?" Of course, you try to persuade her that you are her daughter, but she replies, "No way; my daughter was just a tiny little thing, bald as a cue ball—not at all like you, whoever you are."

As Liu Xun says, commenting on the passage from Zhuangzi some six hundred years later (exemplifying, incidentally, what we said earlier about the philosopher's use of a rich tradition of previous philosophizing),

> A moment of time can never be held up; in a flash something has happened and something has ceased to happen. That is why the shadow of a flying bird is never seen to move and the wheel of a chariot does not touch the ground. Hence the removal of the fly-whisk was not a removal; how then could there have been a "reaching"? Likewise, since the reaching did not reach, how could there have been a removal?

> (Liu Xun, in Fung, *History*)

At the opposite extreme, Gong-Sun Lung (Chinese, fourth century B.C.E.), like the Greek philosopher of the same period, Plato, argued that whiteness itself is eternal and unchanging. A yellow house can be painted white, but whiteness can never be anything but white—that is, the idea or concept of whiteness is always whiteness. A stone, Gong-Sun Lung says, seems to be made up of different parts—there is whiteness and hardness, and these are quite different from one another, since we can see but not feel the whiteness and feel but not see the hardness, and also, perhaps, stoneness. So, is the stone one thing (a stone), or two (whiteness plus hardness), or three (whiteness plus hardness plus stoneness), or four (whiteness plus hardness plus stoneness plus the actual stone itself)—or what? But the whiteness of the stone is also the *same* whiteness of the paper, so it is not clear whether the whiteness is spreading itself out into all of the many white things there are all over the world (but in that case, how can it be the *same* whiteness in each and not just a small part and a different part in each?).

The Indian Nyaya logicians, as we have already seen, also had a theory of immaterial, eternal "universals" ("cow" in general, in addition to the particular cow, Bossy). Plato similarly wondered whether beauty could exist at all in the physical world. There are lots of good-looking people, but are any of them absolutely, perfectly beautiful (a perfect "10")? If not, then what are we talking about when we talk about "beauty"? We must have some idea of beauty, otherwise we wouldn't know that he or she falls short of a perfect 10. But if this perfect beauty cannot be a physical thing, then what is it? It is something we can think about, something that does not change (like the best-looking guy from high school who is now getting bald and fat—and is not yet thirty!). Like Gong-Sun Lung's whiteness and hardness, beauty seems to be shared in some sense by many physical things, though never perfectly. Perhaps as Plato said, these physical things imitate and approximate the real, nonphysical beauty, in varying degrees (an "8" or a "7 1/2," and so on), but unlike beauty itself, which is always perfect and never changing.

Although there are many references in Chinese texts to Hui Shih as being one of the best known of the "Ming Jia" (the logicians known as the "School of Names"), none of his sayings has survived, except those mentioned by Zhuangzi.

Hui Shih . . . examined the meanings of things and said,

The greatest has nothing beyond itself, and is called the Great Unit; the smallest has nothing within itself, and is called the Little Unit.

That which has no thickness cannot be increased in thickness, yet in extent it may cover a thousand miles.

The heavens are as low as the earth; mountains are on the same level as marshes.

The sun at noon is the sun declining; the creature born is the creature dying.

A great similarity differs from a little similarity. This is called the little similarity-and-difference. All things are in one way all similar, in another way all different. This is called the great similarity-and-difference.

The South has no limit and has a limit.

I go to the state of Yueh today and arrived there yesterday.

Connected rings can be separated.

I know the center of the world; it is north of Yen [in the North] and south of Yueh [in the South].

Love all things equally; the universe is one."

(Zhuangzi 1994)

Perhaps the most famous paradox of Hui Shih is the third one: "The heavens are as low as the earth; mountains are on the same level as marshes."

When does a tall thing start being tall, and when does it stop being tall (suddenly becoming short)? But, like many pairs of words, "small, large," "young, old," these are relative concepts—everything in the world (except the Great Unit and the Little Unit) is both small (relative to one thing) and large (relative to something else)—and at the same time! Only one thing is absolutely large—the Great Unit, that is, the universe as a whole, and only one thing is absolutely small—the Little Unit, that is, an atom. Everything else is only relatively large and relatively small—and at the same time. So judging from these relative concepts, individual objects do not seem to remain the same (large or small) for any length of time within the class of large things or the class of small things (as compared to persons lasting seventy to eighty years, trees upward of 200 years, butterflies just a day or so, cigarette smoke rings just a few seconds, and so on).

Even if we specify the *kind of object* we are talking about, the object still lasts much longer (as a thing of that kind) than it remains small, short, and young (a small, short, young person is still a person when she is forty-five years old, 5'9", and weighs 150 pounds). And does this not imply that things are not so different from one another as we normally suppose? If things are really so different from one another, then what is the difference between them? If it turns out that everything is both tall and short, fat and skinny, young and old, all at the same time, does this not suggest that everything is more or less the same? As the Greek philosopher Heraclitus said, "It is one and the same thing to be living and dead, awake or asleep, young or old." And as Zhuangzi said in one his most paradoxical assertions, "The universe is a finger; all things are a horse." And if that is the case, then, as Hui Shih said in his aforementioned last paradox, how can we discriminate among things, preferring one over another? Should we not love them all equally?

The fifth century B.C.E. Greek philosopher Zeno also loved to put forward paradoxes. One of his paradoxes states that in a race between a hare and a tortoise, it is impossible for the hare to ever catch up to the tortoise if the tortoise is given a little head start, because as soon as the hare gets to the place from which the tortoise started, the tortoise has moved on farther, and as soon as the hare gets to this second place, the tortoise has moved still farther, and so on, forever. In a similar paradox, Zeno denies that it is possible for a man to run the length of a field, because before he can reach the end he must reach the halfway point and before he can reach halfway to that halfway point, he must go half that distance, and so on, to infinity—therefore, he will never reach the end. Compare this paradox of Zeno's with a similar Chinese Ming Jia (School of Names) puzzle: "Take a stick one foot long and cut it in half everyday and you will never exhaust it even after ten thousand generations." Other Chinese paradoxes also resemble those of Zeno: "The wheel never touches the ground"; "The shadow of a bird never moves"; "The arrow is flying so fast there are moments when it is neither in motion nor at rest." In Indian philosophy, the Buddhists argue that because we can only understand the present moment in terms of what has gone immediately before it (the past) and what immediately comes after it (the future), the present therefore does not exist!

> There is no present time because when a thing occurs, we can know only the time through which it has occurred and the time through which it will yet occur.

Some philosophers love these paradoxes and love confounding common sense (Hui Shih, Gong-Sun Lung, Zeno), but most philosophers step forward to defend common sense against the paradox mongers (Aristotle, Xunzi, later Mohists, the Nyaya logicians)—and here is where logic is born. To solve these puzzles and paradoxes, in other words, logic is created, in Chinese, Indian, and Western philosophy. China's first philosopher, Kongzi (or Confucius, as he is known in the West), insisted that the first responsibility of the philosopher is "the rectification of names." The first philosophers recognized that universals and particulars were different sorts of things, so what could be said of one could not be said of the other. But because the same words (e.g., "cow" or "pen") are used to refer to both universals and particulars, paradoxes can be created that require special logical analysis to correct.

"A white horse is not a horse" (Gong-Sun Lung) is the most famous of the early Chinese paradoxes. The story goes that as Gong-Sun Lung was about to pass a border post on his white horse, he was told by the guard that no horses were allowed to cross the border, to which Gong-Sun Lung replied, "Oh, but a white horse is not a horse," and he proceeded to ride through the gate. Gong-Sun Lung's paradox turns on a failure to make clear whether we are talking about physical objects or concepts. Among all of the things that exist in the world, there are many horses, and some of these horses are white in color. But these large animals are quite different from the *words* "horse" (Chinese "ma") and "white" (Chinese "bai") that are used to describe them. But if we are not careful to differentiate word and object, paradoxes and puzzles will crop up. Is "white horse" synonymous with (i.e., have the same meaning as) "horse"? Is the concept "horse" identical with the mixture of the two concepts "whiteness" plus "horseness"? Is the mixed concept "white horse" an actual horse (i.e., a particular) that you could saddle up and ride out of town? In each of *these* senses, the white horse is not a horse, but since in ordinary speech the white horse obviously is a horse, an acute sense of philosophical perplexity is created. In the quotation from Gong-Sun Lung that follows, we will capitalize the concepts—Whiteness, Hardness, Horseness—to indicate the way in which Gong-Sun Lung tries to differentiate them from actual physical objects, stones and horses, and their physical properties, white and hard (although in ordinary Chinese, just as in ordinary English or Greek, there is no way to indicate linguistically the concept horse from an actual horse—both are referred to as "ma").

> The words "white horse" mean Horseness and Whiteness, but Horseness and Whiteness is not an actual horse. Therefore I say that "A white horse is not a horse." Horseness without Whiteness is still a horse. Whiteness without Horseness is still white. Furthermore, Horseness combined with Whiteness is known as a white horse, but when not combined, we can no longer call it a white horse. Therefore we cannot say that a white horse is the same as a horse. That which you mistook for being a horse is really Horseness which you keep confusing with an actual horse. However, you cannot call Horseness a horse.
>
> Whiteness is white in itself; otherwise how could it make a stone and other things white? Hardness is not hard because it is present in a particular stone, it is also common in other things. If it is not completely present in things yet there is still Hardness, this Hardness must be hard in itself. This Hardness is not the hardness of this or that stone, but it is hard in itself. Whiteness is not any particular white thing, because there are many white things. A thing which is white does not define Whiteness. A thing which is hard does not define Hardness. As such, Hardness does not exist in the world; it lies concealed. Concepts are not of this world; things, on the other hand, are of this world. And yet without concepts there would be no things [of this or that kind]. Yet though they are separate, they do not exclude one another. Without Whiteness we cannot see a stone. Without Hardness we cannot feel a stone. So, Whiteness and Hardness and stone do not exclude one another.

(from Discourses of Gong-Sun Lung)

If we shift from words to objects, it becomes clear that the group of white horses is surely part of a larger group of horses. Of all the millions of individual animals in the world, there is a large group known as horses, and some of these are white in color. But even when talking about the groups or classes of objects, say, horses and white horses, we still cannot say that these two groups are *identical*. If we say that the class of white horses is the *same* as the class of horses, then, once more, Gong-Sun Lung is right—in that sense (the class of) white horses is not (the same class as the class of) horses. When we say a white horse is a horse, we have to make it clear that the "is" in this case is the "is" of class inclusion, as when we say dogs are mammals (the class of dogs is included in the larger class of mammals), and not the "is" of identity, as when we say "a puppy is a young dog" (where "puppy" and "young dog" are simply different names for the exact same class of objects). (In the fifth-grade school textbook "Harry Stottlemeir's Discovery," Harry Stottlemeir rediscovers what Aristotle had discovered 2,000 years earlier, that from "all white horses are horses" we cannot reverse this and conclude that all horses are white horses—only some of them, and that this works for all sentences of the form "all s is p".) But if we are careful to specify that we are talking about objects and the inclusion of one group of objects in another group of objects, then a white horse is a horse—in *this* sense (talking about objects rather than concepts), a white horse certainly *is* a horse. Too bad the border guard hadn't taken a course in logic!

Gong-Sun Lung's paradox of the white horse also helps us see the point Aristotle and other philosophers make when they insist that we must carefully distinguish the different roles played by nouns, adjectives, and other parts of speech (what Aristotle called "predicables"). When we talk about a white horse, we are not talking about two different things, the white and the horse, but only one thing that has many different properties (white, seven years old, likes apples, cannot speak Chinese, and so on, which we can predicate of the horse). In language, we use nouns to refer to things in the world, and we use adjectives to describe the properties those objects have. In the case of Gong-Sun Lung's paradox, we first pick out an object existing in the world and then begin to describe it. Primarily it is a horse; that is what it is essentially, or basically. And then we can go on to describe other properties of the horse without, however, contradicting the fact that it is essentially, first and foremost, a horse, and so we describe its color as "white," its age as "seven years old," its speed as "slow," and so on. And of course the horse could remain a horse but change some of its properties—it used to be a fast, gray, three-year-old, but it is now a slow, white, seven-year-old. Given this analysis, it is clear that a white horse is white and a white horse is a horse, just as a small, hungry, slow, white horse is small, hungry, slow and is white—since all of these are properties we attribute to the same thing—the horse.

Gong-Sun Lung is generally referred to by his ancient Chinese critics as a trickster, wasting our time using logic to confound and confuse us. But in his book, it is clear that he has a serious purpose in using logic to further Kongzi's (Confucius's) "rectification of names." In several passages, Gong-Sun Lung criticizes the rulers of his day for serious political mistakes that they have made by failing to keep the meaning of words clear. His most famous paradox, "A white horse is not a horse," at first seems silly, but in his conversations with various political rulers of the time, Gong-Sun Lung uses this statement about the white horse to point out serious political mistakes these leaders were making.

For example, one of the rulers says he wants to find scholars to employ in helping him to run the country, but he cannot find any. Gong-Sun Lung gets the ruler to agree on the definition of a scholar. But then it turns out that the ruler also prefers *bold* scholars and dislikes *timid* scholars. But this is a confusion, Gong-Sun Lung points out. A scholar is a scholar. If you want a scholar, then you should be happy to accept any genuine scholar—bold or timid. But it turns out that the ruler does *not* want a scholar *simpliciter*; he only wants a *bold* scholar—and now we can see that there is an important difference between a scholar and a bold scholar, just as there is a difference between a horse and a white horse—"a bold scholar is not (the same thing as) a scholar."

In another example from Gong-Sun Lung, a king accidentally leaves a hunting bow behind and later decides to give it to the local people ("let the Chu people have it," he says). But the king is criticized for preferring the Chu people. Why not let *anyone* have it who finds it? Why just the *Chu* people? Again, there is a difference between people and the Chu people, just as there is a difference between a horse and a white horse—"the Chu people is not (the same thing as) the people." In the American Declaration of Independence, certain unalienable rights are attributed to "all people." Was this meant to include African slaves? Or women? The language is unclear. Gong-Sun Lung would say that there is an important difference between adult, white, free, male people and people, just as there is a difference between white horses and horses.

Later in his discussion, Gong-Sun Lung extends this criticism to the confusion government leaders create by their contradictory talk about "right," "wrong," "punish," and "reward." These leaders create confusion and do the country great harm when they say that it is right to fight back when insulted (dueling), but they also say it is wrong to engage in personal fighting (dueling). They say it is right to *reward* with government appointments the brave, noble ones who fight back against personal insults, but they also say it is right to *punish* these same people for breaking the law and disturbing the peace. Obviously this is inconsistent and can easily lead to confusion and misunderstanding. These harms are caused by failures to "rectify names"—names like "right," "wrong," "punish," "reward," and so on.

There also was a serious side to Hui Shih's paradoxes. His last paradox is, "Love all things equally; the universe is one." According to Hui Shih, all things are changing and all things are relative; what is big (a person compared to a cat) is also small (a person compared to an elephant), what is young (a child) is also old (compared to a butterfly), one thing (a leaf) is part of another thing (a tree, which is itself part of yet another thing, a forest, and so on). Hui Shih concludes from this that there are no fundamental differences between things. All of the ordinary differences we detect in the world are illusory; our verbal system of classification that divides the world into distinct compartments (large things and small things, heavy things and light things, and so on), simply does not capture the way things really are. The world resists these divisions we have verbally imposed on it. In the end, all is one, so we should love all things equally and not prefer one thing to another.

When Buddhism was first introduced into China, between the second and fourth centuries C.E., many of its initial adherents were Taoists who naturally tended to understand and explain Buddhism in terms of Taoism, especially the

Buddhist rejection of the reality of any permanent objects. Unlike most philosophers who tend to conservatively defend common sense against counterintuitive paradoxes, these Taoist–Buddhists used them to defend Buddhism and defeat common sense. Seng Zhau (384–414, barely thirty when he died!), for example, argued that the idea of objects changing from the past into the future (you, for example, growing from a baby to a twenty-something young person) was an illusion—not just a verbal trick, but really false—according to the Buddhists, you are simply not that tiny baby born twenty years ago. The object in the past remains in the past, he says, and the object that follows it is a *different* object that did not exist in the past and will not continue on into the future. This is a more serious use of Zhuangzi's playful argument we saw earlier, that if a thing is constantly changing, then it is a different thing from one moment to another and therefore not the same thing that changes from one moment to another, and therefore there is nothing that changes from one moment to the next ("The shadow of a flying bird never moves, and the wheel of a chariot never touches the ground"). As Seng Zhau put it in his famous article, "On the Immutability of Things,"

> What people mean by change is that because things of the past do not reach unchanged to the present, they are therefore said to change and not remain static. But what I mean by static is that because things of the past do not reach to the present, they are therefore static and do not change. . . . If we look for past things in the past we find that they have always been in the past and never left the past. But if we demand that they move from the past into the present, we find that they never exist in the present. The fact that they never exist in the present shows that they do not reach the present. . . . Past things are in the past and do not go there from the present, and present things are in the present, and did not get there from the past. . . . That is to say, the raging storm that uproots trees is in fact perfectly still and quiet. Rivers which compete with one another to inundate the land do not flow. The blustery wind that blows about is not moving. The sun and moon, revolving in their orbits, do not turn round.
>
> (Seng Zhau, "On the Immutability of Things," in Chan)

This sounds a lot like Zeno's paradoxes. Paradoxically, while Parmenides held that nothing can change or move, and Heraclitus held that all things are in flux, one way to analyze the constant change in objects, as we have seen, is to break them up into many unchanging, static individuals. As Ludwig Wittgenstein said, once we begin to philosophically reflect on ordinary language, the ordinary rules of language usage are thrown to the winds and language goes "on holiday," and then everything is up for grabs!

There was a serious side to Zeno's paradoxes, too. Zeno used his paradoxes to defeat the critics of his teacher, Parmenides. Parmenides had said that reality could not change in any way.

Never shall it be proven that not-being is. From that path of inquiry restrain your mind. Do not let custom, born of everyday experience, tempt your eyes to be aimless, your ear and tongue to be echoes. Let reason be your judge. . . . The one way, that It Is and cannot not-be, is the way of credibility based on truth. The other way, that It Is Not and that not-being must be, cannot be grasped by the mind, for you cannot know not-being and cannot express it. . . . Accordingly, all the usual notions that mortals accept and rely on as if true—coming-to-be and perishing, being and not-being, change of place and of color—these are nothing more than names. . . . What can be thought and what can be are the same.

If a thing changes, say from a seed to a ripe apple, which is eaten and destroyed, or even changes from small to large, or from green to red, or from being there in the tree to being here in my hand, then it goes from not-being an apple (when it is a seed) to being an apple to not-being an apple again (when it is eaten), and from being small and green to not-being small and green, and from being there to not-being there, that is, from what is to what is not, from being to not-being, and that is impossible to think and to be. So, Parmenides concludes, nothing can change in any way. It may *appear* to sense experience that things change, but reason tells us otherwise. But this was hard to accept, since it seems so obvious to common sense that things clearly do change. So Zeno's paradoxes are designed to show that Parmenides is right (by showing that his opponents are wrong), despite the commonsense evidence that things obviously do change.

> If anything is moving, it must be moving either in the place in which it is or in a place in which it is not. However, it cannot move in the place in which it is [for that place is exactly the same size as the thing and so there's no room for it to move], and it cannot move in the place in which it is not [because it's not there]. Therefore, movement is impossible.

Nonetheless, despite the serious intent of some of the creators of paradoxes and puzzles, they do not really convince anyone. As Chinese critics said of the Ming Jia,

> They could easily attract and always overcome everybody with their great eloquence, yet they were unable to convince. This was their weakest point. Their teachings are strange and they confused the people with their queer ideas. They are severe in their criticisms and pay no attention to what is useful. Their arguments are not practical. With all their bustle they accomplish nothing. However, what they maintain seems reasonable, so are their teachings with which they try to mislead the people who are ignorant.

(Zhuangzi 1994)

As Aristotle said of Zeno, "His arguments seem irrefutable, though his conclusions are impossible to accept." Most philosophers, like most of us, are conservative defenders of common sense. We never for a moment accept the wild and crazy conclusions of these arguments (that things cannot move, that a white horse is not a horse, and so on), so we feel there must be something wrong with the argument—though it is not immediately clear what is wrong with it. We are puzzled, in other words, but not convinced; we cannot see the mistake in the reasoning, but neither can we embrace the conclusion. Logic often arises in response to such conceptual puzzles in an effort to resolve them.

In the Indian tradition, the Nyaya philosophers developed a sophisticated system of logic, in part to refute what they regarded as attacks on common sense, like the Buddhist argument we saw earlier, that the present does not exist. Here the Nyaya use a kind of "argumentum ad absurdum," arguing that if there is no present then there cannot be any past or future, nor can there be any sense perception and thereby any empirical knowledge; but since the past and future obviously do exist, and since we clearly do have empirical knowledge by means of sense perception, it follows that the present does exist.

> There is, some [the Buddhists] say, no present time because when a thing falls, we can know only the time through which it has fallen and the time through which it will yet fall. But if there is no present time, there will, it is replied, be no past and future times, because they are related to it. The past and future cannot be established by a mere mutual reference to one another. Moreover, if there were no present time, sense perception would be impossible, and therefore no knowledge would be possible. Yet we can know both the past and the future, since we can conceive of a thing as having been made and as about to be made. Moreover, perception is brought about by the contact of the sense organ with the object; and that which is not present . . . cannot be in contact with a sense organ.
>
> (Nyaya Sutra, in Radhakrishnan and Moore, *Sourcebook*)

Although Chinese logic did not develop beyond an early stage, there are nonetheless interesting examples of logical analysis that resemble some of those in Indian and Western logic. Since most of the paradoxes involve confusions in the relation of words to objects, the first step in logic is to work out the proper relationship of words to objects which they name or refer to. Kongzi (Confucius, Chinese, sixth century B.C.E.) spoke of the need for the "rectification of names." He said, "Let the ruler be ruler, the minister minister, the father father, and the son son" (*Analects*, p. xx). But how can a father fail to be a father? Only in the sense that a biological father may fail to fulfill the expectations, duties, responsibilities, and, in short, the conception or definition of what it *means* to be a father. And so for a ruler. A person may usurp power and call himself "emperor" but utterly fail to live up to the duties, responsibilities, and definition of a "ruler." As the twentieth-century Chinese philosopher Fung Yulan points out,

> Every name contains certain implications which constitute the essence of that class of things to which the name applies. . . . The essence of a ruler is what the ruler ideally ought to be. . . . If a ruler acts according to this way of the ruler, he is then truly a ruler, in fact as well as in name. There is an agreement between name and actuality. But if he does not, he is no ruler.

(Fung Yulan 1966)

Mengzi (Mencius, Chinese, fourth century B.C.E.) follows this line of thinking a step further. He raised the question of whether it was ever permissible to murder a king. His answer was that if the individual properly fits the definition of a king, or true ruler, then it is wrong to murder the person, but if the individual is merely a "king" in name only, but in reality is a usurper, a tyrant, and a bandit, and not a true and benevolent king, then it is permissible under certain circumstances to kill him. As he says, "Killing the tyrant Zhou [the last emperor of the Shang dynasty] was not murdering a king."

> King Xuan of Qi asked, "Is it true that . . . King Wu marched against Zhou?"
> "It is so recorded," answered Mencius.
> "Is regicide [killing a king] permissible?"
> "He who mutilates benevolence is a mutilator; he who cripples rightness is a crippler; and a man who is both a mutilator and a crippler is an 'outcast.' I have indeed heard of the punishment of the 'outcast Zhou,' but I have not heard of any regicide."

(Mengzi, *Mengzi (Mencius)*, in Chan, *Source Book*)

Of course, there is something very puzzling about Mengzi's claim. Zhou, after all, was the king; the question about the justification for killing a king only arose because Zhou was a king who had in fact been murdered. To put the point a different way, one problem with Mengzi's "rectification of the name 'king' " is that it does not allow us to talk about a *bad* king. According to Mengzi's new and reformed definition of "king" (in Chinese, "wang"), only a good king counts as a king. A "king" is defined in terms of the correct performance of the proper duties of a king; one who fails in this respect is simply not a king. But when we write about or talk about kings, we want to be able to distinguish the good kings from the bad kings.

In a sense, we may say Mengzi went too far. While he has correctly recognized the normative, evaluative meaning of words like "king," he need not have gone so far as to exclude all of those from being called kings who failed to live up to those normative, evaluative standards, because the word "king" includes a factual or descriptive element in addition to the normative and evaluative element. A "king" is someone who is selected to perform the normative and evaluative role of a king (serving the people, and so on). The person thus selected can either fulfill those expectations or fail to do so. The first is a good king and the second a bad king—but both are kings.

A similar problem confronts the definition of many other words today, such as "work of art." Like Mengzi, some aestheticians (philosophers of art) define "work of art" in such a way that there cannot be any bad works of art (saying, for example, that a work of art is a man-made object that produces aesthetic experience), and that seems counterintuitive (since many works of art fail to produce any aesthetic experience). Like "king," "work of art" has both descriptive and evaluative elements. A work of art, we might say, is any object made by someone with the purpose of producing aesthetic experience. Some such objects will succeed in this regard, and some will fail, so we can continue to talk, as we normally do, of good and bad works of art.

If we do wish to follow Mengzi's lead, then at the very least we must come up with a new word for bad kings (and by analogy, for failed art works). That is, if we decide to reserve the word "king" for only the good kings, then we must come up with another word for bad kings. During the Warring States period there was in fact a word for military tyrants (ba), who did not qualify as true kings (wang). Mengzi himself calls them tyrants, so we could say, "Zhou was a tyrant, not a true king." But even here, we have to say "*true* king" or "*real* king" since we know that other people do not accept our convention of limiting the word king to good kings but continue to speak of kings in the old way as both good and bad, including the bad king, Zhou. Similarly, we could differentiate "real art" from mere "decoration, illustration, entertainment, pretty pictures," and the like, although this would have the consequence of even more damning criticism of failed art: "it's not just bad art, it doesn't even qualify as art at all!" This is what some people do when they distinguish between "statesmen" (of whom there are few) and "politicians" (of whom there are far too many!).

When philosophers discover that the source of contradictory and paradoxical assertions is the result of a serious ambiguity in our ordinary ways of speaking, as in the aforementioned case, they generally try to resolve the paradox and ambiguity by drawing a distinction between two different senses of the word. Clearly, in the case just mentioned, we need to distinguish the descriptive and the normative (or evaluative) senses of the same word. "King" descriptively means the person designated to perform a certain task (job/role), but "king" normatively means someone who has actually performed that task (job/role) well (up to a certain acceptable standard). But there are many ways of drawing such a distinction. We can say with Mengzi that Wu was a king and Zhou was a tyrant; that is, we use the word "tyrant" to refer to a bad ruler and "king" to refer to a good ruler. Or we could choose instead to use words like "good," "bad," and "designated" to modify the concept of "king," so we would say that after Zhou was crowned or designated king, he later turned out to be a bad king, whereas after Wu was crowned (designated) king, he proved to be a good king.

Socrates and Thrasymachus raise a similar question in Plato's *The Republic*. Is justice merely what is in the interest of the stronger, as Thrasymachus claims?

> So entirely astray are you in your ideas about the just and unjust as not even to know that justice and the just are in reality another's good; that is to say, the interest of the ruler and stronger. . . . The just is always a loser in comparison with the unjust. First of all, in private contracts: wherever the unjust is the partner with the just you will find that, when the partnership is dissolved, the unjust man has always more and the just less. Secondly, in their dealings with the State; when there is an income tax, the just man will pay more and the unjust less on the same amount of income. . . . But all this is reversed in the case of the unjust man. . . . My meaning will be most clearly seen if we turn to that highest form of injustice in which the criminal is the happiest of men, and the sufferers of injustice or those who refuse to do injustice are the most miserable—that is to say tyranny, which by fraud and force takes away the property of others.
>
> (Plato 1945)

As we saw with the word "king," so in the case of "justice" there is both a factually descriptive sense of the word and an evaluatively normative sense. As a matter of *fact*, what goes by the name of "justice" is often just what Thrasymachus says it is (the strong exploiting the weak); but nothing that truly satisfies the *definition* of "justice" (which includes the evaluative and normative sense as well) could be so described. Indeed, using words according to their established meanings, it would be contradictory and absurd to say that taking advantage of the weak simply in order to pursue one's own interests was just— that sort of activity is precisely what we normally mean by *injustice*.

In the first part of Thrasymachus's aforementioned statement, where he defines justice as what is in the interest of the stronger, he tries to substitute the descriptive sense of the word for the usual normative sense of the word. But in the rest of the quoted statement, he slips back into the ordinary, normative sense of the word, now claiming, not that the strong exploiting the weak is "justice," but that while such exploitation is indeed "unjust," it is nonetheless "better" in the sense of being more profitable (at least for the stronger). Socrates' argument against Thrasymachus is basically that Thrasymachus cannot arbitrarily change the meaning of the word "justice," and therefore although what people call justice is often in fact the strong exploiting the weak, that does not make it just.

In other words, Socrates defeats Thrasymachus, because Thrasymachus has not clearly distinguished between the descriptive and the normative senses of the word "justice." Had Thrasymachus said that whereas "justice in the conventional sense" (justice-1) was to treat everyone equally, "justice as it is actually practiced" (justice-2) was in fact almost never like that—and furthermore, that what we ought to do is accordingly redefine the word "justice" to better conform to actual practice, so that in our new sense of justice, "justice is the legitimate right of the stronger to rule the weaker" (justice-3). We already recognize in daily life, Thrasymachus might point out, that there is something "good" about being unjust in the conventional sense (that is, that injustice-1 is "good," and justice-1 is "bad"), in the sense that "nice guys finish last." If it is "good" to finish first, then it is bad to be just-1. Of course, what we mean is that from a strictly self-interested point of view, it is often smarter to be unjust than just (without of course getting caught). Still, it sounds strange to say that it is good to be unjust and bad to be just (like saying that it is good to be bad and bad to be good)—and it is just this strangeness by which Socrates trips up Thrasymachus. But since we recognize that those in power simply describe as "justice" whatever suits them, and since we also may respect the natural right of the stronger to rule (it is their rightful place), Thrasymachus thinks we could straighten out all of the strangeness in his position, simply by redefining the word justice to mean a completely open and honest power play. Nice guys come in last; the race goes to the swiftest— we simply acknowledge this fact of life and embrace it, rather than hypocritically pretending it does not exist—or worse, trying to reverse it to favor the wimps! (But wait! If all us wimps join together, then aren't we "the stronger"?)

But even if Socrates has won the argument and shown that, using words in their customary way, taking advantage of the weak cannot be what we mean by "justice" but must be considered unjust, Thrasymachus can still claim to have made the more important point that whatever we mean by words like "justice" and "injustice," it seems far better and smarter to be "unjust" than to be "just." As the other participants in the discussion, Glaucon and Adeimantus, wonder, apart from the fear of getting caught, why would anyone want to be just? That is what Socrates tries to answer in the rest of *The Republic* (which we will return to in chapter 5).

Like Socrates, Mozi (Chinese, fourth century B.C.E.) similarly distinguishes the normatively correct meaning of yi (righteousness) as "right" and the descriptive, factual understanding of yi as "force."

> What does it mean to regard righteousness [yi] as right? If one is in a large state, he will not attack a smaller state. If one is a member of a large family, he will not bully

a small family. The strong will not oppress the weak; the eminent will not lord it over the humble; the cunning will not deceive the stupid. . . . But a man who regards force as right is different. His words and actions will be directly opposed to these, as though he were galloping off in the opposite direction. If he is in a large state, he will attack a small state. If he is a member of a large family, he will bully small families. The strong will oppress the weak; the eminent will lord it over the humble; the cunning will deceive the stupid. . . . And . . . the foulest names in the world will be given to such a man, and he will be called an evil king.

(Mozi, *Mozi*, in Burton Watson, ed. & trans., *Basic Writings*)

Like Kongzi (Confucius) and Mengzi (Mencius), Socrates restricts the sense of the word "ruler" to what is meant by that word—one who leads, is a shepherd, a helmsman, one who looks after his people, and so on, and not one who merely *calls* himself that and has the power to force others to call him that. Mozi, on the other hand, as we see from the last sentence in the previous quotation, allows for "an evil king"—one who fits the descriptive sense of "king" but not the normative.

Xunzi (third century B.C.E. Chinese Confucianist) also discusses the "rectification of names." Xunzi was the last of the Warring States (700–200 B.C.E.) philosophers, therefore was in the enviable position to learn more from his predecessors and incorporate and synthesize their views. We described in chapter 1 the way in which philosophy builds on its past traditions—not by any agreement or consensus in their beliefs and theories, but in their terminology, logical apparatus, and in general what we called "the tools of the trade." During the reign of the feudal lord of the state of Chi, King Xuan (who ruled from 342 to 324 B.C.E.) set up a kind of university research institute, inviting scholars from all over China, offering them salaries, living accommodations, and honorary titles to pursue their studies, expound their theories, and debate with one another. Mengzi (Mencius) spent some time there, as did Xunzi a generation later (sometime around 264 B.C.E.), toward the end of its heyday.

Xunzi draws an important distinction between classes of things and classes of classes. Things may be grouped under broader and broader classes, just as Aristotle said in discussing species and genus, ending finally, Xunzi says, in the largest class of all, "things"—Fido is a dog; dogs are mammals; mammals are vertebrates; vertebrates are animals; animals are living things; living things are things. Names are conventional, Xunzi held, but once we have accepted the convention then we must stick to it, and so the convention thereafter becomes a standard of correct and incorrect thought and speech.

In the chapter of his book called "On the Rectification of Names," Xunzi argues that knowledge is a correspondence between name and thing. Like the Indian Vaisesika tradition and much of Western philosophy, Xunzi holds that knowledge is a product of sense perception and intellectual classification and interpretation of sense perception. That thing we see with our five senses, what should we call it, "father," "king," "son"? That is, what is the right word to use to refer to that thing? Once that is agreed upon, then, to avoid confusion, as Aristotle also said, we should call different things by different names, and similar things by the same name. And whatever name we agree to call a certain kind of thing, we should all agree on a common definition of that word. Thus, errors in judgment, mistakes in knowledge, result in two ways—either we fail to correctly classify the object (I think the bird overhead is a hawk but it is really an eagle), or we misuse words (I mistakenly say a glass of ale is not beer, not knowing that the meaning of the word "beer" includes both lager and ale). Whatever linguistic conventions we agree upon, we should stick with those and be consistent in their usage.

John Locke (seventeenth-century Englishman) was similarly concerned with correcting errors in judgment by a "rectification of names."

> When it is considered how much all sorts of knowledge, discourse, and conversation are disordered by the careless and confused use and application of words, it will perhaps be thought worthwhile thoroughly to lay it open. And I shall be pardoned if I have dwelt long on an argument which I think, therefore, needs to be inculcated, because the faults men are usually guilty of in this kind are not only the greatest hindrances of true knowledge, but are so well thought of as to pass for it. Men would often see what a small pittance of reason and truth, or possibly none at all, is mixed with those huffing opinions they are welled with; if they would but look beyond fashionable sounds, and observe what ideas are or are not comprehended under those words with which they are so armed at all points and with which they so confidently lay about them. I shall imagine I have done some service to truth, peace, and learning, if, by an enlargement on this subject, I can make men reflect on their own use of language, and give them reason to suspect, that . . . it is possible for them to have sometimes very good and approved words in their mouths and writings, with very uncertain, little, or no signification.
>
> (Locke 1989)

Ideally, we should agree to use the same words to refer to the same things; if I use a word to refer to one thing and you use the same word to refer to something else, we will create all sorts of confusion, error, and falsehood. At first this may seem too obvious to be worth mentioning. Obviously, when I talk about a rattlesnake, I should mean the same thing everyone else does by "rattlesnake." It would, of course, be a mistake, but an absurd mistake, if I meant by "rattlesnake" a Persian cat. You claim that rattlesnakes are poisonous, and I say rattlesnakes are not. But our disagreement lies in the fact that we are talking about completely different things—you are talking about a particular kind of reptile of the American Southwest, and I am talking about a kind of small domestic feline. In this case it is hard to see how such an absurd verbal mistake could ever occur. But in other cases we can see that such mistakes are indeed quite common.

Suppose now that you and I are both referring to the exact same thing when we talk about "rattlesnakes"—both of us are talking about the slithering reptile with the "rattles" on the end of its tail. But suppose now that you say the rattlesnake is poisonous, and I claim it is not poisonous. Wherein does our disagreement lie? Is it a factual disagreement? That is, does one of us know something the other does not? Or is it a disagreement over words and their meanings? Perhaps you mean that the *bite* of the rattlesnake is poisonous, and I mean that the rattlesnake is safe (and good) to *eat*—if the rattlesnake bites you, it is poisonous; if you bite the (cooked) rattlesnake, it is not poisonous.

Clearly, this kind of mistake is prevalent. Almost every country in the world today (since the United Nations Charter of 1948) claims to support "human rights," and almost all countries today claim to be "democratic" and to support "liberty," "equality," and "free and fair elections." Yet when we look at the actual practices of these countries, we see very different interpretations of these concepts. Some countries interpret freedom and rights to mean that each person should have the right to be free to do as he or she pleases, as long as they do not interfere with the equal rights and freedoms of others. That is, freedom and rights are interpreted to mean that individuals have the right to be largely free from any governmental interference in their private affairs. But other countries interpret freedom and rights differently, to mean that everyone has the right to be free from hunger, poverty, homelessness, and lack of health care. These are clearly quite different interpretations of rights and freedoms (which we will examine in chapter 6). In the first case, governments should do nothing but prevent anyone from violating the individuals' rights, while in the second case, the government must become heavily involved in redistributing the nation's wealth (taking from the rich to give to the poor) in order to provide food, clothing, housing, health care, and so on. In the United States today, the question arises whether censorship of pornography is a violation or a protection of human rights. Does it violate the rights of free speech, or does it protect the rights of women? Does legally outlawing abortion protect the rights of the unborn or violate the rights of women? In cases like this, verbal agreement (we all agree to support human rights, democracy, and so on) masks real disagreement over what these words should mean. Here then is the continuing need for the "rectification of names."

Xunzi used his theory of the rectification of names to analyze what he regarded as some of the fallacies of his opponents, especially those who created logical paradoxes. There are three main fallacies, he said, which result from failures in the rectification of names: confusing names with names, names with things, and things with names. As an example of the first (confusing names with names), Xunzi criticizes Mozi's claim that, "To kill a robber is not to kill a man." Mozi had claimed that we should love everyone equally (my mother as much as your mother). But his critics wondered how the Mohists could also consistently justify punishing a thief (by capital punishment, that is, killing him). If you punish the robber by killing him, do you really love him as much as you do your own mother? Mozi offered the aforementioned reply, "To kill a robber is not to kill a man." If the class of robbers is included in the class of men, then, Xunxi argues, Mozi is wrong—it logically follows that killing a robber is necessarily killing a man. The class of men includes the entire class of robbers, so whatever is true of the class of robbers must also be true of some men—though not the reverse, as Harry Stottlemeir discovered: All robbers are men, but not all men are robbers (fortunately).

Even so, Mozi might reply that he is thinking of one's *intention*, which is part of the action—in killing a robber, it is not our intention to kill a human being per se but only to punish someone who has wronged us by robbing us. In defending this position, Mozi might point out, for example, how odd and unfair it would be to refer to the executioner (out of context) as someone who "goes around killing people" (Mozi might even be supported by a follower of Gong-Sun Lung—a robber person is not a person). If we are thinking simply of all the things in the world and how they are classified, then we would certainly agree with Xunzi, that in that sense all robber men are men (just as all white horses are horses). But if we are thinking of the *meaning* of these universal terms, then we might want to defend Mozi (and Gong-Sun Lung) in claiming that what is meant by killing a man is not the same as (not synonymous with) what is meant by killing a robber and that what is meant by buying a horse is not identical with the meaning of buying a white horse. If these expressions had the same *meaning*, then we could substitute one expression for the other in any sentence without changing either the meaning of the sentence or its truth value. But we obviously cannot substitute one for the other in the case of the robber and the white horse.

Suppose you are the state executioner and you are told to kill a robber in the morning; but in the morning you go out and kill another man to whom you owe a lot of money. Could you defend your action by saying, "You asked me to kill the robber man; but a robber man is a man, and I did kill a man—so what's the problem?" Surely we would respond, "But we didn't ask you to kill just any man—your job as state executioner was to kill this convicted robber duly sentenced to die." Similarly, suppose we are filming an old-fashioned Western movie, but when you send me out to get a white horse for the hero of our film, I return with a black horse. When you criticize me, I reply, "But a white horse is a horse, and I brought you a horse—what's the problem?"

As an example of the second fallacy (confusing names with things), Xunzi attacks the argument of Hui Shih and Zhuangzi, that "mountains and valleys are on the same level." While it is true that an exceptionally high valley might be higher than an exceptionally low mountain, nonetheless, the name, or concept of mountain and valley, indicates the class as a whole, not the individual mountain or valley, and so refers to the *typical* member of that class, in which case mountains and valleys are *not* on the same level. Or, we might say, since valleys are formed by mountains, this *particular* valley formed by that *particular* group of mountains is always and necessarily lower than those particular mountains.

Similarly, Aristotle tried to resolve the apparent paradox that a small thing could be large and a large thing small by analyzing the meaning of relative terms.

> A man might argue that "much" is the contrary of "little" and "great" is the contrary of "small." However, this is not quantitative but relative. Things are not great and small absolutely, they are so called rather as the result of an act of comparison. For instance: A mountain is called "small" in virtue of the fact that this particular mountain is smaller than all the others.
>
> (Aristotle, Richard McKeon, ed., *Introduction to Aristotle*)

As an example of the third fallacy (confusing the thing with the name), Xunzi attacks the Mohist claim that "an ox and a horse is not a horse" (reminiscent of Gong-sun Lung's more famous paradox "A white horse is not a horse"). Although it is true that the names (the words "ox" and "horse") are not synonymous (that is, identical in meaning), the class of horses is included within the class of things that includes both oxen and horses (large, four-legged, hoofed, grass-eating, domesticated animals), and in that sense a horse certainly *is* all of those things (a class consisting of both oxen and horses).

Other examples of Chinese logicians trying to solve the paradoxes of the Ming Jia are found in the later Mohists, that is, Chapters 40 through 45 of the book *Mo Zi*, which were in all probability not written by Mozi himself but by his followers many years later. Many of the paradoxes we have seen spring from the failure to distinguish different senses in which things may be said to be "the same" (in Chinese "tung"). In Chapter 40, the Mohists try to draw some useful distinctions that will resolve some of these paradoxes. "Tung: there is that of identity, that of part-and-whole relationship, that of co-existence, and that of generic relation." Then, later, in Chapter 42, these different senses are defined. "That there are two names for one actuality is identity. Inclusion in one whole is the part-and-whole relationship. Both being in the same room is co-existence. Having some points of similarity is generic relation."

So, for example, when Hui Shih (and Zhuangzi following him) says that "all things are alike" or even that "there is no difference between things and that all things are one," and so on, this, the Mohists say, is merely generic similarity, not identity. In a trivial sense, as Xunzi also noted, all things are similar to one another in the sense that they all belong to the class "things," just as everything is *dis*similar to everything else in the sense that each is an individual thing. It is only by sliding over the generic/identity distinction that Hui Shih and Zhuangzi make it seem that they have established the far more radical and mysterious (and paradoxical) claim that all distinctions are unreal, that there are no differences between things, that all things mysteriously blend into one. Or, when philosophers claim that "heaven and earth are one," they are only saying, truthfully, according to the later Mohists, that they are both parts of the same whole (universe), not that they are identical, which is absurd.

In these chapters, the Mohists also attack the Taoist claim that "learning is useless," that (as Zhuangzi said) "there can never be agreement, right or wrong, in an argument," that "all speech is perverse." Like the liar's paradox in Western philosophy ("I am lying"—is that statement true or false?), if these claims are true, the Mohists point out, they apply to themselves, thus refuting and undermining themselves (or if they *do not* apply to themselves, then they are not universally true as claimed, and so again are falsified). How, for example, can Zhuangzi assert that words do not assert anything? If no words assert anything, then Zhuangzi's words also assert nothing; but if Zhuangzi is asserting this claim, then some words at least do assert, and it is false to say that no words can assert anything. As the later Mohists say, "'All speech is perverse' is itself perverse." This is similar to Aristotle's refutation of skepticism—by claiming he knows there is no knowledge, the skeptic contradicts himself; either knowledge is impossible, and the truth of the skeptical claim cannot be known, or the skeptical claim can be known, in which case knowledge is possible—what the skeptic cannot consistently say is that he knows there is no knowledge.

Of course, the Taoists were talking about a completely different sort of knowledge in which there are no distinctions among things in the world, and therefore no categories or classes of things, and moreover no distinction between knower and known, a kind of knowledge whose goal is not information but to become one with everything. But how can we use logic and ordinary forms of speech to discuss such a thing? As the Taoists themselves admit, we cannot ("those who know don't speak; those who speak don't know"). They are referring to a kind of experience that goes beyond ordinary speech and ordinary forms of thinking. As they themselves say, ordinary speech and knowledge are useless for discussing this all-embracing reality. But since philosophy is a reflection on ordinary ways of thinking and speaking, this means to go beyond philosophy itself.

And so, as a *philosophical debate*, Xunzi and the later Mohists clearly win. There is only one way to debate, and that way favors ordinary ways of thinking and speaking and experiencing, which are universal in all human beings.

Even if the Taoists are right (and they might be), it is hard for them to argue for their position. How could they convince us? Only by showing us another way, beyond reason and common sense and philosophy, perhaps through mystical intuition and meditational practices. (Only in his skeptical argument can Zhuangzi possibly score a few points. That is, if he can convince us that knowledge in the ordinary sense is impossible, then he may be able to convince us to take a chance on an alternative sort of mystical knowledge. But to embrace complete skepticism is to abandon philosophy altogether, and few philosophers are willing to go that far.)

Greek philosophers like Plato and Aristotle tried to resolve paradoxes in a similar way (to that of Xunzi and the later Mohists) by analyzing different senses in the verb "to be." When we say Beijing is the capital of China we are using the "is" of identity—"the capital of China" and "Beijing" refer to one and the same thing which goes by these two different names. But when we say Beijing is a city in China, we are using the "is" of inclusion—Beijing is one of many cities in China. And of course when we include something in a larger class of things, we are at the same time, at least implicitly, *excluding* it from many other classes of things. So when I say that Fluffy is a cat, I am at once *including* her in the class of cats and *excluding* her from the class of dogs, tuna fish sandwiches, volcanoes, triangles, and so on. And this gives us a way of answering Parmenides's and Zeno's puzzling claim that it is impossible to talk or think "what is not." When I say that Fluffy is not a dog, I am not talking about something that "is not" (Non-being); I am simply saying that Fluffy belongs in the category of cats and not in the category of dogs. There is also the "is" of existence, as when we say (in 1998), "There is an underground train system in Shanghai," or (after 1911), "There is no Emperor of China." Thus, Greek logicians would have solved the white horse paradox much like Xunzi did, by pointing out that while a white horse is not identical with a horse, white horses certainly are included in the larger class of horses.

3

Epistemology, or Theory of Knowledge

*P*HILOSOPHY, we have said, is a critique of commonsense, traditional views. But how can philosophers convince others? As we saw earlier, before we can criticize traditional knowledge claims, we need to become clear about exactly what knowledge is, how it can be attained, and why some knowledge claims have a better right to be believed than others. Before we can hope to convince others about any particular issue, we first must answer the questions: How do you *know?* What is good evidence? What counts as proof or justification? Preliminary to other work in philosophy, then, is work in logic and theories of knowledge. Whatever their ultimate interests in gaining knowledge, Indian, Chinese, and Western philosophers have all recognized the paramount need to first become clear about the nature of knowledge. This is the branch of philosophy known as epistemology, or theory of knowledge.

The goal of epistemology, or theory of knowledge, is to discover the standard or criterion for knowledge as opposed to mere belief. What is the difference between knowledge and belief? Like most philosophical questions, this is a normative distinction. Belief can be true or false, whereas knowledge is always true and can never be false. If you really know something, you cannot be mistaken (though it is hard to know whether we really know something or merely believe it). So knowledge is "better" and more reliable than mere belief, so we want to know the difference between the two.

In every branch of philosophy, there are "skeptics" who say the philosophical goal is impossible to achieve. So in the case of epistemology, the skeptic claims that there is no difference between belief and knowledge—except conceit. "I know it" just means the speaker believes it and is overconfidently claiming he or she knows it. According to the epistemological skeptic, in other words, there is no objective and universal way to tell which beliefs are true (correct) and which are false (incorrect). It is therefore impossible to differentiate knowledge from mere belief. But those philosophers who think it is possible and have tried to achieve the goal of epistemology—a universal and an objective criterion for differentiating knowledge from mere belief—do not agree among themselves but have come up with different answers, which we will examine in this chapter.

Let us begin with what we learned from the last chapter on logic and language. We can already see the connection between logic and epistemology (just as we will see, in the next chapter, the connection between logic and metaphysics, the theory of what really exists). In logic, we become aware of the difference between the particular individual things in the world and the concepts, categories, and ideas by which we classify those things (a distinction normally disguised and confused in ordinary speech where the word "cow," for example, can refer either to the individual cow or to the concept "cow"). This leads to the desire in epistemology to make sure there is a reliable connection between words (concepts) and objects, that is, that our language accurately and reliably represents reality, providing knowledge and truth. If I know that this individual thing belongs to the general category of cow, then I know that it is not something I can saddle up and ride out of town, nor is it something likely to attack and eat me, but rather something that eats grass and produces milk.

How then do we know that our words truthfully match, or correspond, with reality, giving us genuine knowledge of the world? At first the solution might seem to be a two-track approach—using sense perception to tell us what the individual thing is (that is, that the individual thing is correctly classified by a particular word or concept), and then using logic to extend perceptual knowledge by working out the logical relations among the meanings of the general concepts themselves. If our words are to have any bearing on the real world, they must connect with reality at some point through sense experience. *If* that is a guppy, then certain inferences are allowable. *If* that is a cow, we know what to expect. But *is* it a guppy? *Is* it a cow? Here we can only look and see. In our earlier example, I can see just by looking that Judy is a guppy; and then, by the meanings of words and their logical relations, I can extend that knowledge: guppies are fish; fish cannot live outside of water; so, if Judy is a fish, she is in big trouble being carried around in my shirt pocket—on the other hand, if I see that Judy is a cow, then although cows can live outside of water, they are a little big to fit comfortably in my shirt pocket.

Nonetheless, as we will see, there are problems with this initially appealing approach. First, because sense perception always involves an element of classification, it is therefore always liable to error. To see something, we must see it as this or that, as a snake, for example, but then it may turn out not to be a snake but only a piece of rope, and so we were mistaken. Second, the logical connections among our general concepts may not be completely reliable, either, leading to errors in logic as well. To judge that the hill is on fire because we see smoke is a valid inference, only if smoke is always accompanied by fire, but this may *not always* be the case (the fire might have been put out, although the brush is still smoking). And if we are in some doubt, we can only go and look more closely (walking over to the hill we can see for ourselves whether the hill is on fire or not)—thus checking the reliability of our logical inferences by further sense experience.

In the history of philosophy, this sort of reflection on our ordinary intuitions has led to two different approaches to the theory of knowledge—the first, empiricism, looking for the element of greatest certainty and reliability in sense perception, and the second, rationalism, looking for the element of greatest certainty and reliability in logical relations among the meanings of abstract general concepts. Still other philosophers have argued that knowledge requires *both*. In this chapter, we will see how Chinese, Indian, and Western philosophers have tried to find the balance between sense experience and logical inference in answering the question, what is knowledge, and how can we attain it?

As Indian, Chinese, and Western philosophers began to reflect on our ordinary, intuitive, commonsense notion of knowledge, they all came to the initial conclusion that reliable knowledge generally comes either from sense experience or from a logical extension of sense experience by means of reasoning. Reflecting on ordinary commonsense intuitions, most philosophers agree that the most reliable evidence is our own direct sense experience. As China's second-great philosopher (after Kongzi, or Confucius) Mozi (fourth century B.C.E.) said,

> The way to determine whether something exists or not is to find out whether people actually know from the evidence of their own ears and eyes whether it exists, and use this as a standard. If someone has actually heard it and seen it, then we must assume that it exists. But if no one has heard or seen it, then we must assume that it does not exist. If this is to be our method, then why don't we try going to some village or community and asking [whether people have seen or heard it]?
>
> (Mozi, *Mozi*, in Watson, *Basic Writings*)

Or, as the Indian Nyaya logicians put it,

> Perception, inference, analogy, and verbal testimony—these are the means of right knowledge. Among these four kinds of cognition, perception is the most important.

. . . When a man has once perceived the thing directly, his desires are at rest, and he does not seek for any other kind of knowledge.

(from the *Nyaya Sutra*, in Radhakrishnan and Moore, *Sourcebook in Indian*)

Like the Nyaya philosophers just quoted, most philosophers also believe that we can reliably extend (generalize) our knowledge from direct sense experience by logical inference (you do not have to actually jump from a twenty-story window to know that it will hurt!). A month-old infant can see the book I am holding, but she does not yet know that it is a book, and this involves correctly classifying the thing she sees into the properly labeled category ("That thing I am seeing is what we call a book, and since it is a book I know that even though it is now closed it can be opened onto pages with words on them"). In a famous example from traditional Indian Nyaya logic (fourth century B.C.E.), we begin by seeing smoke on a distant hill, and we reason that since smoke is caused by fire, the hill must be on fire (although we cannot actually see the fire).

The Indian Nyaya and Vaisesika schools of philosophy debated over whether there were more than these two sources of knowledge—for example, eyewitness testimony, which is important in criminal court proceedings, and also for authenticating holy scripture (that is, where a particular religious report, say of a miracle, might seem strange and otherwise unbelievable, except that some very reliable person reports actually having seen it). But is this third kind of knowledge (eyewitness report) really different from the second kind of knowledge, where we reason from what we have directly experienced to something beyond our own immediate sense experience? For instance, we tend to believe Susan's testimony, even though we never actually saw the thing she is describing. Why? Well, she has always told the truth in the past, so we reason that she is probably telling the truth now. Of course, people do sometimes tell lies, but we also know from our past experience *why* people tend to tell lies, and in this particular case we have no reason to think that Susan stands to gain anything by telling a lie. We are simply using reasoning to go beyond our own sense experience. So we probably can reduce knowledge by eyewitness testimony to the second kind of knowledge by logical extension of sense experience.

Can we go still further, reducing these two kinds of knowledge to only one? In the history of philosophy, empiricists have attempted to reduce all knowledge claims to those based on sense experience alone, while the rationalists have tried to reduce all knowledge claims to those based on reasoning alone. According to John Locke (English, seventeenth century), the first in a long line of British empiricist philosophers, including George Berkeley and David Hume, all knowledge ultimately reduces to ideas implanted on the mind through the five senses (plus a kind of sixth sense, called "reflection," by which we can introspect the operations of our own mind). The empiricist view is that while the mind can arrange and rearrange its simple sense ideas into more and more complex notions, all ideas must nonetheless be trace-able, ultimately back to simple sense impressions ("ideas") of yellow, bitter, cold, and so on. That is the only source of knowledge.

> All ideas come from sensation or reflection. Let us then suppose the mind to be, as we say, white paper, void of all characters, without any ideas; how comes it to be fur-nished? Whence comes it by that vast store, which the busy and bondless fancy of man has painted on it with an almost endless variety? Whence has it all the materials of reason and knowledge? To this I answer in one word, from experience; in that all our knowledge is founded, and from that it ultimately derives itself. . . . Our senses, con-versant about particular sensible objects, do convey into the mind several distinct per-ceptions of things, according to those various ways wherein those objects do affect them; and thus we come by those ideas we have of yellow, white, heat, cold, soft, hard, bitter, sweet, and all those which we call sensible qualities; which when I say the senses convey into the mind, I mean, they from external objects convey into the mind what produces there those perceptions.
>
> (Locke 1989)

At the empiricist extreme, the Indian Carvacan school (sixth century B.C.E.) rejected any source of knowledge except direct sense experience—if you do not actually see the fire on the hill, then the Carvacans say you do not really know whether the hill is on fire or not. The Carvacans were strict mate-rialists; only matter exists, they held, and therefore there is no soul or God or life after death, and for that reason, we should enjoy whatever physical plea-sures we can in this life.

> Only perceptual evidence is authority; the elements are earth, water, fire, and air; wealth and enjoyment are the objects of human existence. Matter can think. There is no other world. Death is the end of all.
>
> (the Carvacans, in Radhakrishnan and Moore, *Sourcebook in Indian*)

The Carvacan rejection of inference, however, would very severely restrict knowledge, since almost all ordinary, commonsense knowledge relies on our ability to generalize beyond our actual direct sense experience (for example, your knowledge that putting your hand in the fire will hurt you, that jumping out of a twenty-story building will probably kill you, and so on). As a child, I remember burning my finger once in the flame of a candle, and I remember how much it hurt; I now assume that all fire will similarly hurt, so I never again deliberately stick my hand into the fire. I have learned from my experience, but this clearly involves *going beyond* my own direct sense experience (of being burned that one time as a child).

As the Indian dualists, the Samkhya, pointed out, the Carvacans seem to contradict themselves when they say that we can know that other people are mistaken, for this implies that we know what they are thinking, and how can we know that except by inference from their words and actions (you cannot actually see or hear another person's thoughts)?

> When the materialist affirms that inference is not a means of knowledge, how is it that he can know that a man is ignorant or in doubt or in error?
>
> (*Samkaytattvakaumudi*, in Radhakrishnan and Moore, *Sourcebook in Indian*)

The eighteenth-century Scottish philosopher David Hume points out that practically all of our knowledge of "matters of fact" is based on generalizations from experience, which he calls reasoning from "cause and effect."

> All reasonings concerning matter of fact seem to be founded on the relation of cause and effect. By means of that relation alone we can go beyond the evidence of our memory and senses. If you were to ask a man why he believes any matter of fact which is absent, for instance, that his friend is in the country or in France, he would give you a reason, and this reason would be some other fact: as a letter received from him or the knowledge of his former resolutions and promises. A man finding a watch or any other machine in a desert island would conclude that there had once been men in that island. All our reasonings concerning fact are of the same nature. And here it is constantly supposed that there is a connection between the present fact and that which is inferred from it. Were there nothing to bind them together, the inference would be entirely precarious. The hearing of an articulate voice and rational discourse in the dark assures us of the presence of some person. Why? Because these are the effects of the human make and fabric, and closely connected with it. If we anatomize all the other reasonings of this nature we shall find that they are founded on the relation of cause and effect.
>
> (Hume 1977)

Let us consider Hume's example. You hear a voice in the dark. That is your present sense impression. And you reason that there is someone in the room who is producing that voice (as Hume would say, someone who is "causing" that "effect"). When we stop to think about it, we can see that Hume is right; without this ability to generalize from sense experience (cause and effect), our knowledge of the world would be extremely limited.

Hume's analysis of causality is quite typical of philosophy at work. We have said that philosophy is a reflection on our commonsense intuitions. But sometimes it is difficult to get beyond "the obvious." It seems so obvious that we just see things and that is all there is to it! We often need some device to help stimulate our powers of "reflection"—in this case, specifically on the reasons why sense experience alone cannot explain everyday knowledge. Typically, these "devices" will include thought experiments: we might try to imagine the experience of a newborn baby, or we could (like David Hume) imagine what the experience of a space alien might be like; we could (like John Locke) try to think of the mind as someone inside a "dark closet" inside the brain receiving messages from the outside world (through the five senses); or finally, we could try to think of the difficulties involved in programming a computer to recognize physical objects of a certain kind, and to "learn" the causal dispositions of different types of physical objects.

The object of any of these thought experiments is to recognize the contribution of the "mind" or "brain" or "reasoning" powers of thought (i.e., that which is *not* empirical) to our ability to organize our sense impressions into semi-permanent physical objects, our ability to classify physical objects into kinds, types, categories, and classes, and our ability to construct causal laws, causal regularities, and causal dispositions about what these kinds of physical objects can do to us or for us (positively or negatively).

With that in mind, try this thought experiment. Imagine a person with excellent sensory perception but suffering from a complete loss of memory. First, would such a person be able to even *recognize* what he sees as *fire*? If he has lost all memory, will he even remember what it is he is looking at? Of course, like a month-old baby, he sees something, but will he remember that this thing that he now sees resembles that thing that hurt him many years ago? And even if he can somehow recognize that it is fire (that is, even if he recognizes that this thing he is now looking at resembles things he has seen before, which he *also* remembers are called "fire"), will he remember that many years ago the fire burned and hurt him? If he has lost all memory, it is difficult to see how he could know *any* of this; in all likelihood, he would probably simply see a bright shining thing and have no idea what it is or what it can do.

Now, although this is more difficult, try to imagine a person with excellent sense perception and good memory, but who is unable to generalize ("cause and effect" rules) from his past experience. Climbing down a mountain one day he sees fire blocking his path; he recognizes that it is fire, and he remembers being burned and hurt by the fire years ago. But will that knowledge have any bearing on *this* fire, here and now? Not unless he can formulate the causal rule that things of the same kind generally behave in the same way, so that the present will in general always resemble the past, and that since the fire burned and hurt him once, it is likely to burn and hurt him now on this occasion. But can he formulate this rule of cause and effect if, as we said, he is unable to generalize from his past experience? No; if he lacks the ability to generalize from experience, he is likely to see the fire in front of him as fire, remembering how he was burned by fire once before, but now wondering what the fire will do to him this time. This is a person with five senses and memory, but no intellect. How can such a person live? He will obviously have to be institutionalized. He is obviously not a normal human being (although there are such severely handicapped people). Without the ability to generalize from past experience and to reason reliably from that to new situations, we could never *learn* from our sense experience; every experience would then be totally new, and the world would forever be a strange and surely a frightening place.

So a pure empiricism divorced from all reasoning seems impossible. At the opposite extreme of empiricism is rationalism, the view that knowledge depends entirely and only on reasoning, and not at all on sense experience. But it is equally hard to imagine a pure rationalism entirely divorced from empiricism. Of course, like empiricism, rationalism has something to be said for it. If we reflect on our commonsense intuitions about knowledge, we can see that we ordinarily think that to really know something we must be sure. We would not ordinarily say, "I know she is coming, but I'm not sure." If we are not sure, we would say, "I think (believe) so, but I'm not sure." Only if we are certain do we say we know, "I know it; I'm sure." To be sure means having very good reasons for believing something, reasons that justify us in believing it. But *how* sure or certain do we have to be? How good do the reasons justifying belief have to be in order to qualify as knowledge? This is where philosophers, in this case the rationalists, depart from common sense.

In everyday life, we try to be reasonably sure, perhaps 70 to 80 percent certain. Rationalist philosophers argue, however, that if a thing is worth doing it is worth doing right—no halfway measures! To be certain, they say, means being 100 percent certain. Anything less than that (even 99.99 percent certain) is mere belief—not knowledge. As Descartes said, to know something it must be beyond the possibility of doubt, something we are so certain of we cannot even imagine how it could conceivably be mistaken. To discover what he knew beyond the possibility of doubt, Descartes developed a reflective "device," his famous "method of doubt," in which he would ask himself for every belief he held if he could imagine how it might turn out to be mistaken. Even in cases where we feel reasonably sure, as in Hume's example of the letter from a friend abroad, or hearing a voice in the dark, we can nonetheless imagine how these might be mistaken (a forged letter, a tape recording).

There is no novelty to me in the reflection that, from my earliest years, I have accepted many false opinions as true, and that what I have concluded from such badly assured premises could not but be highly doubtful and uncertain. From the time that I first recognized this fact, I have realized that if I wished to have any firm and constant knowledge in the sciences, I would have to undertake, once and for all, to set aside all the opinions which I had previously accepted among my beliefs and start again from the very beginning. . . . I will therefore make a serious and unimpeded effort to destroy generally all my former opinions. In order to do this, however, it will not be necessary to show that they are all false; . . . because, since reason already convinces me that I should abstain from the belief in things which are not entirely certain and indubitable no less carefully than from the belief in those which appear to me to be manifestly false, it will be enough to make me reject them all if I can find in each some ground for doubt.

(Descartes 1979)

But that is a tough standard. What can we know by such a strict criterion? Do I know with absolutely certainty that a letter is really from my friend who is now vacationing in France (to use Hume's example)? No, the letter might be forged, or perhaps it is really from my friend who is bragging that she is in France when she never actually left Columbus, Ohio. Even the voice in the dark might come from the radio or a tape recorder. It is even possible, Descartes argues, that we could be dreaming.

Everything which I have thus far accepted as entirely true . . . has been acquired from the senses. . . . But I have learned by experience that these senses sometimes mislead me, and it is prudent never to trust wholly those things which have once deceived us. But it is possible that, even though the senses occasionally deceive us about things which are barely perceptible and very far away, there are many other things which we cannot reasonably doubt, even though we know them through the senses—as, for example, that I am here, seated by the fire, wearing a winter dressing gown, holding this paper in my hands. . . . Nevertheless, I must remember that I am a man, and that consequently I am accustomed to sleep and in my dreams to imagine the same things that lunatics imagine when awake. . . . How many times has it occurred that the quiet of the night made me dream that I was here, clothed in a dressing gown, and sitting by the fire, although I was in fact lying undressed in bed! It seems apparent to me now, that I am not looking at this paper with my eyes closed. . . . But I am speaking as though I never recall having been misled, while asleep, by similar illusions! When I consider these matters carefully, I realize so clearly that there are no conclusive indications by which waking life can be distinguished from sleep that I am quite astonished. . . . So let us suppose now that we are asleep and that all these things are merely illusions; and let us think that perhaps our hands and our whole body are not such as we see them.

(Descartes 1979)

Descartes concluded that only the fact that "I think therefore I am" is absolutely certain and beyond all doubt—I cannot be mistaken in thinking I am thinking!

I suppose . . . that everything that I see is false; I convince myself that nothing has ever existed of all that my deceitful memory recalls to me. I think that I have no senses; and I believe that body, shape, motion . . . are merely inventions of my mind. What then could still be thought true? Perhaps nothing else, unless it is that there is nothing certain in the world. . . . But at the very least am I not an entity myself? But I have already denied that I had any senses or any body. However, at this point I hesitate, for what follows from that? Am I so dependent upon body and the senses that I could not exist without them? I have just convinced myself that nothing whatsoever existed in the world, that there was no sky, no earth, no minds, and no bodies; have I not thereby convinced myself that I did not exist? Not at all; without doubt I existed if I was convinced of this. Even though there may be a deceiver of some sort, very powerful and very tricky, who bends all his efforts to keep me perpetually deceived, there can be no slightest doubt that I exist, since he deceives me; and let him deceive me as much as he will, he can never make me be nothing as long as I think that I am something. Thus, after having thought well on this matter, and after examining all things with care, I must finally conclude and maintain that this proposition: I am, I exist, is necessarily true every time that I pronounce it or conceive it in my mind.

(Descartes 1979)

Other philosophers added statements like "all bachelors are unmarried," "either it will rain or it won't," which are true beyond all doubt but trivially true by definition. But even with these additions, that does not get us very far. And if our standard is 100 percent certainty, it will have to exclude all sense perception, which can never achieve such complete certainty.

Our senses sometimes deceive us, but we can never be mistaken in reasoning that two plus two is four, or that all bachelors are unmarried, or that it is either raining or it is not raining, or that if Judy is a guppy and guppies cannot live outside of water, then Judy cannot live outside of water, and things of that sort. So it might seem (and has seemed to many philosophers) that rationalism (reasoning alone) provides the best (most certain) kind of knowledge. But there are problems with this approach as well. The fact that all bachelors are unmarried and that tomorrow it will either rain or not rain does not really tell you much about the world or provide you with much useful information (whether this young man is married or not, or whether we should take an umbrella when we go out this evening).

Imagine a person planning to raise unicorns. Before buying the unicorns, she wants to make all of the necessary preparations. She knows from the meaning of the word that a unicorn is much like a horse (except that it has a horn which a horse does not). So, she knows that unicorns probably eat grass, and she accordingly fences in a large area of grassland. Thus she is all set, right? Well, no. Actually, there is a big problem she has ignored. There *are* no unicorns! The word "unicorn" is meaningful and can be defined, but it does not represent anything existing in the world. So even the most accurate logical derivation from the meaning of the word "unicorn" (that it is like a horse, eats grass, etc.), will not result in reliable knowledge, since the word does not describe anything actually existing in the world.

Therefore, it looks like we need *both*—sense experience and reasoning from sense experience. As the eighteenth-century German philosopher Immanuel Kant said, knowledge without reasoning is blind, and knowledge without sense experience is empty. To learn something about the world, we need both, Kant said; we must use words to refer to things in the world that we can actually experience and then reason from the meaning of these words to further experiences that we have not actually had but could conceivably have. Seeing smoke on the hill, I reason that the hill is probably on fire, and although I cannot actually see the fire, I can walk over to the hill and actually observe it (or not—perhaps the fire has been put out, though the area is still smoking).

> There can be no doubt that all our knowledge begins with experience. . . . But though all our knowledge begins with experience, it does not follow that it all arises out of experience. For it may well be that even our empirical knowledge is made up of what we receive through impressions and of what our own faculty of knowledge . . . supplies from itself. If our faculty of knowledge makes any such addition, it may be that we are not in a position to distinguish it from the raw material, until with long practice of attention we have become skilled in separating it. . . . Our knowledge springs from two fundamental sources of the mind; the first is the capacity of receiving representations (receptivity for impressions), the second is the power of knowing an object through these representations (spontaneity in the production of concepts). Through the first an object is given to us, through the second the object is thought in relation to that representation. . . . Intuition and concepts constitute, therefore, the elements of all our knowledge, so that neither concepts without an intuition in some way corresponding to them, nor intuitions without concepts, can yield knowledge. . . . Without sensibility no object would be given to us, without understanding no object would be thought. Thoughts without content are empty, intuitions without concepts are blind.
>
> (Kant, Immanuel, *Critique of Pure Reason*, Norman Kemp Smith, trans.)

Hearing what sounds like rain on the roof outside, I grab my umbrella and walk outdoors. First I hear sounds, which I then describe as "rain," and then, using the meaning of the word "rain," I reason that if I go out without my umbrella I will get wet (which I do not want), so I grab my umbrella as I leave the house. (Of course, once I get outside, I may discover that the sound I heard was *not* rain after all but only some tree branches scraping against the roof. Although my logic is not foolproof, in most cases my reasoning will be confirmed by seeing and feeling the actual raindrops as I open the door to go outside.)

So in the end it seems reasonable to conclude that there are at least these two sources of knowledge—sense experience and reasoning from sense experience—and that we really need both. Nonetheless, the ancient Indian Carvacans (and their Western empiricist counterparts) do raise a serious question about knowledge based on inference. How do we know that the hill is on fire? Because we see the smoke, and smoke is always accompanied by fire. But is it really true that smoke is *always* accompanied by fire? As in our previous example, might not the fire have gone out, although the charred brush continues to smoke? Is it not also possible that it is not smoke at all, but steam coming from a factory just out of sight? Or maybe a geyser? Perhaps the Carvacans are right after all, and all we can say for sure is that the hill is *probably* on fire.

For reasons of this sort, Hume was skeptical of our most ordinary knowledge of the world, arguing that we really have no good reason to make such causal inferences. No matter how hard we look, he says, we can never observe any causal connection, that is, we never actually see the productive force that causes the effect. All we can see is the temporal succession of the cause followed by the effect. When we have observed such a temporal succession many times we are simply habituated to expect the effect whenever we see the cause.

> Suppose a person, though endowed with the strongest faculties of reason and reflection, to be brought on a sudden into this world; he would, indeed, immediately observe a continual succession of objects and one event following another, but he would not be able to discover anything further. He would not at first, by any reasoning, be able to reach the idea of cause and effect, since the particular powers by which all natural operations are performed never appear to the senses; nor is it reasonable to conclude, merely because one event in one instance precedes another, that therefore the one is the cause, the other the effect. The conjunction may be arbitrary and casual. There may be no reason to infer the existence of one from the appearance of the other and, in a word, such a person without more experience could never employ his conjecture or reasoning concerning any matter of fact or be assured of anything beyond what was immediately present to his memory or senses. Suppose again that he has acquired more experience and has lived so long in the world as to have observed similar objects or events to be constantly conjoined together. . . . He immediately infers the existence of one object from the appearance of the other, yet he has not, by all his experience, acquired any idea or knowledge of the secret power by which the one object produces the other, nor is it by any process of reasoning he is engaged to draw this inference. . . . There is some other principle which determines him to form such a conclusion. This principle is custom or habit.

(Hume 1977)

According to Hume, we have no more reason to believe in causal connections than the rooster that Bertrand Russell (twentieth-century British philosopher) tells us about who found that when he crowed early each morning the sun would come up and so, by "custom and habit," the rooster assumed that he was *causing* the sun to rise each day. But then one day, sadly, the farmer wrung his neck and roasted him for supper and the sun continued to come up each day just as before! Or we can think of Pavlov's dog. Pavlov conducted an experiment in which for several months he rang a bell each time he was about to feed the dog. After some time he would ring the bell without putting out any food and the dog continued to salivate just as before.

But are we really as stupid as the rooster and the dog? Do we have no better reason for expecting things to happen than the fact that they have always happened that way in the past? We think the sun will rise tomorrow, but why? Is it just because we have seen it come up every morning in the past, or is it also because we know something about *why* the sun "comes up" every morning, that is, the earth's rotation and the probability that this and the light and heat from the sun's atomic fusion will continue for a long time? Suppose one day we observe the mating behavior of a particular pair of birds. How many times do we have to see this to conclude that this is how all birds of this species engage in mating? Once is probably enough. Why? Because we have many other sorts of information indicating that the ways in which the members of a species behave are similar to one another in certain respects, including mating behavior. Hume is not taking into account the way in which many beliefs, theories, and pieces of information are interconnected.

Or consider the reverse. Suppose that one day a tree began talking to you. Would you believe this was really happening? Suppose it happened several times a day for a couple of weeks. Would you believe that a tree was talking to you, or would you still think it was probably a trick of some sort (or that you were going crazy)? Why? Is it not because this sense experience of yours (of the talking tree) just does not fit in with all of your other beliefs—beliefs about how it is possible for something, like a person, to carry on a conversation and beliefs about trees, which you know do not have that sort of equipment?

But even if we reject the skeptical challenge of Hume and the Carvacans and acknowledge that there are these two ways of knowing (sense experience and causal inference, based on sense experience), is this *all* we are capable of knowing? What about knowledge of God, of the soul, of life after death, of the ultimate, underlying reality of the universe? Can this be known simply by means of sense experience and its extension by logical inference? Some philosophers have indeed argued that we can infer the existence of God from the order we find in the world (like Hume's example of inferring the existence of a watchmaker from the existence of a watch). And some philosophers have argued that we can infer the existence of an invisible soul within each person from observations of human behavior, as well as speculation about what happens when a person dies (the body is still there but something seems missing—perhaps, we reason, it is the soul that animates a living body, without which a body is dead and lifeless).

But how good are these indirect arguments by analogy? It all depends on how good the analogy is, that is, how similar the two things being compared really are. Hume himself thinks it is just as reasonable to suppose that the world grew like a plant as it is to think it was planned and constructed by an intelligent being such as God. Similarly, one might argue that it is just as reasonable to assume that all of the evidence for an inner mind or a soul is just evidence for an extremely intricately constructed body (like the super-computer Hal, in the movie, *2001*). The point is, without some more direct and certain knowledge of such "transcendent" and nonempirical matters, whether from revealed scripture or mystical experience, all of these philosophical arguments from "analogy" seem pretty weak.

We often are told that "Eastern" thought has a very different concept of knowledge from that which we find in Western philosophy. Unlike Western theories of knowledge, which draw a sharp distinction between the knower and the known, that is, between the person who knows and the objects which that person knows, as well as distinctions among the *kinds* of objects which can be known (horses, fire, etc.), there are no such distinctions, we are told, in Eastern theories of knowledge. In Eastern thought, it is said, the knower becomes one with the known, and the reality we thereby come to know is one in which all distinctions disappear—all is one.

Although Indian, Chinese Taoist, and Buddhist thinkers do indeed espouse a kind of knowledge of an absolute undifferentiated reality that transcends ordinary experience, they also recognize, as we saw in the aforementioned discussion, a more ordinary kind of knowledge in everyday, mundane situations, a commonsense knowledge in which the subject seeks to know a distinct object compartmentalized by limiting categories (a book and not a tuna fish sandwich; a horse and not a cow, etc.).

As philosophers, we can only discuss the more ordinary kind of knowledge. Why? Because that is the only way to establish objective rules of evidence and logical validity. In other words, this is the only way reason operates in all human beings, universally and crossculturally, and philosophy, as we have been saying, is only a reflection on our most common, everyday experience. Few human beings have had the kind of mystical experiences in which the knower becomes one with the known and distinctions among the objects and kinds of objects known disappear, but everyone can appreciate the Nyaya argument that the hill must be on fire because of the smoke we see. If there is some other kind of knowledge, it cannot be known by ordinary sense experience and reason and therefore lies outside of philosophy. We cannot philosophically transcend reason. We may, like Kant, use reason to philosophically recognize the limits of reason, but we cannot use reason to go beyond reason.

How, then, if indeed it is at all possible, can we go beyond reason? Only by a kind of intuitive religious or mystical experience, available on rare occasions to a few individuals. But, as legitimate as this may be, it cannot form part of philosophy. Think of different human approaches to reality—science, religion, philosophy, and art. Each is different; each has its own particular strengths and weaknesses. There is no need to choose one over the others; most of us will want to utilize all of them in our lives.

Finally, it is simply not true that the distinction between a mystical intuitive knowledge and an ordinary sort of knowledge is a distinction between Eastern and Western theories of knowledge, since both sorts of knowledge occur in both the East and the West. That is, there are Western as well as Eastern religious mystics who claim intuitive insight into a unified reality in which all is one, and, as we have seen, there are Eastern as well as Western philosophers who analyze ordinary knowledge of everyday life. So the supposed difference between Eastern and Western theories of knowledge is really just the difference between a *philosophical* account of knowledge based on universal principles of human reason and the possibility of a *religious* knowledge transcending those limits (and thereby stepping beyond philosophy itself).

It is true that the philosophical analysis of knowledge has been motivated by somewhat different cultural concerns in Eastern and Western thought, although the analysis of knowledge itself is rather similar. Basically, the motivation of Western philosophers was to defend commonsense belief in the (perhaps limited) existence of ordinary physical objects, while Indian and Chinese religious thought (though for different reasons) was motivated to discredit this commonsense belief in favor of the more radical, religious claim, either (in Hinduism and Taoism) that all is one, or (in Buddhism) that nothing exists, that all is empty. Even so, we should not exaggerate these broad cultural differences. Western philosophers have always been very much divided among themselves, some arguing against the commonsense notion of the existence and knowledge of everyday physical objects, and some Indian and Chinese philosophers arguing for their existence and our knowledge of them.

It also is true that since the rise of modern science in Europe in the seventeenth century, Western philosophers have become less interested than they once were in mystical claims to knowledge and more interested in the everyday sorts of knowledge that can lead to science, while this is less true of Eastern philosophers, who continue to be interested in both sorts of knowledge. Indeed, reacting to eighteenth- and nineteenth-century colonial domination by the Western powers, Eastern thinkers have tended to defend their cultures by exaggerating differences between their culture and those of the West. Instead of feeling inferior because they did not develop science and technology and a capitalist market economy, Eastern cultures toward the end of the colonial era (late nineteenth and early twentieth centuries) began to criticize the violent, wasteful, crass materialism of the West and, in contrast, to praise their own more spiritual, balanced, holistic culture.

Since many of us in the West are equally critical of the excesses of our own culture, especially during the past hundred years or so, we tend to agree with our Eastern critics. Nonetheless, a closer look at both Eastern and Western cultures reveals a more complex picture lacking in such stark black-and-white contrasts, a grayer picture in which both Eastern and Western cultures over the past 2,000 years have sought both ordinary, scientific, and technical knowledge and also mystical, religious knowledge.

Because of differences in the rate of scientific and technological development, the cultures of the East and the West have today become somewhat different—though that is rapidly changing, as we can see especially in the case of Japan. As India and China take their place in the modern technological "information age," the contrasts between "Eastern" and "Western" culture become less pronounced and obvious. Of course, cultural differences remain, just as they also remain between America and Europe, and Germany and Italy (and also between India and China and China and Japan). But as we remarked at the end of chapter 1, these general cultural differences do not translate directly into differences in philosophy.

To illustrate this point, let us look at an interesting debate within Indian philosophy between Ramanuja and Shankara about what we can and cannot know. Both offered different interpretations of Hindu Vedanta philosophy, based on the early sacred texts known as the Upanishads. As we indicated in chapter 1, religious texts often are ambiguous and lend themselves to radically different interpretations. The Upanishads are no exception. They can be read as a kind of nontheistic monism in which everything is part of an impersonal One known as Brahman; and they also can be read as a kind of theism in which a personal God is distinct from individual human souls and from the material world.

According to the first (nontheistic monism) interpretation of the Upanishads, all distinctions are ultimately illusory; there is no difference between the person who knows and the object which that person knows, and no differences among the objects known, that is, no differences between trees, mountains, cows, and horses (or between oak trees and maple trees, or between this horse and that horse, this oak tree and that oak tree); and finally no difference between the thinking, knowing person and God and the world—all is one undifferentiated whole, known as Brahman. According to the second (theistic pluralism) interpretation of the Upanishads, there are sharp and clear distinctions between the knower and the known, between God and the world, and between things in the world and between types of things in the world (trees, mountains, cows, and horses).

We can see in this debate a very interesting example of the intersection between philosophical debate and more general aspects of the culture at large. Even without any philosophical debate, Shankara and Ramanuja could have fought over the Hindu religious doctrine of the nature of Brahman—whether the Vedas and mystic vision support the view that Brahman is a personal God who creates and rules the world (as Ramanuja held), or whether the Vedas and mystic vision support the view that Brahman is the impersonal totality of the entire universe (as Shankara held). But as soon as philosophy is brought into the debate, a new dimension is added, which we see in the debate between Shankara and Ramanuja.

Shankara (ninth century) interprets the Hindu texts in the first way, known as advaita, which means nonduality, and Ramanuja (twelfth century) interprets these same texts in the second, theistic, and pluralistic way. Let us first look at Shankara's interpretation.

> Brahman, the non-differentiated pure Consciousness, is the only reality, and all this manifoldness [we see about us in everyday life] is simply imagined . . . and is false. . . . The texts [the Upanishads] show that Brahman is bereft of all differences; . . . that Its nature is essentially opposite to what we generally experience in this world. . . . This illusion [of the diversity of things in everyday life] disappears when the identity of the individual soul and Brahman is realized. . . . It might be said [on the contrary] that since direct perception, which is the best of all proofs, affirms this world of manifoldness, it cannot be overturned by scriptural knowledge of unity. . . . [But] scriptural knowledge of unity can overturn the knowledge of manifoldness based on direct perception, because scriptures which are eternal and of divine origin are free from all defects while direct perception is defective [and can lead to error]. . . . It has been shown already that when there is a conflict between direct perception or other means of knowledge and the scriptures, that the latter are of greater force. But actually no such contradiction exists between direct perception and scriptures, for it is only the non-differentiated Brahman, which is Existence Itself, that is directly perceived in all objects of perception. . . . Consciousness which persists in all our cognitions is real and therefore identical with Existence. . . . And because it is consciousness, it is self-evident . . . and eternal, for it cannot have a beginning or end. . . . Therefore consciousness is devoid of all plurality, and, as a result, it cannot have any "knower" (self) behind it which is different from itself.
>
> (*Brahma Sutra with Bhasya of Ramanuja*, trans. and ed. Swamis Vireswarananda and Adidavananda)

Now let us look at Ramanuja's refutation of Shankara.

> Brahman cannot be, as the Advaitins [Shankara] say, non-differentiated pure Consciousness, for no proof can be adduced to establish non-differentiated objects. All sources of knowledge prove the existence only of objects qualified by difference. Non-

differentiated objects cannot be established by one's experience either, for such experience is only of objects qualified by some characteristic difference, as is shown by statements like "I saw this," where "I" and "this" are both differentiated objects. . . . It is certain qualities of the object that exclude other qualities and thus help us to distinguish it from other objects, and so a non-differentiated thing [such as Brahman] cannot be established. Consciousness or knowledge is by nature such that it reveals an object to a knower . . . therefore, consciousness always involves the cognition of difference [between knower and known]. . . . Scriptures, too, cannot prove a non-differentiated entity. A word consists of different roots and endings, and so all words denote difference. . . . Scriptures, therefore, which consist of words and sentences, cannot denote a non-differentiated entity. Direct perception, too, cannot denote non-differentiated things. . . . In determinate perceptions we experience objects qualified by attributes like generic character, as for example, when we see a cow we see the object as qualified by the generic character of a cow. . . . In [so-called] non-determinate perceptions the determining attributes are not experienced and the subject and object are [supposedly] merged into each other. Such knowledge, it is said, is beyond sense-perception. . . . [But all such perceptions] are denied by experience and are impossible. All our experience is of the kind—"this is such and such," that is, as qualified by difference. . . . Inference also denotes only objects qualified by difference, for inference depends upon the invariable relation between two things [e.g., fire and smoke in the inference, "we know the hill over there is on fire because we can see the smoke rising from the hill"] which are objects of perception [e.g., hills and fire and smoke], and perception deals only with objects qualified by difference. . . . Therefore, no proof—whether from scriptures, direct perception, or inference—can be adduced to establish a non-differentiated object. . . . It is not true, as the Advaitins say, that Being alone is experienced through perception, for, as shown already, perception has for its objects only things qualified by differences. . . . common to all things of a class. . . . Further, if we experience only Existence in all perceptions, then statements like "there is a pot," "the cloth exists" will be meaningless. Moreover, why does one who goes to buy a horse not return with a buffalo? Again, if we do not experience difference, why do we not use the word "elephant" or "cow" when we see a horse, since all words would have the same object, viz., Existence, and therefore these words would be synonymous, referring to the same object? Moreover, when we see in sequence a horse and then an elephant, the latter knowledge (about the elephant) would only be a remembrance [the horse again, and not the perception of a second, different object, the elephant]. . . . And finally, if Existence alone is perceived in all perceptions, then blindness, deafness, etc. will not be handicaps, for a single perception by any one sense alone will suffice to experience everything, since there is no difference among objects. . . . Again consciousness cannot be Existence, for the latter is an object of consciousness, and as such the difference between the two is quite palpable.

(*Brahma Sutra, ibid.*)

This is an excellent example of the distinction between philosophical and religious knowledge. Insofar as philosophy reflects upon and analyzes our ordinary, commonsense experience, it can never be used to justify the kind of knowledge we find in Shankara, which radically contradicts all commonsense experience of daily life. Philosophy, as we have been saying, is a reflection on our ordinary, commonsense intuitions, and absolutely central to these commonsense intuitions is the intuition that the knower is distinct from the object known, that there are many different things in the world, that these different things belong to different categories that define what these individual objects are and what they can do, that there are larger categories encompassing smaller categories, and so on. This is the way the world appears to us as human beings, and this is where philosophy starts and beyond which philosophy cannot go.

Philosophically, therefore, Ramanuja clearly wins the debate, since logic and all of our forms of objective reasoning spring from a base in common sense. But this does not mean Shankara is wrong. The way the world appears to God may be very different from the way it appears to us, and since God is by definition unlimited and human beings are limited in our outlook, this means that in that case God's view is correct and our view is incorrect. But as long as we are human beings (and not God or gods), there is no way we can know this, so we are stuck, at least for now, with the human perspective (and the philosophical articulation of that human perspective). So to say that Ramanuja wins the philosophical debate does not mean that Ramanuja is right and Shankara is wrong (perhaps Shankara has caught a glimpse of the world much closer to a "god's eye view"). It only means that Shankara must look beyond philosophy to prove his claim. The proof he needs will lie in mystical intuition, guided by the discipline of meditation and religious devotion (and perhaps revealed scriptures, the Vedas).

As we saw earlier, the same point could be made about Taoism and its Chinese critics. When the Taoists (Laozi and Zhuangzi) claim that reality cannot be described or known, that no argument is better than any other, that assertions (whether true or false) are impossible (that, like the chirping of birds or the wind in the trees, they fail to represent or make claims about an external world and so are neither true nor false), or that all is one, they are talking about a kind of extraordinary religious, mystical insight, while their critics (Xunzi and the later Mohists) in denying this are talking about the ordinary sort of knowledge we find in everyday experience.

To explain this distinction, the early San Lun Buddhist scholar Chi Tsang (fifth to sixth centuries) developed a doctrine of "two truths" (er ti)—one ordinary and relative truth (in which we differentiate real, individual things) and the other absolute and transcendent (in which we say there are no separately existing entities at all and therefore all is one), both of which are valid in the appropriate context—the first when the Buddhist nun goes out to buy garlic and the second when she is meditating later that night on the ultimate Reality. There are similar debates within Western philosophy on the possibility of mystical knowledge beyond philosophical analysis.

In conclusion, we have seen that knowledge (or at least ordinary com- monsense knowledge of everyday life, which we can analyze philosophically) requires both sense experience and reasoning. For 2,000 years, that is, until the rise of modern science around 1500, philosophy was concerned with both, that is, with empirical investigation as well as logical analysis. Indeed, from 500 B.C.E. until 1500, philosophy included all branches of knowledge— biology, physics, and astronomy, as well as logic and metaphysics. But with the rise of modern science, the empirical sciences broke away from the main body of philosophy and one by one became independent entities. So today we see that empirical investigation has been taken over by science, leaving to philosophy the task of reasoning and logical analysis.

But since, as we have seen, all sense experience involves conceptual clas- sification, we cannot really separate the two. How can I empirically investigate the different races of human beings in the world today without clarifying what I mean by "race"? Surely before I can empirically study the art of Native Amer- icans or Africans before contact with Europeans, I have to know what the word (concept) "art" means and whether it even applies to these cultures. Similarly, in the case of the study of religions, how can I decide whether Confucianism or Taoism is a religion until I first define what I mean by "religion"?

In the Indian Nyaya–Vaisesika tradition, sense experience itself involves an element of conceptual classification. At first it might seem that percep- tion occurs in two distinct stages—first I see the thing and then I classify it. But the Nyaya–Vaisesikans argue that you cannot do the first without also doing the second. To see something, you must see something "definite" or "determinate," and to do that, they point out, one must not only see *some- thing*, but see that something *as* this or that determinate or definite kind of thing—to see it, for example, as a snake (and not a worm or a piece of rope or an electric cable or a garden hose). And that means to see the universal (kind) in the individual object.

> What is denoted by the word "cow" is not the mere individual by itself, without any qualifications, and as apart from the universal to which it belongs, but the individ- ual as qualified by and along with the universal.
>
> (*Nyaya Sutra*, in Radhakrishnan and Moore, *Sourcebook in Indian*)

To see something as a snake, the Nyaya–Vaisesika philosophers say, we must perceive the "form" of snake in the object, that is, we must see that this par- ticular object has the form of a snake, a form shared by other snakes. But to see it as a snake involves a conceptual classification (classifying what you see as belonging to the category of snakes, knowing that the "form" of the object you see is the form of "snake"), and this is where error can creep into your perception—for example, if in the dark you mistake a piece of rope for a snake, mistakenly seeing a rope as a snake.

The Indian Samkhya philosophers similarly recognized that in order to perceive an object we must not only perceive an object but recognize what that object *is*, that is, what *kind* of object it is, and that while the initial experience of the object is a matter of sensation, the classification of that object as a recognizable kind is a conceptual operation of the mind.

> Mind is defined by observation; when a certain object has been just vaguely apprehended by a sense organ as "a thing," there follows the definite cognition in the form "it is such and such a thing, and not some other"; and it is this observing, i.e., the perception of definite properties as belonging to the thing apprehended, that is done through the mind.
>
> (the Samkhya philosophers in Radhakrishnan and Moore, *Sourcebook in Indian*)

Also in the empiricist tradition of Western philosophy, beginning with Aristotle but coming to full development with the British empiricists in the seventeenth and eighteenth centuries, error enters sense perception at the level of "judgment" as to what it is we are seeing or hearing. I know I hear *something*, and there is no way I could be mistaken about that. But *what* do I hear? If I say I hear rain falling on the roof, but in fact it is only branches of the tree blowing in the wind and scraping against the top of the house, then, of course, I am mistaken and my sense perception is in error—just as in the case of misperceiving the rope as a snake (or in our earlier example, mistakenly seeing the steam as smoke).

And of course these initial mistakes in conceptual classification can lead us, by the logical implication of the words we use, to expect certain consequences that also may prove wrong. Judging the sound on the roof to be rain, I rush outside to roll up my car windows, only to discover that it is not raining at all! But assuming we have correctly classified what we are perceiving, then we must also be careful to use words in describing that object in the same way other language users do—otherwise we are liable to a second type of error in using the wrong word to describe what we have correctly perceived.

But there is a problem in the Nyaya–Vaisesika account of perception, just as there is a problem in the Western empiricist account. On the one hand, Indian and Western empiricists want to say that immediate sense experience is infallible (I cannot be mistaken that I am seeing something red right in front of me), as long as I do not go further to make a conceptual judgment or classification of *what* this red thing in front of me is. That is, if I go on to say that it is a plum, it may turn out on closer inspection to be a tomato—and so I was initially mistaken. The problem, however, is that perception itself seems to involve some conceptual, classificatory element. In other words, there does not seem to be any perception that does not involve classification. Unless I can say I see an apple, or smoke, and so on, how can my sense experience give me knowledge? And if I don't know what I am seeing, have I really perceived anything? ("What did you see?" "Well, I saw something." "But, *what?*") But wherever there is conceptual classification there is room for error, and so, it seems, sense experience is *not* infallible after all. If it is classificatory, it is not infallible, and if it is not classificatory, it is not really perceptual knowledge.

We can see this dilemma in the following passage from the *Nyaya Sutra*.

> Perception is that knowledge which arises from the contact of a sense organ with its object, and which is determinate [well defined], unnameable [not expressible in words], and non-erratic [infallible and unerring].

But how can perception be both determinate and nonerratic? By determinate, the *Nyaya Sutra* states that it is the perception of some definite kind of thing, a plum, for example, rather than a tomato. Otherwise, it provides no knowledge ("What do you see?" "I don't know, something reddish but I can't tell what it is"—which is not knowledge but ignorance).

> When the man observes from a distance and sees something he can't make out rising from the earth, the cognition that he has is in the doubtful or uncertain form— "this may be smoke, or again it could be dust." Inasmuch as this doubtful cognition is also produced by the contact of the sense organ with the object, it would have to be regarded as genuine sense perception, if this were defined simply as "that which is produced by the contact of the sense organ with the object." With a view to guard against this, the author of the above definition of perception has added the further qualification that the cognition should be "determinate, or well-defined."
>
> (*Nyaya Sutra, ibid*)

But if the perception is determinate, then the perception cannot be "nonerratic," that is, in that case it cannot be infallible.

To avoid the possibility of error through classification, the sutra therefore says that the perception is "unnameable," that is, prior to linguistic classification—I am seeing something, but I have not yet determined or said what it is—that is, have not yet classified it. But in that case, how can it be "determinate"? Perhaps you know what it is, but just do not have a word for it, but in that case you could very well be mistaken—it is not what you thought it was. Child psychologists have recently reported that even before they learn to speak, children always see individual objects as belonging to some definite kind or class of things with predictable properties. An infant may hear what she thinks is her mother coming down the hall (though she does not yet know the word "mother," or "mama"), but then she is surprised to see that it is not her mother but the baby-sitter. The point is that while there may be classification before linguistic labeling, there is nonetheless no perception without some classification, linguistic or otherwise.

Other Hindu philosophers (of the Purva Mimamsa Hindu school) argue that we *can* perceive things in an indeterminate manner and also in an unnamed manner—that is, we see something simply as an individual object, but we are not sure what it is, either because we cannot decide whether it is smoke in the distance or a cloud of dust, or because we simply have never seen any thing of this sort before and have no idea what it might be. As with many philosophical disputes, part of this disagreement is simply a matter of definition. The disagreement turns on the question of whether we insist on defining perception as a kind of knowledge (in which case, by definition, it must correctly classify the object), or whether we want to define perception as including erroneous and mistaken perceptions. In fact, words like "see" are ambiguous in ordinary English usage. If someone says, "I saw a body of water," we usually take that to mean that the speaker thinks that there was indeed a body of water and that the statement is true and the speaker was not mistaken. But we also sometimes say, "I saw a body of water" in describing a mirage.

Remember that philosophy is a reflection of our ordinary commonsense intuitions. In Shakespeare's play *Macbeth*, Macbeth says, "Is this a dagger I see before me . . .", when we know that Macbeth is hallucinating and that there is no dagger there at all. Now, ask yourself, did Macbeth see a dagger or not? Do you not feel the tendency to say, well, yes and no? Now analyze that intuition—yes in what sense, and no in what sense? Well, yes in the sense that he *thought* he was looking at a dagger, although in fact he was mistaken; and no in the sense that you cannot see a dagger unless there is a dagger there to see. This means that in ordinary English, there is an ambiguity in the word "see"; sometimes it is limited to correct, true perception and other times it is extended to incorrect, false perceptions. Sometimes the false perceptions are known only to the outsider, not the person having the perception, as in the case of Macbeth. But sometimes we know that our own perception is mistaken and untrue, but nonetheless use the language of seeing simply as a way of describing what we mistakenly perceived. "I was driving along when I saw this huge lake right in the middle of the highway! Of course, when I got closer I could see it was only a mirage." In most cases we try to avoid this ambiguity by making it clear that, unlike Macbeth, we are not ourselves under some sort of illusion, and so we say something like, "I saw what appeared to be . . .", or "I thought I heard . . .", "At first it smelled like . . .", or "It tasted like. . . . "

The philosophers we have been looking at are trying to sort through this confusing mess, analyzing it into its component parts—first we have a visual sensation, which we then classify as being an object of a certain kind, and which we generally go on to put into words; if it later turns out that that conceptual and linguistic classification is mistaken, we have to retract our verbal claim, but if it later turns out that we were correct, then we consider this an important form of knowledge—in most cases, when we say we saw or heard this or that, we mean that we were not mistaken, so our statement about perception is a knowledge claim. Many Western empiricists try to avoid this ambiguity by distinguishing "sensation," which is the experience of the immediate given, from "perception," which is the correct classification of that "sensation." So they would say, while Macbeth "sensed" something (that is, had some sensation), he did not "perceive" a dagger.

Look at how the Nyaya philosophers defend their definition of sense perception.

> If we don't include 'non-erratic' in our definition of sense-perception, then the apprehension of water in the case of a mirage would have to be regarded as 'sense-perception.' That cognition is erroneous in which the thing is apprehended as what it is not; while, when a thing is perceived as what it is, the perception is not erroneous.
>
> (from the *Nyaya Sutra, ibid*)

In the second sentence in the aforementioned quotation, the Nyaya philosophers admit that, of course, there can be erroneous perception (as in the case of a mirage or Macbeth's dagger), but the first sentence indicates quite clearly that for purposes of epistemology, they want to limit the definition of sense perception to nonerroneous cases.

Empiricists always want to have it both ways—saying that perception is both determinate and also infallible; but how can it be both? The same dilemma haunts most Western empiricist accounts of knowledge. The sensory given, they want to say, is prior to any classification and therefore immune from error. But in that case, the sensory experience provides no knowledge. To provide knowledge, the perception must involve classification (whether conceptual or linguistic or both), and then it is liable to error. Suppose someone says, "At this moment I am having an experience of what appears to be a dagger in front of me (or a pool of water in the middle of the road)." It is true that unless the speaker is lying, there is a sense in which she could not be mistaken—that she really is having this daggerlike, or waterlike sensation. But that does not tell us anything about the existence of a real dagger or a pool of water out there in the physical world, outside of her experience. And in order to talk about a physical dagger or pool of water is to make a classificatory claim that may well be mistaken (as in the case of Macbeth, or in the driver seeing a mirage—"Put on your swimming suit, I see a lake just ahead").

It is interesting to see both Indian and Western empiricists struggling with the same knotty problem. If sense perception is to yield genuine knowledge, then it must involve classification, and that means inference beyond the immediate given—it looks like a snake but later turns out to be just a piece of rope. What we see in immediate sense experience is not the whole object but only part of it; so when we go on to say that we have seen the whole object, we are inferring this—and this is what may turn out to be mistaken. This is why the Carvacans reject inference as a form of knowledge.

> If we see a river swollen, we infer that there has been rain; if we see the ants carrying off their eggs, we infer that there will be rain; and if we hear a peacock scream, we infer that clouds are gathering. These inferences are not necessarily correct, for a river may be swollen because it has been damned up, the ants may carry off their eggs because their nests have been damaged, and the so-called screaming of a peacock may be nothing but the voice of a man.
>
> (from *Nyaya Sutra*)

The Nyaya philosophers reply that "what is not an inference has been mistaken for inference," that is, these so-called inferences are not really inferences, or at least not very good inferences (there are many reasons a river may be swollen or ants move their eggs). But even the Nyaya's own best argument, which they use over and over again, that we know the hill is on fire because we see the smoke, is not much better, as we have seen. So inference can go wrong in many ways. But if inference is an inevitable part of every perception, then it is hard to see how the problems of inference can be removed from perception.

Look at how the Nyaya philosophers try to overcome the Carvacan problem of inference. First, the objection:

> When the observer cognizes the tree, what he actually perceives is only its part nearest to himself; and certainly that one part is not the "tree." So that when the man cognizes the "tree" as a whole what happens is that there is an inference from the part he sees to the rest of it which he does not see, just like the inference of fire from the apprehension of smoke.
>
> (*ibid.*)

And the Nyaya answer to the Carvacan skeptical objection:

> There is, some say, doubt about the whole because the whole has yet to be established. But, if there were no whole, it is replied, there wouldn't be any perception.
>
> (*Nyaya Sutra*)

The Nyaya reply is just that any so-called perception without some inferential classification is not going to be called perception by their definition. Perception has been defined, in other words, such that in order to perceive something one must classify that object in terms of inferences that are not falsified in the immediate future. If you say, "I see something that looks like the outer surface of one side of a tree and which I suspect may belong to a tree, which I will find out very shortly," the Nyaya philosophers reply that this is not a case of genuine perception. To perceive something, they say, you must specify what it is you see—for example, a tree—and you must be right about that—that it is indeed a tree as confirmed by subsequent experience (walking around to see the other side of the tree, feeling its bark, and so on).

In summary, we can see that the history of philosophy has led to two different approaches to the theory of knowledge, the first, empiricism, looking for the element of greatest certainty in sense perception, and the second, rationalism, looking for the element of greatest certainty in logical relations among the meanings of abstract general concepts. But as Kant pointed out, knowledge requires both. As we saw with the Carvacans, sense experience alone (without some conceptual generalization) cannot yield knowledge, and, as we just saw, logic alone cannot assure us that our words are eventually connected with reality.

Certainly, we need both. I see something, but if this is to qualify as knowledge, I must classify what I see as belonging to this or that kind (e.g., I judge that it is a fish). But by the meaning of the word "fish," certain logical inferences can be drawn (if it is a fish, it cannot live outside of water). And this, in turn, leads to certain expectations (if Judy is not put back in the water, she will soon die). And that expectation can be directly tested in my immediate future sense experience (a little later, I can see Judy is now dead, just as I expected). Or if those expected consequences are undesirable to me, I can do something to try to prevent their occurring (I run to get a glass of water and put Judy in it). And this also leads to further expectations, based on the logical inferences of the meanings of words like "fish," and "aquatic," and these expectations also can be directly tested in sense experience (expecting and hoping to see Judy swimming happily about, I look at the glass of water to see if that is in fact the case—which I am pleased to see it is). So, starting with sense experience (I see something), we come full circle, through a process of desires and logical inference and actions taken to get what we want and avoid what we do not want, ending at last once more in sense experience (I can see Judy is alive and well).

This means that our knowledge is motivated by pragmatic desires and ends—knowledge that guides our action to the things we want in life and away from the things we do not want. I see something which I judge to be an object of the kind that can help me or hurt me and which I therefore want to have or to avoid, so I take steps to get or avoid the object. In the process, I either confirm or falsify my initial perception. Hearing what sounds like rain on the roof, I rush out to roll up my car windows, only to discover that it was not rain but the branches of the trees scraping against the house. Seeing what looks like an apple, I walk over to the tree, confirming that it is indeed a ripe apple, and by picking it from the tree and biting into it, I further confirm that it is indeed a sweet, ripe, and delicious, though somewhat tart, apple.

An interesting account of the pragmatic nature of knowledge comes from the seventh-century Buddhist writer Dharmakirti.

> Knowledge is cognition not contradicted (by experience). In common life we like-wise say that (a man) has spoken truth when he makes us reach the object he has first pointed out. Similarly (we can also say) that knowledge is right when it makes us reach an object it did point to. . . . Therefore (we say) that an object has been pointed out by sense-perception, when it is cognized as something directly perceived. Inference (or indirect cognition, differs) in that it points out the mark of the object and by thus (indirectly) making sure (of its existence) submits it as an object of pos-sible purposive action. . . . (Sentient beings) strive for desired ends. They want that knowledge which leads them to the attainment of objects fitted for successful action. The knowledge that is investigated by the theory (of cognition) is just the knowledge they want. Therefore knowledge is cognition which points to a reality (which) is capable of satisfying purposive action. And that object alone which has been pointed out by such knowledge can be "reached". . . . Success is the (actual) attaining or avoiding of the object. When success is achieved by causes, it is called production. But when it is achieved by knowledge, it is called behavior. It consists in avoiding the avoidable and attaining the attainable. Behavior consisting in such activity is called successful action. . . .
>
> (Stcherbatsky 1962)

In short, we cannot know anything without such a combination of sense experience and logical inference. But since error occurs by mixing the two—going beyond merely seeing something to classifying what I see (classifying my present sense experience as an example of smoke and reasoning further that smoke is generally accompanied by fire, both of which can be mistaken), it seems that the goal of absolute certainty must always elude us.

Perhaps absolute certainty is impossible; perhaps the best we can hope for is what Plato describes in the *Theaetetus* as varying degrees of certainty. Plato says in that dialogue that "right opinion with rational definition or explanation is the most perfect form of knowledge." But how good does this explanation have to be? Perhaps the best answer is, "As good as possible under the circumstances, and given the time allowed in which to make a decision."

4

Metaphysics

*J*UST as almost all philosophical questions presuppose and require logic and some theory of knowledge, so almost all philosophical questions presuppose and require some theory of what exists and is real—an ancient branch of philosophy known as metaphysics. In any discussion of the philosophy of religion, for example, the question naturally arises whether God, the soul, and Heaven and Hell actually exist. Or consider ethics, or moral philosophy (which we will look at in the next chapter). In order to know whether values are culturally relative or crossculturally universal, we need to know what kind of thing values are—whether they really exist out there in the world (in which case they could be crossculturally universal) or are only feelings or ideas within the hearts and minds of human beings (in which case they probably are relative to different cultures or even to different individuals). And just as epistemology asks the normative question, what is knowledge and how does that differ from mere belief, so metaphysics asks the normative question, what is reality and how that differs from mere appearance?

The two questions are related and have important practical as well as theoretical consequences. Everyone has a right to their own opinions, of course, but if you want to survive, or at least be reasonably successful in life, your opinions had better correspond more or less to reality! Is this really a good investment? Is he or she really a friend? Is he or she really innocent (or really guilty)? Is it really true that there are good-paying jobs in this field for which I am studying so hard?

Before we can determine which things in the world are real and which only seem to be real but are not, we must first define what we mean by "reality." What are our standards or criteria for what is to count as reality? Then, using this definition (criteria or standard), we can look to see what sorts of things meet or fail to meet that definition. Applying our criterion of reality, we might conclude, for example, that only matter is real according to our definition, or only minds, or both. Many philosophers, both Eastern and Western, have a very similar definition of reality, that only what is permanent, unchanging, and uncaused can be real. But if that is so, then most of the things we experience in daily life are *not* real, and that seems an odd and extreme view to take, just as, in the last chapter, we saw how little could be known by the rationalist's absolute 100 percent certainty criterion of knowledge.

Interestingly, the same arguments are routinely used in both Eastern and Western philosophy against commonsense realism (the belief that physical objects are real and exist as they ordinarily appear to us, independent of consciousness). These arguments may be said to be of roughly two types: those that have a more "objective," or metaphysical, thrust and those of a relatively more "subjective," or epistemological, slant. The more "objective," metaphysical argument is that supposedly real objects of everyday life (like the chair you are sitting on) are not real because they are not eternally unchanging, completely independent of other objects, and are not uncaused by other objects (that is, they are not uncaused or self-caused).

This argument is generally supplemented, again in both Eastern and Western philosophy, by the more "subjective," epistemological argument that the supposedly real objects of everyday life (trees, mountains, persons, the chair you are sitting on) are not real because our knowledge and experience of them varies from culture to culture, individual to individual, and even from moment to moment in the life of the same individual, depending on both external and psychologically internal conditions of perception. The "objective," metaphysical side of the argument claims that ordinary objects of everyday life cannot be real because they change and are dependent on other objects; the "subjective," epistemological argument claims that these same objects cannot be real since our experience of them changes and is causally dependent on other factors. What is similar to the two versions of the argument, then, is that such objects cannot be real because they change and are causally dependent.

This argument is extremely odd, however, in whatever version it is formulated, first, because it is so widespread, common to both Eastern (especially Indian philosophy and Chinese Buddhism) and Western philosophy—and more so, because the conclusion is so sweeping and devastating, despite the fact that the evidence adduced are simply well-known, commonsense facts of everyday life that no one would presumably want to deny. The universally held, deep-seated assumption that we live in a world of real objects that we can experience and come to know is denied simply on the grounds, known to everyone, that things change and appear differently to different people at different times and places and under different cultural influences. How could such ordinary, everyday facts lead to such a shocking and sweeping conclusion?

The form of the argument seems to be aimed at some presumed standard of reality, namely that in order to be real, an object must be unchanging, independent, uncaused (or self-caused), and perceived just as it is in itself. All the antirealist argument does is point out the obvious fact that ordinary physical objects are not real in that sense. We first are simply reminded of the standard of reality we all presumably adhere to, in terms of which it is then pointed out that none of the things we ordinarily think of as real are real by that standard. The realist position that is being challenged can be analyzed, then, as two separate claims—the first is a definition or criterion of reality (that in order for something to be real, it must be unchanging, uncaused, etc.), and the second is the claim that ordinary physical objects meet that definition or criterion. Together we could call the two the "realist thesis" of common sense.

But stated so baldly, the "realist thesis" is wildly counterintuitive. Indeed, it is so completely contrary to our most common everyday experience that we have to ask whether anyone holds such a preposterous view. Does *anyone* hold, or did anyone *ever* hold such an outrageous position? Whoever claimed that objects in the world of ordinary experience are real in the sense that they do not ever change, are completely independent of other things in order to exist and to continue to exist, and exist just as we experience them? Perhaps this is simply what logicians call a Straw Man argument, in which you describe your opponent's position in a ridiculous way which makes it easy to defeat.

Certainly no philosopher ever held such a view. More likely, the antirealist argument is directed against the "plain man's" (or "plain person's") commonsense view, or assumptions of naive realism. Philosophy, we have said, is a reflection on commonsense intuitions. Metaphysicians, therefore, cannot just come up with their own personal standard of reality. Instead, they claim to be articulating what the ordinary person, the nonphilosopher, has in mind when they say something is real. But is this what the "plain person" believes? Does the ordinary person (i.e., the nonphilosopher) really believe that ordinary physical objects are real in the extreme sense proposed in the antirealist argument? Well, yes and no, we may say—yes, people ordinarily suppose physical objects are real, but no, they do not suppose they are unchanging, completely independent of other objects and conditions, and exist just as we ordinarily perceive them. That is, the "plain person" holds that physical objects are real, but does not seem to endorse the claim that such objects conform to the extreme realist criterion or definition of reality. But if so, then where does this realist criterion come from?

Perhaps the philosophers are to blame. Perhaps if we search through the history of philosophy, East and West, we could turn up some culprits, that is, some philosophers who first concocted this strangely counterintuitive standard of reality and then wrongly attributed that bizarre notion to the poor, unsuspecting "plain person" (who does not read philosophy books and so does not realize how they are being caricatured). Have there been philosophers who argued that this is the criterion of reality which the plain person ought in all honesty to accept and, charitably interpreted, does accept?

In the seventeenth century, both Descartes and Spinoza defined reality as "substance," and they defined substance as something completely independent and uncaused. As Descartes put it, "When we conceive of substance, we merely conceive an existent thing which requires nothing but itself in order to exist." Descartes argued that there were three substances by that definition—God and two created substances (that is, substances which God had created), Mind and Matter. Spinoza objected that "created substances" was a contradiction in terms; if they were *created*, then they could not be independent and uncaused and therefore could not really be "substances" as Descartes himself had defined the term. For Spinoza, therefore, there was only one substance—only one really real thing in the world—God!

Actually, Descartes agrees with Spinoza, that strictly speaking, only God meets the definition of substance. Nonetheless, he thought we could speak of Mind and Matter as substances in a secondary and weaker sense, since they do not depend on anything except God.

> To speak truth, nothing but God answers to this description [of substance] as being that which is absolutely self-sustaining, for we perceive that there is no other created thing which can exist without being sustained by His power. This is why the word substance does not pertain in the same sense to God and to other things. . . . Created substances, however, whether corporeal or thinking, may be conceived under this common concept [of substance]; for they are things which need only the concurrence of God in order to exist.
>
> (Descartes 1979)

Here we find another interesting intersection between the logical requirements of philosophy and the dictates of the general culture in which that philosophical debate appears. When Christianized Europeans began (from the fourth century) to incorporate Greek philosophy into the Christian (and Jewish) belief system, they naturally had to make certain adjustments. Greek philosophers had all held that matter was eternal, for example, so any Christian philosophers wishing to utilize the Greek conceptions of matter had to alter the Greek view to say that matter was not eternal but had been created by God—but after that, matter was pretty much off on its own and could be described by physics without any further theological interference. Also, Greek philosophers differed in their opinions of the soul, Socrates and Plato favoring the idea of an eternal immaterial soul, while the atomists and others embraced a thoroughgoing materialism in which the mind is simply part of the body (the brain and nervous system).

But for Christian philosophers, the soul must be sharply distinguished from matter. And finally, while some Greek philosophers believed in one or more gods, others were atheists or agnostics, and some thought of God as being somehow part of the physical world. Christians, on the other hand, did believe in God and could never identify God as part of the physical world but as independent and "transcendent" of the world (which God created). So Christian philosophers in the medieval period had to carefully select those pre-Christian Greek philosophical views that were compatible with biblical teachings and discard the rest.

This is part of the background of the disagreement between Descartes and Spinoza. Descartes realized that, strictly speaking, created substances could not be substances if "substance" was defined as something completely independent of everything else. But Descartes was also trying to bring his philosophy into line with the broader Christian culture of his time (seventeenth-century France), and this led him to attempt to reconcile the two with his doctrine of "created substances." Apart from God's creating them and keeping them in existence, both mind and matter are for all intents and purposes separately existing substances. Spinoza, though deeply religious (often referred to as the "god-intoxicated man"), nonetheless espoused a philosophy that directly contradicted major tenants of the Jewish faith (of the transcendent nature of God as creator of a separate material world), and for this Spinoza was permanently "excommunicated" for life from the Jewish community (and so changed his name from the Jewish "Baruch" to the non-Jewish "Benedict").

Another seventeenth-century philosopher, Gottfried Wilhelm Leibniz (1646–1716), who incidentally was the first European philosopher to realize that ancient China had produced at least three philosophers—Kongzi (Confucius), Mengzi (Mencius), and Zhu Xi—also rejected Descartes's idea of "created substances," but went in the opposite direction from Spinoza. If every substance must, by definition, be completely independent from every other, then the only way to avoid Spinoza's rejection of the commonsense belief in a *multiplicity* of substances is to say that there are many individual substances that are totally independent of one another. Turning the key does not really cause my car to start, as it seems to, but like two clocks in the same room, my desire to drive into town and my car each has its own separate and independent, though parallel, identity and separate causal history! If we ask how all of these independent series of events could be brought into such apparent harmony, Leibniz's answer is that only God could arrange such a preordained order.

But all of this is fairly late in the history of philosophy. Where did this idea of reality as something completely independent and unchanging originally come from? Plato (Greek, fourth century B.C.E.) is a likely candidate. It is certainly true that Plato is one of those philosophers who argued against the reality of ordinary physical objects, saying that such objects are not real because they cannot meet the strict realist criterion. Plato certainly endorsed and made use of the realist criterion or definition of reality, and in light of that criterion quite rightly (and rather easily) pointed out that ordinary objects that we encounter in sense experience in daily life, existing in space and time, cannot meet this standard and so are not real. But if we ask *why* Plato proposed the strong realist criterion, that is, what arguments he adduced to persuade us to accept this strict standard, we strangely find no argument whatsoever.

There is a kind of argument in early Greek philosophy (before Socrates and Plato), which we mentioned in chapter 2, why the origin of everything, the "first cause," must be eternal and uncaused, namely, that otherwise we can always ask of any supposed "origin" where it came from, what caused it, like the child who asks his mom, "If everything comes from God, then where does God come from?"

> The poet [Hesiod], who writes,
>
> > *First of all came the Chasm; and then wide-bosomed*
> > *Earth, the eternal seat of all . . .*
>
> refutes himself. For if someone asks him what the Chasm came from, we will not be able to answer.
>
> (from Sextus Empiricus, *Against the Mathematicians*)

The argument is something like this: If you say that A is the "first cause," then you must tell us what caused A, and if you say B caused A, then once more we will ask you what caused B, and if you say C, then we will ask the same question once more, and so it will go on and on to infinity. This is what is known as an "infinite regress" argument. In order to stop such an "infinite regress," the argument continues, you must assert that the first cause is eternal and therefore not caused by anything else. Most philosophers have wanted to avoid an "infinite regress." But why? What is wrong with saying that A was caused by B which was caused by C which was caused by D, and so on to infinity (where none of the items in the list, A, B, C, and so on need be eternal or uncaused)? There seems to be a hidden and an unargued presumption that there *must* be something eternal, uncaused, completely independent of every other thing.

As Kant (German, late eighteenth century) pointed out in his famous "antinomies" in the *Critique of Pure Reason*, whatever we say about this will seem strange. Suppose we say that the universe is infinitely old. That is certainly hard to grasp! But it is just as odd to say that the universe began at a particular point in time, since it is too easy to imagine what was going on just a few minutes before that point in time. Perhaps as Kant said, there are some things that are just beyond our capacity to comprehend—a good example of which is when did the universe begin and what was the first cause? Nonetheless, the fact is that most early philosophers, whether Greek, Indian, or Chinese, assumed that there must be something eternal, unchanging, uncaused, and completely independent from which everything else springs. Why?

In the *Seventy Stanzas*, "Explaining How Phenomena Are Empty of Inherent Existence," Nagarjuna (Indian Buddhist philosopher, second century) simply says again and again that "all phenomena are devoid of inherent existence and are therefore empty." The only reason he offers is that ordinary objects of daily life (which we normally take to be real) are dependent on other objects and conditions and so cannot be absolutely unchanging, self-caused, and permanent. As he says, "because things arise in dependence on one another they do not exist inherently as permanent phenomena." If they are permanent, then they would never change and so would not have ever changed or evolved into their present form. "Whatsoever has already arisen will not be able to arise. Whatsoever has not arisen will not arise. Either a phenomenon has already arisen or else it will arise; there is no other possibility beyond these two."

The main idea (or definition) of reality, namely, that for a thing to be real it must be uncaused, unchanging, and therefore completely independent and permanent, just seems to be taken for granted! All Plato and Nagarjuna do is work out the logical implications of that definition of reality for ordinary physical objects. If that is your definition of reality, they seem to be saying, then obviously everyone will have to acknowledge that ordinary physical objects cannot be real in this sense, since they obviously are changing and dependent on other objects. As Nagarjuna says, "If a phenomenon were to exist inherently it should be permanent. If a phenomenon were to exist inherently it would either exist permanently or else undergo complete disintegration: it cannot occur in a way which is different from these two." The idea that an object might be constantly changing and dependent on other objects and yet be real is never even considered.

Even Nagarjuna's critic, Vaibhasika, actually *assumes* this very definition in his objection, "If you assert that phenomena don't exist inherently then you are asserting that they don't exist at all." Nagarjuna easily turns this argument on his opponent:

> When you assert that phenomena exist inherently it is you who are asserting that they do not originate in dependence on causes and conditions and thus that phenomena do not exist. For if phenomena do not depend on causes and conditions, then they should have independent existence throughout the three times [past, present, and future].

(Nagarjuna 1987)

This exchange is quite revealing. Vaibhasika seems to be saying that existing inherently is a necessary or defining condition for anything existing at all. If it does not exist inherently, he seems to be saying, then it does not exist at all. Vaibhasika clearly intends this statement as a kind of argumentum ad absurdum (defeating one's opponent by showing that absurd consequences follow from the opponent's theory), that since Nagarjuna claims that nothing exists inherently, it follows that nothing exists, and that is patently absurd. What Vaibhasika does not allow (any more than Nagarjuna) is that something could exist and yet exist dependently on other things.

Nagarjuna's response also is interesting. By claiming that existing objects must exist inherently, Nagarjuna says (in effect) to Vaibhasika, "It is *you* who are saying that ordinary things don't exist, since you agree with me that they certainly don't exist inherently—that is, completely independent and unchanging. If you define real existence as independent and unchanging, then it is you who will have to admit that no ordinary physical object meets that standard." It just does not seem to occur to anyone, even Nagarjuna's opponents, that something could exist and be real and yet dependent, changing and impermanent.

As Parmenides (fifth century B.C.E. Greek) said, this kind of talk (that real, existing things could change) just does not make sense. Despite what our five senses seem to tell us, *reason* tells us that any talk of change means that thin things become fat and therefore not thin, and that involves talk about nonbeing (things that are not thin), and any talk about nonbeing, of things not existing, is just plain nonsense. It makes no sense to talk about something which is not ("What are you talking about? There is no such thing!"). And if something is, then it can never *not* be—which means it can never change and *that* means it can never affect or be affected by another entity. Change is therefore simply an illusion. As one of Parmenides's students, Melissus, put it,

> In our everyday life we assume that we see and hear and understand more or less rightly; nevertheless we believe that what is warm becomes cool and what is cool becomes warm, that soft things become hard and hard things become soft, that what is living dies and that each new living thing is born out of non-living materials—in short, that all things are changed, and that there can be a vast difference between what they formerly were and what they are now. . . . In such ways we show our ignorance of things as they are. . . . [For in reality] anything that ever was must always have been and will always be. For if it had come into being, then before its coming-to-be it must have been nothing. But if ever there was nothing it would have been impossible out of nothing for anything to arise.
>
> (Melissus, in Windeband, *History*)

Parmenides and his followers argued from the strict realist criterion of reality, that only one thing was absolutely unchanging, uncaused, and independent and therefore real—a static, never changing One—everything else was simply an illusion. Another Greek philosopher around the same time (fifth century B.C.E.), Heraclitus, argued from the same strict realist criterion of reality, that therefore *nothing* was real in that sense—since *everything* is constantly in flux. The illusion of permanence, Heraclitus argued, is the constancy of the pattern. Although the water in a fountain is constantly changing, the shape of the water spout remains the same and thus gives the illusion of permanence ("Things find repose in changing," he said).

> Everything flows and nothing abides; everything gives way and nothing stays fixed. You cannot step twice into the same river, for other waters and yet others go ever flowing on. Cool things become warm, the warm grows cool; the moist dries, the parched becomes moist. It is in changing that things find repose. . . . It is one and the same thing to be living and dead, awake or asleep, young or old. The former aspect in each case becomes the latter, and the latter becomes the former.
>
> (Heraclitus, in Windeband, *History*)

So, at least from Nagarjuna's and Plato's standpoint, the definition of reality as something unchanging and independent is not a philosophical claim put forward and defended by them, but is merely presented as the ordinary, commonsense criterion or definition of reality whose disastrous implications for ordinary phenomenal objects Nagarjuna and Plato carefully and mercilessly analyze. Indeed, they act as though this is the only logically possible position and so the only one that common sense can accept upon reflection. No alternative definition or conception of reality is ever put forward.

Since similar arguments appear at all times and places in the history of philosophy, both Eastern and Western, it begins to appear that the realist criterion is a widespread, perhaps universal, human assumption, "hard-wired" crossculturally into the *Homo sapiens'* brain. It certainly could not be an inductive generalization from ordinary sense experience (which reveals constantly changing objects!). It is presented, rather, as an *a priori* assumption—that is, prior to all sense experience. Ordinary people do not "believe" this realist criterion as an actual, or "active" belief. That is, if asked, they would not readily assent to it as one of their firmly held convictions. Nonetheless, they (and we) do seem to *assume* it and rely on it as a general and largely unnoticed background assumption, organizing and guiding much of our thought and experience.

The eighteenth-century German philosopher Immanuel Kant argued that certain general concepts were "hard-wired" universally and crossculturally into the brain of every human being. In order to experience anything at all, Kant argued, you must, if you are a human being, organize your many different sensations into semipermanent physical objects that can be classified into kinds or categories with predictable causal consequences. If you are a human being, you have no choice but to see in front of you a semipermanent physical object with a causal disposition to behave in predictable ways—a tomato with seeds inside, a book with paper pages with print on them, fire that will burn you and hurt you if you touch it, and so on. It is interesting to note that contemporary psychologists are beginning to find empirical evidence that children, even before they learn to speak, perceive individual things as semipermanent objects of a certain kind (as a rattle, as a person), with predictable properties and dispositions.

Of course, we do not have to suppose that these objects are absolutely eternal but only semipermanent, but at least the seeds of realism have been planted. All the philosopher does is push the limits of this idea of permanence. (Just as in the analysis of knowledge, the philosopher does not invent but pushes to the max the commonsense notion that knowledge requires being sure.) How permanent do objects have to be to be real? For the ordinary person, just reasonably permanent (with no clearly fixed degree of permanence), but for the philosopher, the more the merrier—the more permanent the more real. Which is more real, a drop of water or the hydrogen and oxygen atoms the water is made of? If you say that the atoms of hydrogen and oxygen are more real, *why* do you think that is so? Is not your intuition that they are more real because the atoms are more permanent than the drop of water? And is not that an extension of the commonsense belief in semipermanent physical objects? The seventeenth-century Spanish Jewish philosopher Spinoza took this argument one more step—if God created matter (the atoms), then is not God more permanent and independent and uncaused than matter, and if so, then is not God more real than anything else—indeed, the only fully real thing in the world!

Or consider what you think about yourself—who do you think you are? Many people find it natural to think of themselves as an immortal soul that will live on eternally after the death of the body. Before Christianity, many people (including Socrates and Plato) found it natural, for these very same reasons, to think of themselves as souls that had already existed eternally in the past and would also continue to exist eternally into the future. Is not the intuition or assumption here that if something is real it will continue to exist from the infinite past into the infinite future? It is only in attempting to reconcile that notion with the biblical idea that God has created everything, including our souls, that we tend nowadays to think of ourselves as a soul that is more or less the same age as ourselves but that will continue long after we die. The point is, if this is your intuition, then do you not share the strong realist definition of reality as something that is permanent?

The question is, is the realist criterion a background assumption of ordinary people, or is it only the philosopher's supposition? One reason for affirming that this is indeed what most of us ordinarily assume is the extreme ease with which ordinary people fall into the philosopher's trap. That is, when they are shown that the object under consideration changes and may not exist just as we perceive it, most people tend to agree that it is therefore not real, or not fully real. Now, unless we attribute an extreme gullibility to ordinary people, does this not indicate that the ordinary person does in fact embrace, however unconsciously, the realist criterion?

It is just because this assumption has not been consciously considered or reflected on that the mere reminder that ordinary physical objects are, after all, subject to change, are dependent on all sorts of other objects and conditions, that they are seldom, if ever, perceived just as they are in themselves, and so on, is all that is required to completely overthrow the universally held and seemingly stubborn belief of common sense that ordinary physical objects are real. The philosophers have not discovered a new standard of reality, nor have they uncovered a hitherto undetected flaw in commonsense beliefs, nor have they made some earth-shaking discovery, for example, that physical objects change—they have simply analyzed and consciously reflected on these commonsense beliefs and then pointed out the obvious fact that these standards are never fulfilled in ordinary human experience.

But to the extent that the realist criterion is biologically "hard wired" into our human brains, necessary, as Kant would say, to any human experience, the argument against the reality of ordinary physical objects seems to go against human nature itself and would therefore seem extremely hard for anyone to accept (or feel comfortable with)—although many philosophers, both East and West, over many centuries, have apparently accepted this anti-realist position. The idea that we directly perceive real objects in the physical world is a view so deep seated, so stubbornly held, that if it is mistaken, it is a fundamental "illusion," as Freud (Austrian Jew, twentieth century) used that term to mean a false belief, which nonetheless continues to appear to be true even when we know it is false.

You remember from chapter 2 how most philosophers tried to solve logical puzzles and paradoxes that the first generation of philosophers posed. And so, in this case, we may ask, how have philosophers responded to this attack on the reality of everyday objects? Well, in many different ways. Some philosophers have, of course, led the attack, delighted to confound and bewilder commonsense with their brilliant paradoxes, and some have genuinely believed that physical objects were not real, but the vast majority of philosophers have sought to defend at least a modified form of realism. Parmenides (Greek, fifth century B.C.E.) argued, quite simply, that reality can only be a single unchanging, eternal One and that anything else (any multiplicity, any change) must therefore be an illusion. Zhuangzi's friend, Hui Shih (fourth century B.C.E.), is an example of an Eastern philosopher who developed the other side of this argument, that since everyday physical objects are constantly changing, none of them can exist as separate entities, and therefore every-thing merges into one (the entire universe with which Hui Shih urges us to identify and "become one").

But this position so radically contradicts our ordinary experience of the world that it is unacceptable to most philosophers. The whole point of doing philosophy is to analyze and make sense of our ordinary experience of the world, the world as it ordinarily appears to us—to simply deny that this world exists therefore defeats the unspoken but very real agenda of human reason and the whole enterprise of philosophy. Most philosophers, both East and West, have therefore tried to "recover" a limited sense in which we may speak of the existence of ordinary physical objects. Ultimately, perhaps Parmenides and Hui Shih are right—nothing can be real in the strict, absolute sense but the unchanging and eternal One (or maybe the Madhyamika Buddhist fol-lowers of Nagarjuna, known in China as San Lun, are right to think that noth-ing is real, all is empty, "sunyata"), but what about all of the many things we find in the world around us? Surely they must exist in some sense or another.

If they are not *fully* real, as Parmenides and Nagarjuna have shown us, how are these other things related to the true reality? How do they, as they must, share at least a pale reflection of that reality which they cannot claim absolutely for themselves? Most philosophers have therefore not been con-tent merely to show that the objects of everyday life cannot be real in the strict sense, but have wanted to go on to discover some way in which these objects that are admittedly not fully real nonetheless have a limited or rela-tive existence by being connected somehow with something else that *is* truly real in the strict, absolute sense. (If you think that the atoms of oxygen and hydrogen are more real than the drop of water, do you not think that the atoms are somehow related to the drop of water, giving the drop of water at least a little reality?)

This is what the Indian philosopher Nagarjuna (second century) meant by "the middle way" (Madhyamika), that is, the middle way between saying ordinary physical objects are real in the strict, realist sense of being permanent, unchanging, and so on, and saying that they are sheer illusions and do not exist at all. This idea was brought to China in the fourth cen-tury C.E. by the Madhyamika Buddhist, Kumarajiva, who established a school of Middle Way Buddhism known as San Lun, which included Seng Zhau (fourth to fifth century) and Chi Tsang (sixth to seventh century). Chi Tsang expressed this "middle way" by his "double doctrine of truth" (er ti), that in the "absolute" sense physical objects are not ultimately real, while in a "relative" (everyday) sense they do exist. Plato similarly develops the dis-tinction between "reality" and "appearance" (the way things really are in themselves, and the way those same things appear to human beings). Although ordinary physical objects do not belong to "reality," neither are they simply nothing; Plato says they "roll about between being and non-being" in the intermediary position of "appearance."

Thus, from the beginning, in both Eastern and Western philosophy, the "middle way" has been sought as the main task of metaphysics. How then have those philosophers who tried to "recover" some limited reality for the ordinary objects of commonsense responded to the attack on the reality of such objects? One response has been to look for some *other* kind of object which *could* fulfill the realist criterion—and to which ordinary physical objects were somehow related (like the atoms of oxygen and hydrogen and the drop of water). Without abandoning the realist standard of reality, they reasoned that if ordinary physical objects are not real in this sense, then perhaps some other sort of object is—through which ordinary physical objects could share some sort of limited, reflected reality.

The Pre-Socratic Greek philosophers (sixth century B.C.E.), along with the Hindu thinkers of the Upanishadic period (eighth to sixth century B.C.E.), assumed that there must be some "ageless and deathless" (that is, permanent and unchanging) ground of being underlying the changing, ephemeral, and hence unreal, world of everyday experience. For Heraclitus, the form, shape, or pattern of changing things satisfies the realist criterion of reality by remaining the same (the river bank remains the same, even though the water is constantly changing). For Plato, the Forms (Ideas) met the realist definition of reality; and for the early Greek atomists (fifth century B.C.E.), it was the atoms.

Plato argued that only the Forms were real in the sense that only they were eternally unchanging, independent of any other object, not caused by anything else, and existed just as they were, cognized in pure intellectual intuition. For Plato, "Forms" (sometimes misleadingly translated as "Ideas") are the objects of intellectual, conceptual thought. When we think about mathematical entities (triangles, circles, lines, or numbers), and groups and classes of objects (snakes in general, the class of birds as a whole), and ideals (perfect beauty, absolute justice, true wisdom), what are we talking and thinking *about?* Certainly we are *not* talking and thinking about anything physical, which we can perceive with our five senses and which exists in space and time. We can draw a "triangle" on a piece of paper, but the interior angles of the "triangle" in this drawing do not equal exactly 180 degrees (because its three sides are not absolutely straight lines—indeed, since a line is made of points, and points have no width, a real line would have no width and so would be invisible—so, the line you can see in the drawing is therefore not really a line and the drawn "triangle" is not really a triangle!).

Let me remind you of the distinction we often draw between the multiplicity of things that we call good or beautiful, and on the other hand, Goodness itself or Beauty itself. Corresponding to each of these sets of many things, we postulate a single Form or real essence, as we'll call it. . . . Further, the many things, we say, can be seen, but are not objects of rational thought; whereas the Forms are objects of thought, but invisible.

(Plato 1945)

If I am a scientist investigating the mating habits of cobra snakes, I am not writing about any particular snakes, such as my pet cobras, Martha and Jeremy, but cobras in general, and the cobra species (the group of cobras as a whole) is not a physical object existing in space that can be perceived with the five senses, like Martha and Jeremy. And, while some people are more beautiful, more just, and more wise than others, none are absolutely, perfectly, 100 percent beautiful, just, or wise, so when I think, talk, or write about beauty, justice or wisdom, I am not talking about anything existing in space that we can see with our eyes, hear with our ears, touch with our fingers, or taste with our tongues.

So, if these objects of intellectual, conceptual thought are not *physical* objects, then what are they? If there are no such objects, then all of our thinking, talking, and writing about mathematics, biological species, and abstractions like beauty and justice is really about *nothing* and therefore meaningless nonsense. But that seems absurd. Perhaps such objects only exist "in the mind," like the objects in a dream. But then they would not exist when no one was thinking about them. But surely triangles and the species of cobra snakes existed before anyone discovered them and began to think and talk about them. So, Plato reasons, these objects of conceptual thought must be immaterial and exist independently of human thought.

Furthermore, Plato argues, since these objects of conceptual thought are permanent and unchanging, while physical objects are impermanent and constantly changing, these objects of conceptual thought (triangles, species of snakes, perfect justice, and so on) are "real," while physical objects that exist in space and time and are perceived by the five senses are not fully real. Indeed, Plato held, the only reality physical objects have is the reflected reality they gain from their relationship to the Forms. Insofar as ordinary physical objects "participate in," "imitate," and "approximate to" the Forms, they, too, share a limited and relative being, "rolling about between being and nonbeing," as Plato said, parasitic on the firm reality of the Forms. Martha and Jeremy "participate in," or are members of, the species, cobra; the triangle I drew on paper "imitates" and "approximates" a real triangle (that is, the lines are very *close* to being straight, and the sum of the interior angles is therefore very *close* to being 180 degrees), and while the grading system in your philosophy class is not absolutely just, it is as just or fair as is humanly possible, and so "approximates to" or "imitates" true justice.

We have already seen how Indian Nyaya logicians developed a similar notion of universals (the word "cow" refers to the particular animal, Bossy, and to the universal Cow, and also to the "form" of cow by which we know that the word correctly refers to this particular animal). This also is quite similar to Gong-Sun Lung's distinction we saw earlier between universal concepts and particular physical objects.

> That which you mistook for being a horse is really Horseness which you keep confusing with an actual horse. However, you cannot call Horseness a horse. Hardness is hard in itself; otherwise how could it make a stone and other things hard? Hardness is not hard because it is present in a particular stone, it is also common in other things. Even if it is not present in things yet there is still Hardness, because this Hardness is hard in itself. . . . A thing which is hard does not define Hardness. As such Hardness does not exist in the world; it lies concealed. Concepts are not of this world; things, on the other hand, are of this world. And yet without concepts there would be no things [of this or that kind]. Yet though they are separate, they do not exclude one another. Without Whiteness we cannot see a stone. Without Hardness we cannot feel a stone. So, Whiteness and Hardness and stone do not exclude one another.

(from Discourses of Gong-Sun Lung)

Zhu Xi (Chinese, twelfth century) held a similar view that was probably developed from an earlier combination of Buddhism and Taoism, that everything in the world is what it is and develops as it does because of its "li," or principle, which it shares with others of the same kind or species. Goldfish are different from bamboo because goldfish have a different li than the li of bamboo. Like Plato and Gong-Sun Lung, Zhu Xi also held that the li exist independently of and apart from individual things; as he says, they are "above (shang) things." And like Plato, Zhu Xi held that the universal and abstract li are more real than the concrete, particular physical objects that are determined by and whose growth is controlled by the li. According to Zhu Xi (and Plato), if you want to understand what people are really like, you must investigate their human li, that is, the universal, permanent, abstract essence of humanity in general.

> What is "above shapes" and has no shape or shadow, is Principle (li). What is "within shapes" and does have actuality and shape, is matter (qi); . . . qi is the material means whereby things are produced. In the beginning, when no single physical object yet existed, there was then nothing but Principle. . . . And because this Principle is multiple [many li], therefore physical objects are also multiple [many different kinds of things]. . . . Hence men or things, at the moment of their production, must receive this li in order that they may have a nature or essence of their own; and they must receive this qi in order that they may have physical form. . . . The bricks of these

steps have within them the Principle (li) that pertains to bricks. . . . This bamboo chair has within it the Principle pertaining to bamboo chairs. . . . Although a certain thing may not yet exist, the Principle for that object is already there.

(Zhu Xi, *Conversation*, in Chan, *Source Book*)

The atomists argued that although ordinary physical objects could not be real because they were subject to change and so on, the smallest constituent parts of these physical objects were absolutely unchanging, independent of other objects, uncaused, and existed just as they were apprehended by logical insight. Of course, today we know that those things which modern European scientists called "atoms" (the smallest units of oxygen, hydrogen, etc.) are not absolutely unchanging or eternal, having been formed from more elemental stuff during the first few seconds of the universe and also capable of being destroyed in a controlled nuclear reaction, but for the ancient Greek atomists this would only show that these entities were not really "atoms" after all. Atoms are defined metaphysically as the smallest units that cannot be further divided. If one imagines breaking up bits of matter, say a drop of water, into smaller and smaller pieces, then logically we can deduce that either this splitting can go on indefinitely (infinitely), in which case there would be no unchanging smallest part, that is, no "atom," or else there is a terminus to this splitting, and we arrive finally at what cannot be further divided, in which case there are atoms. The ancient Greek atomists argued that the former hypothesis was impossible, since in that case ordinary physical objects would be made of infinitely small stuff, that is, reduced to nothing, in which case there would not be any ordinary physical objects, which there surely are, and that therefore only the atomic hypothesis ultimately made sense. So, maybe today we should not call the smallest units of oxygen or hydrogen "atoms," but should reserve the term *atom* for whatever the atoms are ultimately made up of—if it turns out that the parts of the parts of the parts of the smallest units of oxygen or hydrogen cannot be further divided (if, on the other hand, all parts can be divided, then we would have to conclude, if we observe the "rectification of names," that there simply are no atoms in the world). Can we get the physicists to "rectify names" in this way? Probably not.

Insofar as ordinary physical objects were said to be made up of real atoms, they too enjoyed a limited and relative existence parasitic on the reality of the atoms. As we all know, a banana will not last long in the heat of summer. It is constantly changing—from green to yellow to brown, from hard to soft to mushy, from bitter to sweet, and so on. A month ago it did not exist at all, and a month from now it will no longer exist (and somewhere in between it will be a real mess). But it is made out of atoms that have existed for billions of years, if not forever. When these permanently real atoms join together in this particular collection, the banana comes into existence; and when the atoms separate once more from one another, the banana ceases to exist—though the atoms continue on, becoming parts now of the soil, a blade of grass, a dragonfly, a frog, and so on, for another billion years.

We also find proponents of metaphysical materialism (atomism) in Chinese and Indian philosophy. Remember Hui Shih from chapter 2, Zhuangzi's friend? A key player in the Chinese ming jia, Hui Shih is famous for his ten paradoxes. Hui Shih's first paradox is about the Tai Yi (the "big one") and the Shau Yi (the "little one")—where by Shau Yi he can only mean an atom (something than which there is and can be nothing smaller—that is, something which is absolutely small and not just small relative to other things but large relative to others).

> The greatest has nothing beyond itself, and is called the Great Unit [Tai Yi]; the smallest has nothing within itself, and is called the Little Unit [Shau Yi].

> (Zhuangzi 1994)

Earlier we looked at Wang Cheng's (first century C.E. Taoist) arguments against the tendency for us to explain natural phenomenon in an anthropomorphic, or a human-centered manner. We complain that insects are a plague and a calamity to us, but they could say the same of us. Wang Cheng also argues against the existence of anything spiritual or immaterial, such as ghosts or gods. He reasons that there is no good reason to think that human beings survive death when other animals do not. How are animals so different from us, he asks? If dead human beings continue on as ghosts, why are there no animal ghosts? And if there are no animal ghosts, why should we believe that human beings survive death in some ghostly form? The main argument against immortality, Wang Cheng argues, is birth itself (an argument advanced 2,000 years later by American philosopher George Santayana). The fact that we come into existence suggests that we will eventually pass out of existence. If we were really eternal, as Socrates thought, then we would have existed eternally before, as well as after birth (and, of course, Socrates thinks we have existed eternally before, but only as immaterial souls). The very fact that human beings, as well as other animals, are born, is therefore *prima facie* evidence that they are all extinguished at death.

Like their Western counterparts, these Eastern philosophers also worked out the logical implications of materialism for theories of knowledge and morality. The Chinese Taoist Yang Zhu (fourth century B.C.E.), and the sixth-century B.C.E. Indian Carvacans (including perhaps Ajita Kesakambala and Pakudha Kacchatyana, mentioned in chapter 2) argue (as do the fourth to third-century B.C.E. Greek Epicurus and his first-century B.C.E. Roman follower Lucretius) from the metaphysical theory that reality is material, to the conclusion that the only source of knowledge is through the body, that is, sense perception (the theory known as empiricism), and that the only good in life is also through the body, that is, pleasure (the theory known as hedonism). In the *Liehzi* Yang Zhu is reported as saying,

> In life the myriad creatures all differ from each other; in death they are reduced to a single uniformity. In life they may be virtuous or degenerate, honorable or despicable. . . . But in death they will stink and rot and decompose. . . . Who, then, will be able to distinguish them? Let us hasten, therefore, to enjoy our life, for why should we worry about what comes after death? . . . What, then, is the object of human life? What makes it pleasant? Finery and ease, music and beauty. Yet we cannot always sate ourselves with finery and ease, or incessantly enjoy music and beauty. On the contrary, being warned and exhorted by punishments and rewards, urged forward or repelled by fame and laws, we anxiously strive for an hour of empty fame and plan for a glory that will survive our death. . . . Thus we vainly lose the highest pleasures of the present moment, being unable to give release to ourselves for even an hour. How, then, do we differ from a criminal laden with chains? . . . The praise of the world is all for Shun, Yu, the duke of Zhou and Confucius. . . . None of these four sages, while alive, enjoyed a single day of pleasure, yet in death they gained a fame lasting ten thousand years. This fame, however, cannot bring reality back to them. Although you now acclaim them, they are not conscious of it, and although you honor them, they are not aware of it. What is there to distinguish them from a block of wood or clod of earth. . . . If anyone, being concerned about the praise of a future time, therefore tortures his spirit and body, wanting to gain a fame that will endure after death a few hundred years, how will this revive his dried bones or give them back the joy of living?
>
> (Yang Zhu, in Fung, *History*)

(He did not mean you should go out drinking before you finish your philosophy homework, however.) Therefore, as Mencius (Mengzi) said of him, "The principle of Yang Zhu is 'Each one for himself.' Though he might have benefited the whole world by plucking out a single hair of his body, he would not have done it."

Similarly, with the Indian Carvacans (sixth century B.C.E.):

> In this [Caravacan] school there are four elements, earth, water, fire, and air;
> And from these four elements alone is intelligence produced,—
> Just like the intoxicating power from mixing various ingredients together;
> Since in "I am fat," "I am lean," these attributes abide in the same subject,
> And since fatness, etc., reside only in the body, it alone is the soul and no other,
> And such phrases as "my body" are only significant metaphorically.
>
> While life is yours, live joyously;
> None can escape Death's searching eye:

When once this frame of ours they burn [cremation],
How shall it ever again return?

(Sarvadarsanasamgraha, in Radhakrishnan and Moore, *Sourcebook)*

The argument here is not only that the body is all we have and there-fore the only source of value to us, but also that there is no spiritual or other-worldly prohibition to our "going for the gusto." If, like Socrates, we believe in an immaterial soul, which is our real self and our most important posses-sion, or, if, like the fifth-century B.C.E. Chinese philosopher Mozi, we believe in vengeful gods, or fear the torments of Hell, then of course we will want to restrain our egoistic, pleasure-seeking instincts. But if we are convinced of the Carvacan claim that there are no immaterial things (such as souls, gods, Heaven, or Hell), then these religious restraints are removed and we are free to "go for it." Even the more humanistic benefits of living a virtuous and pro-ductive life are not nearly enough to compensate for any loss of pleasure that might entail while we are alive.

Some have argued against hedonism on the grounds that physical plea-sures are always mixed with pain (a head-splitting hangover being just one example). But that is hardly an argument for renouncing all pleasure. As the Greek and Roman hedonists, Empiricus and Lucretius, argued, this only indi-cates the need for a prudent and cautious search for those pleasures accom-panied by the least pain, perhaps, as they thought, gravitating toward the calmer, steadier pleasures of music, good conversation, and the like, and away from the more indulgent pleasures of food, sex, and drink. Certainly the Carvacans did not buy this argument against pleasure!

They [our opponents] conceive that you ought to throw away the pleasures of life because they are mixed with pain, but what prudent man will throw away unpeeled rice which encloses excellent grain because it is covered with the husk? . . . Nor may you say that sensual pleasures are not the end of man because they are always mixed with some kind of pain. It is the part of wisdom to enjoy the pure pleasure as far as we can, and leave aside the pain which inevitably accompanies it. It is not therefore for us, through a fear of pain, to reject the pleasures which our nature instinctively recognizes as congenial.

(the Carvacans, in Radhakrishnan and Moore, *Sourcebook)*

The linguistic argument in the earlier Carvacan passage (concerning expressions such as "I am fat," "I am lean," and "my body") is interesting in that they resemble certain arguments in contemporary British and American "Linguistic Philosophy." If philosophy is a reflection of ordinary, common-sense intuitions, then, say the Ordinary Language philosophers, the assertions of philosophers, ought to be reflected in ordinary language. If we ask whether ordinary language usage supports the dualist doctrine, that a person is both a material body and an immaterial mind, or the materialist doctrine, that a person is only a body (and that what we call the mind is simply part of the body), we find the linguistic evidence mixed. Expressions such as "I am fat," and "I am lean" seem to support the materialist thesis. That is, when we refer to ourselves ("I") in these expressions, what are we talking about? Something that is fat or lean and that is obviously the body, so that seems to support the materialist view that I *am* my body (and nothing else). But expressions like "my body," on the other hand, seem to support dualism in the sense that they seem to suggest that "I" *have, possess,* or *own* a body. Whose body is it? Mine. Therefore, taken literally, such linguistic expressions seem to imply the existence of *two* things—the mind, soul, or self that has, owns, or possesses a body. But the materialists claim, as in the earlier Carvacan passage, that expressions such as "my body" are meant only metaphorically, as when a speaker says, "My time is up."

What do you know for sure, the materialists ask? Only what you can see for yourself, with your five senses. Therefore, there is no evidence for an afterlife of vengeful gods, and therefore it is foolish to sacrifice today's pleasures to seek the rewards and avoid the punishments in a doubtful future life. In a similar way, therefore, all of these philosophers argue from a materialistic metaphysics to an empiricist epistemology to a hedonistic (that is, pleasure-seeking) ethics.

The main difficulty for metaphysical materialism is indicated in the aforementioned Carvacan quotation—"And from these four elements alone (earth, water, fire, and air) is intelligence produced"—the problem of explaining consciousness, thinking, and perceiving on a purely materialistic basis. How can thoughts, plans, dreams, intentions, and feelings, which seem so utterly immaterial, be nothing more than a by-product of atomic interactions? It may actually be true, but it is hard to *understand how* it is possible.

Indian opponents of the Carvacans argued vigorously against the materialist identification of the self or soul with the body. First of all, they argued, even if there is no consciousness without the body, that does not prove that consciousness is identical with the body. After all, they say, light is a necessary condition for seeing, but that does not mean light is identical with sight. Also, they point out, if consciousness is just a property of the body, how is it possible for us to be conscious of our own bodies, as we surely are? If the body is the object of consciousness, then it cannot be the same thing. (Of course, the Carvacans could rebut this argument (and probably did, except that their opponents destroyed all of their books!) by asking how it is possible for the mind to be conscious of itself, that is, for us to be conscious that we are conscious? (Are you awake? How do you know?) Perhaps it is just a peculiarity of consciousness that it is reflexive—that is, that it can be aware not only of other things but also of itself (whether "itself" is mental or physical). Again, the critics point out, if consciousness is simply a property of the body, why can other people not perceive it (as they can perceive other properties of my body, like my sunburned, balding head)? The only body who can perceive your thoughts is your body; the rest of us can only infer from your behavior that you are thinking and are not a robot (unless we simply identify consciousness with behavior, as the twentieth-century American behaviorists, such as B.F. Skinner, did, arguing that consciousness is nothing but outward behavior—but that is not how you know you are thinking and what you are thinking, is it?). Finally, the Indian critics argue, the fact that we are able to move and control our own bodies, at least to some extent, implies that the controlling mind is distinct from the body that we control. But the main problem is simply trying to understand how the body can think.

We can see the same sort of difficulty facing the Greek atomist, Epicurus (341–270 B.C.E.). Look at how he tries to explain sense perception on a purely materialistic (atomistic) basis:

> Moreover, there are images of the same shape as the solid bodies from which they come but in thinness far surpassing anything that the senses can perceive. It is not impossible that emanations of this sort are formed in the air that surrounds a body, that there are thin, hollow films, and that the particles composing them retain as they flow from the solid object the same position and relative order that they had while on its surface. Such images we call "idols." Nothing in nature as we see it prevents our believing that the idols are of a texture unsurpassed in fineness. For this reason, their velocity is also unsurpassed, since they always find a proper passage, and since moreover their course is retarded by few if any collisions, while a body made up of an inconceivably large number of atoms suffers many collisions as soon as it begins to move. Moreover, there is nothing to prevent our believing that the creation of idols is as swift as thought. They flow from the surfaces of a body in a constant stream, but this is not made evident by any decrease in the size of the body since other atoms are flooding in. . . . We must suppose that [what] we see [is] the outer form of a thing when something comes to us from its surface. . . . When, by the purposeful use of our mind or of our organs of sense, we receive a mental picture of the shape of an object, . . . this picture is true, since it is created by the continuous impact of the idols or by an impression left by one of them.

> (from "Letter to Herodotus," in *Epicurus: The Extant Remains*)

What a theory! From the surface of a physical object, tiny transparent films that look like the object fly out in all directions at incredible speeds. Some of these strike the eye, and because they are made of a subtle or fine nature, they can penetrate the eye without our feeling them. And this is what we actually see—not the actual tree but a little picture of the tree inside the eye.

What evidence is there for such a theory? None. Epicurus's theory *requires* this sort of account (what else could he say to explain sense perception?), and the only argument he offers is that there is nothing that *prevents* us from accepting the theory (it is true because there is no contrary evidence, "it's not impossible that . . .").

But of course there are all sorts of problems with the theory. Why do we not see these little "idols" flying out from the objects? How can they enter the eye? (Of course, Epicurus says that they are fine in texture and move fast—but still, the theory seems pretty "ad hoc" (that is, an explanation the only evidence for which is that it would explain a particular difficulty)). The biggest problem, however, is one you have probably already noticed—suppose that this little image does enter the eye or even the brain—does that explain perception? No; this just raises the question of how we see the image or idol inside the head. Suppose the "idol" strikes and enters a fence post; does that mean the fence post sees the tree that produced the "idol" of the tree? If not, then what is the difference between the fence post and you or I? Of course, we want to say, we are conscious, thinking beings while the fence post is not. But as a materialist, Epicurus cannot say that. It is not that Epicurus is stupid or unimaginative; it is just that this is something that it is extremely difficult for any materialist to explain, even today. Every metaphysical theory has its problems—those aspects of our experience that are difficult for that particular theory to explain—and consciousness is the big problem for materialism.

In reaction to this difficulty, idealist philosophers have gone to the opposite extreme, arguing that only mind and its ideas and thoughts are real. In a similar way, but with a more "subjective" and epistemological focus, empiricists argued that if physical objects did not exist just as we perceive them, there must be something *else* that *did* exist just as we perceive them, namely, "sense data," the "immediately given," from which the perception of ordinary physical objects is constructed—that is, a kind of epistemological atomism, which we examined briefly in chapter 3 in our discussion of the British empiricists, Locke, Berkeley, and Hume, and the Indian Nyaya and Vaisesika empiricists.

Outside of my window is a large black walnut tree. If I say "I see a black walnut tree," however, I am liable to be mistaken (it might turn out to be a butternut tree—or as the seventeenth-century French philosopher Rene Descartes argued, it is possible that I am *dreaming* of a black walnut tree and, like Macbeth, hallucinating a dagger, not really seeing any physical object at all!). But in any case, whether mistaken or not, *something* was going on in my mind. If I reduce my claim to "at the moment I am having a vivid sense impression of what looks like a black walnut tree," then there is no way that I can ever be mistaken or proven wrong (if it turns out to be a butternut tree or even if I dreamt the whole thing, I can still truthfully say that I had a sense impression of what looked like a black walnut tree—"I never said it was a black walnut tree; I only said that is what it *looked* or *seemed* like—and it did!")

As we saw earlier, according to John Locke, we never directly perceive physical objects. These physical objects merely cause reactions in our sense organs (a physical object causing air waves producing vibrations in the inner ear, a physical object emitting light waves interacting with the rods and cones of the retina of the eye, and so on), which in turn are converted into electrical and chemical reactions that travel along the nerve endings into the brain, where, in Locke's famous analogy, the mind or self sits like a person in a dark closet receiving messages (from the nerve endings), supposedly from the outside world—messages allegedly about physical objects, but which are not themselves physical objects). A similar theory was developed over a thousand years earlier by the Indian Buddhist philosopher Dignaga (fifth century).

> Though atoms serve as *causes* of the consciousness of the sense-organs, they are not its actual objects, . . . because consciousness does not represent the image of the atoms. . . . Though aggregates of atoms [i.e., ordinary physical objects] are like the image of consciousness, [being solid, three dimensional, etc., they cannot become its actual objects either] because consciousness does not arise from what is represented in it. . . . [For example,] double vision [of a double moon] is perceived [by a person] on account of defects in her sense-organs. But [this perception is not produced by a double moon, since] there exists no such object as a double moon. Similarly the aggregates of atoms [ordinary physical objects], . . . cannot act as the [immediate] causes of consciousness [since it is not the physical objects themselves which, except in the case of touch, come into direct contact with the sense organs]. Hence they are not its actual objects. Thus neither the atoms nor the aggregates of atoms [i.e., ordinary physical objects] can serve as the actual objects of consciousness. . . . The actual objects of consciousness are the objects which exist internally in knowledge itself as a knowable aspect and which appear to us as if they exist externally.
>
> (In Koller and Koller, *Sourcebook in Asian Philosophy.*)

Like Western idealists and his fellow Yogacara Buddhists, Dignaga goes on to argue against the existence of any external causes of sense perception, whether atoms or aggregates of atoms. Why? If the only things we are conscious of and know anything about are internal mental entities, what evidence is there that atoms or indeed anything exists outside of the mind?

The eighteenth-century Scottish philosopher Thomas Reid challenged the metaphysical premise of the empiricists, that all we are directly aware of (the actual objects of consciousness) are internal sense impressions produced somewhere in the mind or brain. Locke, Berkeley, and Hume (and Dignaga and other Yogacara Buddhist philosophers) have argued that when I look out my window what I really, immediately see, is a treelike sense impression occurring

in my own mind, conveyed to my brain by my sense organs and nervous system (which might or might not correspond to a real physical object in the
external world). This was simply too foreign to commonsense for Reid to swallow. What I am looking at outside of my window, Reid insists, is a tree! Even
in my dream, Reid goes on, I was dreaming of a tree (just as when I wish for
a sports car, or plan a trip to the Bahamas, what I am thinking about are real
physical objects in the external world—it is not an imaginary sports car I am
thinking about; I already have that one!).

The mistake of the empiricists, Reid argued, was their failure to
understand the ambiguity in words like "idea." While it is true, as Locke
said, that we have ideas of trees and other things, this does not mean, in
plain English, that sense impressions are occurring in the region of my brain
which look like trees (like a little slide show inside of the brain), but simply
that I have theories, beliefs, opinions, and feelings, that is, "ideas," about
trees—that they are beautiful, are useful for shade and fruit, clog the plumb-
ing, are ecologically necessary, are fun to climb, are messy in the fall, and so
on. Metaphysically, Reid wondered whether "ideas" in Locke's sense (internal
sense impressions) existed at all. Of course, something (chemical and electrical) is going on in the brain, but not little pictures of trees and other
things! Just as we might accuse Plato of inventing a bogus kind of "real
object," the Forms (of triangles, etc.), corresponding to our infallible intellectual knowledge (of triangles, for examples), so Reid accuses the empiricists
of inventing a bogus kind of "real object," sense impressions, corresponding
to our infallible sense knowledge.

Let us take a closer look at this idealist solution (whether in Western or
Eastern philosophy) to the problem, what limited reality physical objects have
(assuming that they are not fully real on the strong realist criterion). This is
the theory briefly explained earlier that physical objects exist but only as ideas
"in the mind." Like objects in a dream, they appear to us but have no existence apart from our being aware of them—for them, as George Berkeley
(British, eighteenth century) said, to be is to be perceived. Idealism arose in
India as a form of Mahayana Buddhism, known as Yogacara (third century
B.C.E.), which influenced the latent idealist tendencies in Chinese philosophy,
especially in Zhuangzi and Mengzi (who said, "All the ten thousand things are
there in me"), and which is prominently displayed in Chan Buddhism (known
in the West by its Japanese name, Zen) and in the Ming dynasty Confucianist,
Wang Yangming (fifteenth to sixteenth centuries).

Idealism is supported by the fact that, by hypothesis, we have and can
have no direct experience of a mind-independent entity. My mind receives
messages only from nerve endings inside of my brain; I can only assume that
these are caused by physical objects outside of my body. As a thought experiment, imagine that your brain has been removed from your body and hooked

up to all sorts of electrodes that can stimulate it, just as it is now being stimulated. What would you think? Since your brain would be receiving exactly the same sensory stimulation you are receiving right now, you would imagine that you are sitting at your desk reading a fascinating philosophy book! How do you know that this is not what is actually occurring right now? Of course, you can see most of your body, and you can pinch yourself if you like, or pound the philosophy book against the chair, but what is that supposed to prove—that is just what we are stimulating your brain to experience. If we can never directly experience external, mind-independent things, idealists argue, then what is the point of talking about them? Do we have any right to even talk about what we have no way of knowing? (Maybe, in addition to ordinary people, there are antipeople that disappear just as you are about to look at them and become intangible just as you are about to touch them—you cannot prove that there are no such antipeople, but how seriously are you inclined to accept the theory—and why?)

Idealism also is strengthened by our knowledge of how much biological, psychological, and cultural factors obviously affect perception. It is only because of our sensory apparatus as members of the human species that we see the particular range of the light spectrum and so little of the possible olfactory information available to dogs, for example. We know from history and anthropology that different groups of people tend to see the world in rather different ways. And we know that individual people will see things differently, depending on their mood, point of view, bias, and so on. We know, in other words, that our perception of the world is to a large extent distorted, and that we are at least partially responsible for the way the world appears to us. But to how great an extent is this true? Could it be 100 percent, in which case we are *totally* responsible for the appearance of physical objects? Not just that we are *mislabeling* or *misconstruing* objects, which nonetheless exist and which we nonetheless do perceive, though in inadequate ways, but that, like the objects in a dream, we completely fabricate such objects that have absolutely no basis outside of our own consciousness.

Surely at least part of what we see in the external world is due to our own minds (that is, it is subjective), but is it *all* "in the mind"? And if it is partly "objective" and partly "subjective," which is which, and how are the two related? The eighteenth-century British philosopher George Berkeley, for example, held that nothing exists independently of minds—"to be is to be perceived," he said. The chair you are sitting on exists only in the sense that you can feel it and see it; the chair exists, in other words, simply as tactile and visual sensations of which you are conscious. Of course, Berkeley worried about what happens to the chair when we all go home at night, the lights are turned off, and the door is locked. If no one is there to see it, does it cease to exist? (This is the origin of the famous puzzle, "if a tree falls in the forest and no one is there to hear it, does it make a sound?") Don't worry; God is always there to perceive it, according to Berkeley.

> *There was a young man who said, God*
> *Must think it exceedingly odd*
> *If he finds that this tree*
> *Continues to be*
> *When there's no one about in the*
> *Quad.*

> *Reply:*

> *Dear Sir:*
> *Your astonishment's odd:*
> *I am always about in the Quad.*
> *And that's why the tree*
> *Will continue to be,*
> *Since observed by*

> Yours faithfully,
> God

(limerick attributed to Ronald Knox. (In Stewart and Blocker *Fundamentals of Philosophy* 3rd ed.)

We can think about idealism in terms of our earlier discussion about the relation of universals and particulars. Aristotle, Zhu Xi, and others thought that there were "natural kinds," that is, that universals, forms, li, or de are real, though abstract entities objectively existing in the world, independently of human minds. For Zhu Xi and Aristotle, it is the li or form of tomato that makes the tomato seed grow into a tomato plant, rather than a snake or a bird. But what if these categories do not represent objective, real, or natural kinds, but only boundaries arbitrarily drawn by human beings?

We know that at least *some* classifications are subjective, culturally relative to a particular language group, created by human beings, for example, the division of the color spectrum into distinct colors ("red," "blue," "green," and so on), or the distinction between what is art and what is craft, or between "seedling," "sapling," and "tree." Could *all* of our categories be humanly created, relative to a human frame or a particular language group, or must we distinguish between subjective categories like "sapling" or "pet" and objective categories like "oak" or "cat"?

Intuitively, we may tend to agree with Aristotle and Zhu Xi, that "cat" is a natural kind, that things are really grouped into distinct species of plants and animals, and that this is based on something objectively real (today we would call this the genetic code), even if the division of the color spectrum into distinct colors is somewhat more arbitrary, subjective, and culturally relative. One way to understand the idealist position is to see it as the view that *all* categories are human inventions, that they are *all* equally subjective, anthropomorphic. Though some may be universal for all human beings and others relative to specific cultures and language groups, nonetheless, all are relative to human beings and do not represent a "God's-eye" view.

As we have seen, Yogacara Indian Buddhists also developed an idealist metaphysics. In opposition to Nagarjuna's Madhyamika Buddhist position, that all things are "empty" (sunyata) of substantial reality, Yogacarans argued that while all things are empty of *material* reality, they are *not* devoid of a *mental* reality. They exist, in other words, like the objects in a dream or fantasy, existing as ideas in the mind.

Strange as this theory no doubt strikes us, it is a natural and logical development from (or "reflection" on) our ordinary commonsense intuitions. Ordinarily we assume that the world consists of three-dimensional semi-permanent objects that exist pretty much as we perceive them. To this we often add the commonsense or intuitive notion of a mind or soul or spirit somehow inside and controlling the body (of animals and human beings). But then when we begin to reflect on the evidence we have for this "theory," we begin to realize that we have no direct knowledge of physical objects apart from the sensory stimulation they produce in our minds. This leads naturally and logically, then, to the idealist notion that the only thing we know *directly* and *for sure* are the ideas that exist in our minds. But now pushing the same sort of reflection to the next level, we begin to see that we have no more direct evidence of a *mind* underlying our sensations than we do of matter underlying the properties of objects.

In Western philosophy, we see this natural and logical development in the evolution of thinking from John Locke (who held the commonsense view that there are physical objects that cause sensations in the minds of human beings) to George Berkeley (who rejected the idea of an unseen material substrate underlying physical entities outside of the mind as an irrelevant and unverifiable hypothesis) to David Hume (who rejected both underlying, unperceived physical *and* mental substances causing and supporting sensations). In Indian philosophy, the same sort of development can be seen in the evolution of thinking, from early Mahayana Buddhism (which rejected the reality of physical objects but supported the reality of their atomic constituents) to Yogacara Buddhism (which rejected all physical reality in favor of idealism) to Madhyamika Buddhism (which rejected both physical and mental reality, embracing instead sunyata, or emptiness).

Locke	early Mahayana Buddhism
Berkeley	Yogacara
Hume	Nagarjuna (Madhyamika)

Of course, there are *cultural* differences between Western and Indian materialism, idealism, and dualism. In the West, materialism is seen as more of a threat to religion and idealism as being more sympathetic to religion. And it is not difficult to see why. Western religions generally assert the existence of immaterial entities (the soul, gods, spirits, etc.). Berkeley sees idealism as a solution to the atheism and egoistic hedonism of materialism. As we saw earlier, the Indian Carvacans certainly saw materialism as the friend of atheism and the enemy of theism. Nonetheless, the historical context of Buddhism and Hinduism is quite different. For one thing, modern materialistic, mechanistic science (seventeenth century) never developed in India as it did in the West (the Carvacans were virtually ignored and forgotten after the fifth century). Of course, most Indian thinkers urge us to look beyond ordinary physical reality, not necessarily toward some immaterial soul or god, but toward a more neutrally conceived ultimate substance, Brahman, which is neither mental nor material. (Or if Brahman is mental, it is nothing like the *ordinary* sort of consciousness that we are familiar with in everyday life, but more like Spinoza's notion of the ultimate substance, God, which is neither mind nor matter but which can manifest itself and be known as both mind and matter, that is, a neutral substance that has both mental and physical attributes.) So, while the great debate in the West (in modern times) is between the idealists and the materialists (with the dualists occupying an intermediate position), the great debate in Indian philosophy is between those who hold the monistic belief in a neutral but substantial Brahman and the Buddhists who argue that there is no ultimate substance of any kind, that all is empty, with the Samkhyas holding a kind of intermediate dualism. Until modern times, and apart from the brief period of the Carvacans, materialism did not hold the terrors for Indians that it did for religious Westerners since the rise of modern science in the seventeenth century.

In a sense, then, the Buddhist Yogacara position resembles that of Berkeley, while Nagarjuna is much like Berkeley's critic, David Hume. This famous debate begins with John Locke's commonsense dualism of mental and physical objects (admitting minds and bodies). Locke supported the commonsense (and scientific) view that while our ideas were experienced "in the mind," they were nonetheless caused by unseen physical objects out there in the external world (affecting the sense organs which carried nerve impulses to the brain where perception actually took place). Berkeley argued against Locke, denying the reality of an underlying material, physical substance. Since all we know directly, Berkeley argued (following Locke's own position on this point), are our own ideas, we have no direct knowledge of any physical substrate *underlying* the properties we perceive with our five senses. I see the red color and the round shape, and I feel the smooth and soft surface, and I smell and taste the peculiarly tomatoey quality, but I have no direct experience of any underlying stuff in which all of these properties reside. I may feel that somehow or other there *must be* some underlying substrate for all of these properties to reside in and which holds them all together as a single physical object, the tomato, but I have no direct experience of any such underlying material stuff—and therefore I have no direct knowledge of it. And since we have no direct knowledge of matter, Berkeley argued, we have no right to talk about it or to pretend that it exists.

But, by the same token, Hume argued (this time against Berkeley), we have no more idea of any *mental* substrate underlying these same properties. Again, it may seem natural to suppose that if I have ideas of the red color, round shape, tomatoey taste and smell, then these ideas must reside in some underlying mental substance I call my mind (after all, we call them "ideas in the mind," just as we speak of "properties of the tomato," suggesting a distinction between ideas and the mind and between properties and the object). If there are ideas, then there must be a mind. But how do you *know* about this mind, asks Hume? Are you conscious of it as you are conscious of the red color or the tomato taste? Or is it just a supposition that ideas *must* reside in some mental stuff called the mind? But if we are not directly aware of our own minds, then we do not really have any basis for knowing or talking about it, Hume argues, on analogy with Berkeley's argument against Locke's material substance. If, as both Berkeley and Locke argued, we only know the ideas that occur to us in consciousness, then since neither mind nor matter can be ideas in this sense, we have no knowledge of *any* underlying substrate, either physical or mental. What, then, *is* the mind or self, and what are physical objects, according to Hume? Simply, "bundles of sense impressions." In that sense, Hume seems to agree with Nagarjuna that objects are "empty" of *any* substantial reality, material or mental.

Idealism is a perennially attractive position. But it faces many problems. First, it is hard to overcome the overwhelming impression that perception confronts us with an independently existing world, that there is an important difference between dream and waking experience. Also, the things we perceive often seem to resist our will and desire, thus to exist stubbornly and independently of us. Also, there always seems to be more to any object we experience than our particular experience of it at any given moment (the tomato you see with your eyes you later find is soft to the touch and still later tomatoey to the taste), and in that way objects seem to transcend, or go beyond, and not be exhausted by, our perceptions of them. Finally, different people seem to be able to look at and describe the same objects in roughly similar ways that would seem to be impossible if each is a fabrication in the minds of these different observers. This is one of the Indian Samkhya arguments against idealism.

Some people have held that it is idea alone that constitutes pleasure, pain, and delusion, and that there exists nothing besides this. . . . In opposition to this view we assert that the perceptual given is "objective," in the sense of "what can be apprehended." That is, it is exterior to the idea. And because it is objective, it is therefore "common," meaning that it is apprehended simultaneously by several persons. If it were nothing more than an idea, then inasmuch as ideas belong specifically to particular individuals, the perceptual given would belong specifically to particular individuals. That is to say, as a matter of fact, the idea of one person is not apprehended by another, the cognition of another person being always uncognizable to me. But in the case of the glance of a dancing girl, we find that many persons continue to stare at it at the same time. This could not be the case if it were a mere idea.

(the Samkhya philosophies, in Radhakrishnan and Moore, *Sourcebook in Indian*)

The implication of this last weakness in the idealist position is that, carried to its logical conclusion, it would make any communication between people impossible. If two people are describing the same object in different ways, then either there is a real object existing independently of their different interpretations of "it," or there is not. If there is no "it" about which their different versions are descriptions, then there is really no disagreement and no possibility of coming to an agreement—each person would then live in a different, isolated world of their own (like a dream world) in which there is no possibility of the relative success or failure of words to correspond to reality. Only in the first case, where an independent "it" exists, can we meaningfully speak of different opinions about the same thing, each of which may be partially true and partially false, with one view more nearly correct than the other, in which two people can genuinely disagree and, more important, in which two people can agree or come to agree.

Even where we disagree, you seeing it one way, I seeing it another way, we at least share a common world—we have different opinions about the same things in the same world. And this means that we do agree on some basic points—that that is a person, for example, though you think it is Taiwo and I say it is Tanya. We also know how to go about resolving our disagreement, that is, *coming to* an agreement, about who the person actually is. We simply take a more careful look at the evidence to be gathered from a shared, public world, correcting our perceptions and coming finally to an agreement (walking over to her, I say, "Yes, you're right; it's Taiwo"). This is not to argue for some sort of epistemological infallibilism. Even if it later turns out that it is neither Taiwo nor Tanya but someone else who looks like or is impersonating Taiwo, that can also be discovered by further investigations of the same, ordinary sort. The point is that at any stage the two of us confront a common world where disagreements are always partial (never total) and can be resolved, step by step, by quite ordinary means, which we both accept and are familiar with from everyday life—and this would be impossible if idealism were true.

A kind of compromise between idealism and materialism is conceptualism. Conceptualism acknowledges that there is an independently existing world and that it is "given" to us in sense experience, but also concedes to idealism that everything we *know* and can *say* or *think* about this sensory given comes from our own conceptual apparatus. The given is merely a formless mass that is given cognitive shape or "form" by the mind.

You can probably see the relation of this theory to Plato's theory of Forms. Corresponding to every common noun or adjective (tree, book, red, and so on) is a universal, or Form (the Form of Treeness, Bookness, Red Itself, and so on). But whereas Plato held that the Forms exist on their own, independently of mind or matter, other philosophers held that Forms could only exist as Concepts in the mind or as Essences in physical objects. Plato's student, Aristotle, argued that universals could only exist in particular objects. What makes an acorn grow into an oak tree, rather than a cobra snake or a mockingbird, Aristotle said, is its inner oak essence. It is this universal form of oakness within the seed that determines its growth into a uniform member of the class of oak trees, all of which have the same oak essence. Early Christian philosophers argued that since God created everything in the world, the Forms could not exist independently of God, as Plato had thought—Forms therefore, they said, existed as ideas or concepts in the mind of God. In His creation of the world, God already has an idea of an oak tree in His mind, and deciding to add oak trees to His creation, God simply instantiates, or actualizes, His idea of oak trees, making them exist as physical objects in space and time.

Later, in the modern period (seventeenth century), some philosophers extended this theory to say that Universals are concepts in the minds of human beings. On this conceptualist interpretation, universals become principles of classification within the human mind, classifying this perception as a tree, that one as a book, and so on. The problem with this position, however, is that it cannot explain why one concept applies to a certain bit of the sensory given better than another concept (or, to put it the other way, why a particular bit of sensory experience is more appropriately classified one way rather than some other). Unless there is some "connection" between the given and the conceptual, that is, something in the given that enables us to establish and apply standards for the correct application of human concepts, then the sensory given contributes nothing to knowledge and is epistemologically useless—and so is not really a "compromise" with idealism after all. This is what the Indian Vaisesika philosophers we looked at in the last chapter meant when they insisted on the perceptible marks and features, form or shape of the cow, as a kind of intermediary between the individual cow, Bossy, and the universal or concept of cow. Unless there is some visual criterion for cowness that I can see in Bossy herself, I can never know how to correctly classify my visual perception as a cow rather than a grasshopper. But if there is some "connection," then it would seem that the sensory given puts some constraints on our conceptual classification of it, a constraint determined presumably by its own character, structure, or form.

But if we acknowledge that there is something in the sensory given that enables us to apply *this* concept rather than *that*, then we are conceding that there are regions of the physical world that can be objectively differentiated from other regions, and, if language is to work at all, that these differences are sufficiently stable and long lasting and determinate to allow a fixed vocabulary and stable concepts to be used. And all of this counts against conceptualism.

The main problem for materialism, as we have seen, is the problem of how to account for consciousness; the main problem for idealism, which we have just been examining, is the opposite problem of accounting for the existence of physical objects. These, say the idealists, are merely ideas in your mind, like the things you dreamed about last night. But that is very hard to swallow, so a third group of philosophers, known as dualists, try to have it both ways, arguing that both mind and matter are real, that a person, for example, is a mind inside of a body. Are we out of the woods yet? Not quite, for dualism must confront the well-known "mind-body problem," how to explain how two such completely different sorts of things, one material and the other immaterial, can act on one another as they obviously do when the mind moves the body to do what it wants and the body brings information through the five senses, for example.

Two of the most famous mind-body dualists of Western philosophy whom we have already discussed are Socrates (as discussed by Plato) and Descartes. For Descartes, as we have seen, mind and matter are two completely different substances. The essence of mind is consciousness, while the essence of matter is its spatial extension in three dimensions. Mind and matter are not only different things but completely different *kinds* of things. The mind-body problem is how two such completely different kinds of things can interact, as we know they do from our own experience. If philosophy is a reflection of our own commonsense experience, then we must try to explain how through touch, for example, our body makes our minds aware of things in the world and how when deciding to leave a boring movie, our minds obviously move our bodies. This is obvious from everyday life. But how is that possible if mind is immaterial and body is material? How can what is material even touch, much less move or influence, what is completely immaterial? And vice versa, how can something immaterial even come into contact with, much less influence what is material? If we really think of mind as immaterial and body as material, then my moving my arm up to ask a question would be as difficult as my lifting the library ten feet off the ground by sheer mental concentration.

A look at some of the proposed "solutions" to the mind-body problem shows us just how intractable the problem is. Descartes tried to solve the problem by saying that mind and body meet in the tiny pineal gland, just under the brain.

> Let us then conceive here that the soul has its principal seat in the little [pineal] gland which exists in the middle of the brain, from whence it radiates forth through all the remainder of the body by means of the animal spirits, nerves, and even the blood, which participating in the impressions of the spirits, can carry them by the arteries into all the members.

(Descartes 1979)

But how can something completely immaterial move ("radiate forth") through different parts of the body? How can something immaterial be "in" any spatial area or location, and how can it move? Whatever "animal spirits" are, according to Descartes's dualistic metaphysics, they must be either material or mental. If they are material, how are they connected to the immaterial soul? And if they are mental, how can this immaterial thing come into causal contact with any part of the body?

There also are famous dualists in Eastern philosophy. We are often told that all Indian thought is monistic. Hegel, for example, says (reducing all "Eastern" religions to one, Hinduism, and reducing all forms of Hinduism to one, the Advaita Vedanta of Shankara), "In the Eastern religions . . . only the one substance is true, and the individual . . . can have true value only through an identification with this substance in which he ceases to exist as subject and disappears into unconsciousness." But in fact a large part of Indian thought is pluralistic, including those forms of Vedanta (Ramanuja and Madhva) which, in opposition to Shankara, differentiate God, individual selves, and physical objects as separate entities, as well as the sharp dualism in Samkhya (and the related school of Yoga) of prakriti (body) and purusha (mind). Though the basic philosophical problem of how two such fundamentally different sorts of things (mind and matter) can interact is essentially the same as we find in Western versions of dualism, the larger cultural context in which this problem appears in Indian and Western thought is very different. For the Samkhya philosophers, the entire physical universe [prakriti] is evolving in order to enlighten the inner self, or purusha, that it is not identical with its body or empirical self, the jiva—and that is a religious doctrine unlike anything we can find in Western culture (at least since the late Greek and Roman period). But, given this religious doctrine, the problem naturally arises of the relationship between purusha [consciousness] and prakriti [the object of consciousness], and when Samkhya philosophers are called upon to shed light on this problem, they talk much like Western philosophers struggling with the Western version of the mind-body problem.

The Samkhyas are dualists, rejecting both materialism and idealism, because they hold that neither consciousness nor the objects of consciousness can exist without the other. Like contemporary European phenomenologists (Edmund Husserl, 1859–1938), Samkhya argue that consciousness and the object of conscious are relative terms, each dependent on the other. Neither can exist without the other, and neither can be reduced to the other. If there is consciousness, then there must be something which that consciousness is conscious of. And if there is an object of consciousness, then equally there must be a consciousness which is conscious of that object.

> Without the 'subjective,' there would be no 'objective,' and without the 'objective' there would be no 'subjective.' . . . Experience is not possible unless there are the objects of experience and also the vehicle of experience in the form of the body. Hence the necessity of the objective evolution. Conversely, that same experience is not possible without the organs of experience, in the shape of the sense organs and the internal organs. . . . There must be someone to experience pleasure and pain. Objects of experience, like pleasure and pain, are felt by everyone as agreeable and disagreeable, respectively. That is to say, there must be something other than these objects of experience, these feelings, to which they can be agreeable or otherwise. There must be something else, and this something else must be the spirit [purusha, the self].
>
> (*ibid.*)

The Samkhya notion of purusha is quite different from the Western sense of mind. The Western sense of mind includes much more of what Indian philosophers think of as the body, while the Samkhya notion of purusha is much more remote from the everyday sense we have of our own minds—that is, the way in which we are ordinarily aware of ourselves as thinking, feeling, perceiving beings, which Western thought tends to identify with mind or soul or self.

Consider the difficulty in trying to draw a sharp distinction between the mind and the body. Pain, for example, is both mental (certainly we are conscious of it) and physical (the pain is in my stubbed toe). What about seeing and hearing? These also seem very much tied to the body. Do you think you could see without your eyes, or hear without your ears? Suppose your soul were separated from your body. Could you see, hear, taste, or feel anything? What about other forms of thought? Many of these involve emotions and feelings, and these too seem intimately connected with the body (could a soul separated from the body feel rage, hunger, sexual desire?) In Western philosophy, we tend to associate mind with whatever we are conscious of, however causally connected with the body. If I am conscious of pain, or a red color, or the taste of a chili pepper, or the sound of a violin, then these are mental entities existing in my mind, whereas in Indian philosophy anything intimately connected with the body is considered part of the body, even though we are aware of it. According to the Samkhya tradition, conscious thought is a modification of the body produced by an object.

What then remains on the subjective side of the equation in Indian thought? Only the self *behind* the conscious mind (the jiva), what Kant called the transcendental ego. Suppose I am waiting at the corner for the traffic light to change. I am aware of the red light, but who is this "I" who is aware of this bright color? At first we may say that we know this "I" as the one we saw in the mirror combing her hair earlier this morning, the one who now remembers her lunch appointment, worries she may be late, but knows she must try to act cool, and so on. But, again, we can ask, who is the "I" who is aware of *all* of this (remembering all of these different things and holding them all together)? The "I" who is aware of the "I"? This is the self *behind* the conscious mind.

As we all do from time to time, suppose you tried to think about yourself ("who am I? what am I like?"). How would you describe your self, personality, character, disposition? Of course, this would be hard to do, but we might try. What are we doing when we think about our selves in this way? Probably we imagine a more "neutral" self analyzing our more everyday self ("yes," we might say, "I tend to be vain, sensitive to criticism, selfish, confident, maybe even conceited, but also soft hearted and even sentimental"). But who is this more "neutral" self that is examining my ordinary self? Whatever else it may be, this is a "self" we have no direct knowledge of. As John Locke said, it is an "I know not what" we assume exists but cannot directly perceive in any way. It is not an *object* of thought since it is the ultimate *subject* of thought; it is not what we think of or think *about* but the one *doing* the thinking. Or, if you do occasionally think about this self behind the self (as you are doing right now), *that* self then becomes an *object* of that thought and not the subject of that thought! I am thinking about the I that is aware of my everyday self! (First I am thinking about the really unfair comments I got on my last philosophy paper; then I am thinking how sensitive I am to criticism; then I am thinking about my whole personality; finally I'm thinking about how I know all of this—each time "I" shifts from subject to object.) So the irony is that this ultimate thinker or self is *not* something we know much about from our everyday experience—and this is what Samkhya philosophers mean by the "Purusha Self."

The result of all of this is that most of what Western philosophers classify as mental, Indian philosophers put on the body side of the equation. The

Samkhya conception of Purusha is completely independent of the body, completely indifferent to the pains, hopes, dreams, wishes, disappointments, worries, and concerns we normally experience. Aloof, independent, unaffected, the Purusha is merely a witness to all of these goings-on. But if Purusha is completely separated from Prakriti, how can it even witness or be aware of Prakriti? Is not being aware of something to be connected with and affected by it in some way, however minimally? This is the "mind-body" problem for Samkhya dualism.

Here we find another example of a typical situation in philosophy. We begin simply reflecting on our ordinary, commonsense intuitions, and at first there is nothing much that is new in this—just a clarification of what we already know, though in an unconscious, assumed, taken-for-granted way. But then as philosophers we tend to "push it to the max," and in the process of doing that we go far beyond our ordinary, commonsense intuitions. In this case, we begin with our everyday notion of our own consciousness—we know what it is like to be thinking, planning, daydreaming, wishing, perceiving things, with the thinking self on the one side and the objects we think about on the other. But as we reflect on this, we begin to see how much of the object is part of the subject and how much of the subject is part of the object and that the subjective self, which is really distinct from the object, would have to be very different from our everyday notion of the self, the one we know from our own experience in everyday life.

Similarly true when thinking about what is genuinely "real." As we saw earlier, we begin thinking of "reality" as something more or less permanent, unchanging, independent, but then in the thick of philosophical development, we push this to the limit—the really real must be 100 percent permanent, unchanging, and independent, and then we wonder what, if anything, can possibly be real by this very strict standard. Is the soul (the empirical mind, self, or jiva) real? Can this eternal, unchanging, completely independent soul (mind, self) be the same self or mind each of us knows from our own experience in everyday life? (the me I know and the you you know intimately and "from the inside"?) Hardly. This everyday self or mind is always changing, and it is constantly affected by other people and things. Our knowledge and attitudes and dispositions change over the years. We are excited by some things and bored by others; some things please us and others disgust us; and so on. If this is not our real self, is there some other "self behind this self"? The transcendental self? But what is this like? Like the atoms, or Forms, we have no direct knowledge of this at all.

Or, again, think about the theological problem of the nature of God. We normally think of God as loving us, caring about us, worrying about us, sometimes disappointed in us, sometimes proud of us, and so on. But when we philosophically reflect on the metaphysical nature of God, we want to say that

God is "real" and therefore permanent, unchanging, and independent. But now our philosophical reflection seems to have led us into a contradiction. Just as we said about the soul (mind, self), if God cares and worries about us, does it not follow that God is affected by what we do and in that case does it not follow that God is not completely independent? Or, turning the argument around, if God is completely independent, would not God be completely aloof, serene, indifferent—as the theologians put it, "impassive"? But who needs an "impassive" God? The God we want to worship is the more human God who can hear our prayers, think about our needs, really care about and worry about our sad situation, and choose to intervene (even if in mysterious ways) and do something about it—a God we can love and who loves us. Suppose you became convinced that God is "impassive" and therefore can do none of these things—would you worship, pray to, or even bother with such a God? Similarly, suppose your soul, which survives death, is not the thing you now recognize as yourself—when you die this soul will not recognize itself as that woman named Mabel Springer, who played softball, worked for many years as a computer programmer, was married twice, had two children, remembers vividly many pleasant and painful memories, as well as many loved and hated people and situations, and so on—that is, the you that you recognize when you first wake up in the morning or after a dangerous operation ("It's me! I made it. I'm still here. I'm alive!"). In that case, would you care about immortality? Is this really immortality?

In some ways it seems that rather than *clarifying* our understanding, philosophy has turned something quite simple and unproblematic into something really mind boggling! Is there any way out of this philosophical impasse? As you can imagine, different philosophers take different approaches. Some philosophers stick with reason and take it to the limit—"God and the soul are not what you ordinarily think they are; the God you love cannot love you back and the soul that will survive death will not be the soul you know now as yourself—sorry!" Other philosophers settle for a less rigorously logical solution, but one that is more satisfying to our ordinary human needs and desires—"No, the God you love loves you and the soul that will be with God for all eternity after death is the soul you know right now as 'your self'—if this seems somewhat contradictory, never mind, it is a mystery we have not yet completely figured out!"

These, then, are some of the problems involved in radically separating mind and body (however we conceive of mind and body). In the history of philosophy, in both the East and the West, we find theories that cannot accept such a radical separation of mind and body. These include the monistic theories of materialism and idealism, of course, but also of "epiphenomenalism," which holds that while the body acts on the mind, the mind does not act on the body. There is also the "double aspect" theory of Spinoza and others, that mind and body are different aspects ("attributes," as Spinoza calls them) of one underlying substance that is neither mental nor physical but the foundation for both—a person, for example, can be looked at physically, that is, as a physical object (if she is overweight, unusually ugly or beautiful, extremely athletic, etc.) or mentally, as a mind or soul (thinking of her as intelligent, with a good sense of humor, very religious, or unusually sensitive and thin skinned).

But there also are theories that accept the radical separation of mind and body and then go on to try to work out solutions to the apparent interaction between the two. These include various sorts of "parallelism," the theory that although mind and body are two different and separate substances that can never interact, they nonetheless *appear* to interact because they run in separate but parallel paths, like two clocks in the same room that have been set to the same time (imagine the first clock has no alarm and the second has no hands, but when the first clock reads 7:30 the alarm on the second clock goes off). In some Western versions of parallelism, God has created such an elaborate preestablished harmony of mind and body, arranging everything in His creation so that just as I am thinking of getting up and leaving a boring movie, my legs quite independently start to move out of my seat and out the door, making me think, wrongly, that my decision made my legs move. In the Indian Samkhya-Yoga system, there is a teleological purposiveness of Prakriti (matter) to do everything for the sake of Purusha's (mind's) enlightenment (ironically deluding Purusha in order to lead it to overcome delusion and strive for enlightenment!). The fact that all of these solutions are pretty farfetched shows how serious the mind-body problem really is.

The underlying problem in both Eastern and Western versions of the mind-body split is how to conceive causal interaction between completely different realities, each of which is, by definition, eternal, unchanging, and above all, uncaused. The Samkhya-Yoga Prakriti-Purusha distinction, for example, is extreme. If the real Self, the Purusha, is completely untouched by anything, then it cannot respond to bodily sensation, emotion, the will to live or succeed, and so will not be conscious in the ordinary sense. And that part of ourselves which is conscious of and therefore in touch with sensations, emotions, feelings, and a sense of self is therefore *not* Purusha but that part of Prakriti known as "jiva." Nonetheless, in the Samkhya system, the Purusha is said somehow to be conscious of Prakriti, and Prakriti somehow acts "for the sake of" Purusha. But how can two such utterly distinct sorts of things have any causal connection to one another?

Nonetheless, despite these apparently insurmountable obstacles, there have been attempts to work out such a seemingly contradictory notion of causal relations between two utterly independent entities. Plato's Forms, for example, do not do anything and they certainly do not act on particulars. Nonetheless, the Forms do play the role of ideal exemplars toward which the particulars strive, like a young person might strive to emulate a famous movie or rock star or famous athlete, and so, even though the superstar did not even know the young person existed and is not consciously doing anything to influence anyone, she might nonetheless exert a considerable influence on the youngster. The early twentieth-century British and American philosopher, Alfred North Whitehead, developed a similar theory of "affective causality" in which A affects B simply by being the ideal model which B loves and strives to emulate, even though A is totally indifferent to B's interests and "does" nothing to affect B.

In the Samkhya theory, the Purusha similarly illumines and reflects physical activity without itself being really affected, as a mirror is unaffected by changes in its mirror images, or as a crystal looks red in red light without really undergoing any internal change. But, really, none of these analogies are very good. The rock star has physically affected the young person (through rock concerts, CDs, radio, and television), and the light does physically interact with the mirror and the rock crystal. These things are not completely independent of one another as mind and body, Purusha and Prakriti, are supposed to be. It is hard to see how any extreme dualism can really solve the problem we started off with—finding the "middle way," that is, a limited reality for ordinary physical objects without denying that the reality is permanent, unchanging, and completely independent of everything else.

Another "middle way" solution for metaphysics is to treat the whole world as one real entity, or substance, whether material, mental, or perhaps, as in Spinoza, something intermediate between the two. Spinoza says that mind and matter are two "attributes" of the one substance (the universe) and that individual physical objects are "modifications" of this one substance under either of its attributes. Like Shankara and the Samkhya philosophers (at least with regard to Prakriti), Spinoza wants to have his cake and eat it too, asserting the existence of one and only one real substance, but also acknowledging as a "middle way" compromise a secondary sense in which there are many changing individual objects in the world. But does Spinoza's compromise really remove the problem? If there are two attributes and millions of modes (from the modifications), then is not the world a plurality and not a monism, many and not one?

According to this version of monism, there is just one real entity, the whole world, and it is eternal; what we call individual physical objects are just parts or modifications or aspects of this one reality. The problem with this theory, however, is the old problem of the "one and the many," how, that is, to explain the apparent diversity of constantly changing things in the world and still maintain that in some sense all is one. As Parmenides said, if there is just one real thing in the world, how can it have parts or change? We might try to visualize the world as a kind of giant organism, like a person with multiple arms, legs, eyes, and so on, able to walk and in general move about, but which was nonetheless just one composite thing—and which, despite all of its movements, never changed into some other sort of object or split into two or more objects or would ever pass out of existence.

Still, it is changing, and it is made of parts. It is hard to see how that can be made consistent with the strict definition of reality (as something eternal, unchanging, and so on). One way to answer this problem of the "the one and the many" was Shankara's advaita (Vedanta) theory that all of this diversity and change is simply an illusion (maya), just as the idealists had described objects of perception as illusions that only exist in the mind. But is not there still a diversity of individual minds? No, says Shankara, this too is an illusion. We are all part of the one reality, Brahman. But what about all of these illusions—all of the different things you experience, and your consciousness of them, as well as those of other people? Even if they are not fully real, they are still something (and not nothing), are they not? The dragon in my dream last night does not exist in real space and time, but it does exist in my dream—it exists at least as a dream object that I can describe and differentiate from other dream objects (it was a dragon and not a helicopter). So, do we not still have a plurality—one substance, Brahman, and many illusory objects? Even if everything is a dream, are there not still many dreamers or at least many dream objects?

You recall that, unlike Spinoza, Descartes was unwilling to draw the most logically rigorous but counterintuitive conclusion from his definition of substance (as absolutely independent), that there could be only one substance, God. In a similar way, Indian philosophers, Ramanuja (eleventh century) and Madhva (1197–1276), rejected the counterintuitive implications of Shankara's radical nondualism (advaita). As we saw earlier, this philosophical debate arises in the broader cultural context of late Hindu Vendanta religion (just as the Spinoza–Descartes debate arises in the broader cultural context of Christian attempts to reconcile as much of Greek philosophy as possible within the Judeo-Christian tradition). (From the time of the major Upanishads until Shankara, Hinduism moves away from theism, the belief in a personal creator, God, toward a metaphysically neutral and impersonal All or One (Brahman), with which everything in the entire universe is identical, including you and I.) It is not difficult to see why this never became a popular religion for the masses of people! Later, beginning in the eleventh century, popular theism makes a dramatic comeback, and the theistic worship of either Shiva or Vishnu have come to dominate Hinduism ever since.

It is this popular theism that Ramanuja and Madhva philosophically support. God, whether Shiva or Vishnu, created and controls the world and cannot therefore be identical with it. For Ramanuja and Madhva, as for Descartes, the world is made up of God, physical objects, and individual selves, who long to be *with* God but not to *become* God. When Indian scholars began to reconstruct Indian philosophy in the late nineteenth and early twentieth centuries, they tended to compare Indian thought with the dominant European philosophy of the time, Hegelianism, in which everything in the world is part of one all-encompassing impersonal mind, which Hegel called the Absolute—something that seemed very similar to Shankara's notion of Brahman. Thus, they tended to favor and privilege the more philosophical, metaphysical, and less theological view of Shankara over that of the more popular religious and traditional theists, Ramanuja and Madhva. But today, those of us standing philosophically "on the outside looking in" should not prejudge the issue and should leave open the possibility that India supported talented and able philosophers of many different perspectives and persuasions. Specifically, while Shankara was undoubtedly a great philosopher, so were Ramanuja and Madhva.

Madhva holds that individual selves and physical objects exist eternally as separate entities, although they are, as Descartes also held, dependent on God for their existence. It makes no sense, according to Madhva, to say that individual selves and physical objects are *identical* with God, that is, the same thing as God.

Let us take a look at Madhva's arguments. First, Madhva argues that if two things are identical then we must be able to meaningfully and truthfully say the same things about them, which we cannot do in the case of God and individual selves, like you or me. If George Washington is identical with the first president of the United States, then whatever we meaningfully and truthfully say about George Washington we should be able to meaningfully and truthfully say about the first president of the United States—"both" were married to Martha and commanded the Continental army, and so on—and so these "two" things are really only one. But in the case of God and individual selves, what we say of the one we cannot say of the other—God, but not the individual self, is omnipresent, all knowing, all powerful; and by the same token, the individual self, but not God, responds to the physical condition of one and only one particular body, feelings its pains, suffering its fatigue, its excitement, and so on, therefore the two are different.

> God is not the embodied self, as it is quite impossible to predicate omnipresence of the embodied self. That is, it is impossible and against fact and reason that one and the same individual self could be in all the bodies at the same time. . . . This is also said in the *Garuda Purana*, "There is no equality in experience between the Lord and the self; for the Lord is all-knowing, all-powerful, and absolute; while the self is of limited understanding and power and absolutely dependent."
>
> (Madhva, *Commentaries on the Vedanta, or Brahma Sutra*)

Neither can the physical world simply be an imaginary idea in the mind (and therefore *part* of the mind, whether an individual mind or the all-embracing

Mind of Brahman), as Shankara held. The fact that we are conscious of objects indicates a distinction between the two—the seer and what is seen. Also, we easily discriminate between dreams and reality. And finally, there is the objection also raised against Berkeley, that mental ideas momentarily come and go as we briefly entertain one idea before turning to other ideas, whereas physical objects continue to exist even after everyone has stopped thinking of them.

> The ignorant say that the world is unreal, for they are really ignorant of the supreme power of God, who, boundless in wisdom, having created such a world of real existence, has become the author of a real world. . . . The non-existence of external things cannot be maintained, on account of our being conscious of them. . . . It cannot be said that as the creatures of a dream are, so also the world is a non-entity; for, unlike the world, the creatures of a dream are perceived differently from real objects, as when we say, "This is a mere dream, this is not a real snake." . . . The world is not vijnana (consciousness) for it is not so perceived. The world is not a mere mode of the mind; for nobody has perceived it as such in his experience. . . . Vijnana or consciousness is only of a moment's duration, whereas physical objects we perceive are permanent. Hence, too, the mind and the world outside cannot be said to be identical.
>
> (ibid.)

Another solution is provided by the Samkhya philosophers, who (although they affirm the duality of Purusha and Prakriti) argue that the material world (Prakriti) is just one gigantic entity evolving out of itself all of the different forms we find in our world (and which at the end of time will "devolve" back into one homogenous entity). This is a kind of monism (at least on the physical reality side) that avoids the problem Shankara faces. By insisting that the one (physical) Reality cannot have parts or change in any way, Shankara is forced into the rather preposterous view that virtually everything we experience in the world is an illusion. The Samkhya philosophers admit plurality and change, but only as modifications of the one Reality. We might think of the way a human being develops from a single fertilized egg—arms and legs form, the brain and sense organs develop, and so on, not as independent entities, but simply as evolving parts of one entity—that particular human being.

But there are problems with the Samkhya approach as well. Perhaps you have already seen it. Samkhya must deny the creation of any new entities in the world. Nothing that appears in the world is really new but is only an evolution from a former state—the seed is just an evolved form of a flower that is just an evolved form of a bud, and so on. But this raises enormous problems about causality. Normally we think causality creates completely new entities. Striking the match brings into existence a fire that never before existed. Having unprotected sex brings into the world a completely new, and perhaps unwanted, baby. But given the Samkhya monistic assumption that the entire physical world is just one evolving entity, Samkhya must deny that causality ever creates any novelty.

Among Western philosophers, the neo-Platonist of the Roman period, Plotinus (204–269), developed a similar view in which the world evolves out of the One. Like the Samkhya, but unlike Shankara and Spinoza, Plotinus denies that the One is all things (or that all things are really One), but that the One *came before* all of the many things. Nonetheless, Plotinus recognizes the problem also confronting the Samkhya philosophers: if the many are contained in the One then the One is not really "one," and if, on the other hand, the many are not contained in the One, then where did they come from? The problem both for Plotinus and the Samkhya philosophers is, how can the One create something and still remain "one"?

For the Samkhya, the kind of constant change we see in the world is not one distinct thing causing another distinct thing, where the first, the cause, ceases to exist as soon as the second, the effect, begins to exist. There is only one real thing in the world, and change is just a modification of that thing— in fact, say the Samkhya philosophers, the effect was already there in the cause all along. How do we make salt from sea water? We just let the water evaporate, and there is the salt; the salt was there, dissolved in the water, all along. So the threads in the shirt existed as threads on the spool before the shirt was made, and even before that the fibers of cotton existed before they were spun into thread, and so on. Of course, the shirt is not *actually* present in the cloth, but, Samkhya say, it exists in the cloth in a *potential* or "unmanifested" state, just as opponents of abortion might say that a person already exists in the fertilized human ovum though only in a potential, or an unmanifested state. The idea here is to picture the apparent diversity and change we find in the world as an unfolding of what was originally present from the very beginning, and so, in a sense, not really fundamentally new.

> Objects have an unmanifested entity for their cause. . . . The jar is found to have, for its cause, clay, in which inhere the unmanifested state of the effects. . . . The cause is that wherein the effect already exists in the unmanifested state.
>
> (the Samkhya philosophies, in Radhakrishnan and Moore, *Sourcebook in Indian*)

Of course, some examples of causality are indeed like that, and these are the examples the Samkhya philosophers like to emphasize. In a sense, the house was already in the bricks and mortar, the shirt was already in the threads, the threads were already in the cotton fibers, and so on. But even in these examples, something new has obviously been created. As we will see in chapter 5, Dong Zhongshu (third century B.C.E.) said a silkworm cocoon is not the same as silk, and threads of silk are not the same as silk cloth, and silk cloth is not the same as a silk dress—and an egg, Dong points out in another example, is not the same as a chicken (imagine ordering roast chicken at your favorite restaurant and being served an egg—by a Samkhya waitress, of course). But Samkhya philosophers must maintain this position or give up their view that the whole physical world is just one evolving thing. Of course, we might admit that the cloth is *potentially* a shirt, that it can be made *into* a shirt, or that it is one contributing factor in making (causing) a shirt—but that is a far cry from saying that the shirt is already there (*actually* there) in the cloth.

Some Buddhist philosophers argued in just the opposite way from the Samkhya philosophers, insisting that every change brings an entirely new entity. But, since physical objects are constantly changing, this means that they really do not exist at all as real, permanent entities. As we saw earlier, you are different than you were yesterday, so, following this Buddhist logic, you are a different person today from the person sitting in your seat yesterday. But since by the same reasoning you are different and therefore a different entity than you were an hour, a minute, a second, a spit second ago, and so on to infinity—there really is nothing left of you. As a real, substantive, permanent entity, you have dissolved into a constant state of flux and change. As a famous seventh-century Tibetan Buddhist, Candrakirti, said, the Samkhya philosophers have got it all wrong (Candrakirti, *Reasoning into Reality*, Lindtner 1987).

> For you [Samkhya philosophers] the distinction of the sprout's shape, color, taste, capacity and development would not be distinct from the seed's creative cause. If after it ceases to exist as a seed and becomes a different entity [a sprout], how could it still be the same thing?
>
> If for you the seed and sprout are not different then, like the seed, the so-called "sprout" would not be apprehended because, if they are the same, the [seed] would be apprehended when the sprout appears. This you cannot assert.
>
> Because the effect is seen only if the cause is destroyed, not even by conventional criteria are they the same. Therefore, to assert that "things arise out of themselves" is incorrect.
>
> If self-production were to be asserted, then product, producer, object, and agent alike would be identical. As they are not identical, you should not assert self-production because of all these objections which have been raised.
>
> Seed and sprout do not exist simultaneously, and if they were not different how could the seed *become* different?
>
> (*ibid.*)

Causality has always been a big problem for philosophers. As we saw earlier, although Hume recognized how important causal connections are to our ordinary commonsense world of everyday experience, he denied genuine knowledge of causal connections because he had no direct sense impression of them. Carvacans were also skeptical about causality. As we saw earlier, they denied any inferential knowledge—and that eliminates any knowledge of an unobserved cause (fire) by observing the effect (smoke). And because they also deny the existence of universals, it is impossible, given the Carvacan assumptions, to be able to generalize from particular instances of fire causing smoke. Monday morning's fire was followed by and accompanied by smoke; and so was Tuesday evening's, and Wednesday's, and so on. Now, having observed and remembered all of these fire-smoke events, can we generalize and say that fire causes smoke or even that smoke always accompanies fire, or even that it usually does? No. Why not? What makes us think this connection will occur the *next* time we see the smoke but cannot see the fire? Only if we think fire and smoke *generally* go together, that the nature or essence of fire is to cause smoke. But we cannot infer that, since we cannot assume generalities, essences, and universals—and besides, we cannot infer!

To understand the following Carvacan quotation, we need to know a little more about Indian logic. In the Indian syllogism, as in Aristotle's syllogism, there are two premises, the major premise and the minor premise, and the key term that appears in both premises is known as the "middle term." The major term is the other term that appears in the major premise, and the minor term is the other term that appears in the minor premise. So, the crucial argument that the hill is on fire because it is smoking goes as follows:

The hill is smoking.   (minor premise)
All smoking is caused by fire. (major premise)
Therefore, the hill is on fire. (conclusion)

In this case, the middle term is "smoking," which connects the hill (in the minor premise) to fire (in the major premise), and the major term is "fire" and the minor term is "the hill."

> Those who maintain the authority of inference accept the sign or middle term [smoking] as the cause of knowledge, which middle term [smoking] must be found in the minor premise and be itself invariably connected with the major term [fire] in the major premise. . . . What then is the means of this connection's being known? We will first show that it is not perception. Now perception is held to be of two kinds, external and internal [as in Locke, the five "external" senses plus an "internal" intuitive sense of our own states of mind]. The former [the external, five senses] is not the required means; for although it is possible that the actual contact of the sense and the object will produce the knowledge of the particular object thus brought in contact, yet as there can never be such contact in the case of the past or the future,

the universal proposition which was to embrace the invariable connection of the middle and major terms in every case [the major premise] becomes impossible to be known. Nor may you maintain that this knowledge of the universal proposition has the general class as its object, because, if so, there might arise a doubt as to the existence of the invariable connection in this particular case. Nor is internal perception the means, since you cannot establish that the mind has any power to act independently towards an external object, since all allow that it is dependent on the external senses.

(the Carvacans, in Radhakrishnan and Moore, *Sourcebook in Indian*)

This later became known among nineteenth- and twentieth-century Western philosophers as "the problem of induction."

Some Eastern (Samkhya) and Western philosophers have argued that causality is always purposeful, and have argued on that basis for the existence of God as the only plausible purposeful cause of the world, while others (Wang Chung and modern Western scientists) have denied purposeful causality apart from human agency.

As we saw earlier, the Taoist philosopher Wang Chung (27–100 C.E.), argued against all anthropomorphic (human centered) explanations (for example, that the floods occurred because the gods were angry with us). Wang Chung opposes all teleological explanations for natural phenomena. Only human beings act purposefully, doing one thing for some reason, to accomplish some end or purpose. Nature acts spontaneously, with no particular concern for the outcome, and certainly without regard for the outcome for human beings.

By the fusion of the yin and yang ethers of Heaven and Earth, all things are spontaneously produced, just as by the union of the fluids of husband and wife, children are spontaneously produced. . . . When Heaven moves, it does not desire to produce things thereby, but things are produced of their own accord: such is spontaneity [cu jan, a Taoist term]. When it gives forth its ether, it does not desire to create things, but things are created of themselves: such is non-activity [wu wei, another Taoist term, meaning without purposeful action by a conscious, willing agent]. . . . The Way of Heaven is one of non-activity. Therefore, in spring it does not act to germinate, in summer to cause growth. But the yang ether comes forth of itself in spring and summer, and things of themselves germinate and grow.

(Wang Chung, in Fung Yulan, *A History of Chinese Philosophy*)

Hence, Wang Chung ridiculed those who thought that nature punishes and rewards us with bad or good weather and that this can be magically controlled by the actions and thoughts of the ruler.

Those who talk about cold and heat say that when the ruler is joyful, there is warmth, and when he is angry, there is cold. How can this be? They say that joy and anger develop within his bosom and afterward find their way to the outside, where they give form to rewards and punishments.... but the Way of Heaven is that of spontaneity, and this spontaneity means non-activity. It may fortuitously happen that the yin and yang principles coincide with human events in such a way that, when a human event occurs, these ethers of Heaven are already present.

(ibid.)

In short, Wang Chung argues, human beings do not occupy any privileged place in the universe—the world does revolve around, and for the sake of, us!

Man holds a place within the universe like that of a flea or louse under a jacket or robe, or of a cricket or ant within a hole or crevice. Can the flea, louse, cricket, or ant, by conducting themselves either properly or improperly, effect changes and movements in the ether that lies under the jacket and robe or in the hole or crevice? The flea, louse, cricket, and ant are incapable of this, and to suppose that man alone is so capable is to misconceive of the principles of things and of the yin and yang ethers.... How can human affairs or the administration of the country have any influence on them?

(ibid.)

The Samkhya philosophers, on the other hand, accept a version of teleological causality, which resembles that of Aristotle. While Samkhya rejects any divine, external agency controlling nature, they hold, somewhat like Aristotle, that nature itself acts purposefully for the sake of Purusha.

Evolution is brought about by Nature itself; it is neither produced by God nor is it an evolution from Brahman; nor is it without cause. This evolution is for the sake of the emancipation of each spirit [Purusha]; while it appears as if it were for Nature's own sake, it is really for the sake of another [Purusha].... Some object that only a sentient being can act either for its own or for another's sake; and Nature, being insentient, cannot act in that way but requires a sentient controller [God behind the scenes]. But we answer, it is a fact of observation that insentient objects also act towards definite ends; for example, the milk, which is insentient, flows for the nourishment of the calf. So Nature though insentient acts towards the emancipation of the spirit [Purusha].

(the Samkhya philosophies, in Radhakrishnan and Moore, Sourcebook in Indian)

Aristotle analyzed four different senses in which we speak of causality—material, formal, final (i.e., teleological), and efficient. The material cause of the pot is the clay; the formal cause is its shape; the final or teleological cause is the potter's plan to make an unusually slim teapot; and the efficient cause is the work of the potter herself. In the aforementioned arguments, Samkhya philosophers stress material causality (the salt already in the sea water), while their critics stress efficient causality (where the tailor clearly contributes something to the cloth that was not there before), and formal causality (where the evening gown is clearly different from the yards of satin cloth).

While final (teleological) causality is certainly necessary in making sense of human action, modern scientists seem to agree with Wang Chung in excluding teleological causality from explanations of physical phenomena. One of the big changes brought about by modern science (beginning in the seventeenth century) was the removal of final, teleological causality—whether of the Aristotelian–Samkhyan or theological sort—from explanations of nature. When Newton was asked why the universe existed at all, or what the final purpose of creation was, he replied, "I propose no hypotheses," meaning that he refused to speculate as a scientist on final, teleological causes. Of course, that does not prevent someone from speculating about the internal purpose of natural evolution or God's plan for the universe on religious or metaphysical grounds, as the great British chemist, Robert Boyle, did in his religious writings.

Another metaphysical "middle way" attempt to "save the appearances," that of Aristotle (Greek, fourth century B.C.E.), was to find some essential correlate *within* ordinary physical objects that satisfied the realist criterion of reality. Although an individual tree changes, is causally dependent, and so on, the "essence" of treeness, or treehood, is unchanging, and causally independent. This theory resembles Plato's theory of Forms, except that Forms can exist on their own, independently of physical objects, while essences can exist only within physical objects. Thus, for Aristotle, we can say that the person we have not seen for ten years is the same person, even though she has changed in many ways, because the "essence" of that person has remained the same, although various "accidental" properties (weight, hair color, muscle tone) have changed. Because changing entities contain a real core of unchanging essential nature, they, too, have a limited and relative existence based on the reality of essences.

The theory of evolution would seem to deny the immutability of essences (the essence of oak has not always existed, for instance). It is possible to patch up the theory by holding that the essences exist eternally awaiting actualization—so, for example, the essence of oak has always existed but was only actualized at that stage of biological evolution when oak trees first began to appear. Before that, say, as the planets in our solar system began to form, oak trees were merely a possibility, or potentiality. But since this means that essences can exist apart from individual physical objects that embody them, this approach amounts to Platonism, which Aristotle would have rejected (but which we are, of course, free to embrace if we like).

A similar theory was developed by the early Taoist, Laozi (Chinese, third century B.C.E.), who argued that every physical object becomes the kind of thing it is (whether a snake, banana, or frog) and grows and develops the way it does because of its internal "de" (as in *Tao De Jing*, the book attributed to Laozi) that it shares with all other entities of that kind (class or species). The reason a frog egg becomes a frog and not a chicken or banana is that, like all frog eggs, it shares an internal frog de that is different from a chicken de or banana de. Like Aristotle's essences, the de spontaneously shape the entity from within and do not exist independently of or separately from individual things (as do the Forms for Plato and the li for Zhu Xi).

As we saw in chapter 2, Chinese, Indian, and Western philosophers have been concerned with the relationship between universals and particulars. Indeed, given the nature of human language and the structure of the human brain, it is hardly surprising that anyone thinking about how we perceive the world would recognize that we see things primarily as members of a group or class, and that this is what tells us what those things will be like. Philosophers, reflecting on this obvious but important fact about human beings, go on to theorize about the nature of universals and how they relate to particulars. Gong-Sun Lung argued that particular objects perceptible to the five senses were composed of abstract universals that were fundamentally different from particular physical objects. The stone, for example, is made up of "the hard," "the white," and "the stoniness." Each of these universals, he argued, is unique and distinct from all other universals, as well as from particular physical objects. Whiteness is different from Hardness, and neither is identical with the stone, which is hard and white. Therefore, he objected to Hui Shih and to the Taoist, Zhuangzi's, view that everything changes into its opposite, so that all distinctions are ultimately illusory. According to Gong-Sun Lung, the distinctions between universals, and between universals as a group and particulars as a group, are very real and fundamental.

At the same time, he was concerned about the problems that this theory generates, namely, how the whiteness in this particular white thing (the white stone) can also be in other white objects (e.g., the white egret). Or, if the white is *different* in each one, then how can we say that particulars are made of the *same* set of universals, in which different individuals share the *same* universals? He also worried about how different universals could be combined in the same object. A stone, to return to one of Gong-Sun Lung's favorite examples, is both hard and white. We can feel but not see the hardness, and we can see but not feel the whiteness of the stone. How, then, are such fundamentally different universals—whiteness, hardness, and stoneness—integrated into one single entity, this particular hard, white stone? And how many things are involved—one (the hard, white stone)? three (hardness, whiteness, and stoneness)? or four (the universals hardness, whiteness, and stoneness, plus the particular stone)?

One of the reasons Aristotle rejected his teacher's (Plato's) theory that Forms existed independently of individual physical objects was what became known as the "third man argument." The reason we say the essence or form of whiteness is in the stone is because the white stone resembles, or is similar to, the white egret in its whiteness. But now if we say that in addition to the stone and egret there also is something else, the Whiteness itself, then we have to ask whether the stone and the egret resemble, or are similar to, this Whiteness, and if so, then would there not be yet another thing, call it Whiteness-2, in addition to the stone and the egret and the original Form of Whiteness (Whiteness-1)? And if that is so, then there will be a Whiteness-3 (the similarity between Whiteness-1 and Whiteness-2), and so on to infinity. (The "third man," of course, is the similarity between men and the essence or Form of Man.) Of course, as we saw earlier, this infinity argument does not absolutely refute Plato's theory, since Plato could simply welcome all of the many new Forms, but it does make the theory seem somewhat ridiculous! (Plato himself records in one of his dialogues, *Parmenides*, Socrates as a young man having to admit to the wise old Parmenides that if there was a Form for every common noun, then, alongside the Forms of Beauty, Justice, and Equality, there would have to be eternal, immaterial Forms of dirt, hair, and garbage!)

Greek philosophers, including the Pythagoreans, Eleatics, Socrates, Plato, and Aristotle, worried about many of the same problems as Gong-Sun Lung. Plato drew a sharp distinction between physical objects that are constantly changing and the concepts by which they are classified. A particular dog, Fido, is constantly changing; he is born, grows from a puppy to an adult dog, leads an active life, then starts slowing down, gets sick, and finally dies. The concept or idea of a dog, that is, a dog in general (dogginess), on the other hand, remains constant, whether referred to by Plato, Confucius, or Shakespeare.

Plato held that these were two completely separate kinds of things—sense particulars, like Fido, and Ideas, or Forms, like the universal Dogness in general. The Song dynasty Neo-Confucian philosopher Zhu Xi also held that abstract principles (li, a different word from the virtue of propriety, discussed earlier, or the Chinese word for profit, which are also spelled "li" in the Roman alphabet) existed independently of sense particulars. And the Indian Nyaya philosophers also held that the "genus" (e.g., animal) is a universal and as such is eternal.

Aristotle agreed with his teacher, Plato's, distinction between particulars and universals, but disagreed that universals could exist apart from particulars. Universals, Aristotle argued, can only exist in particulars—the universal Dog existing in Fido, Lassie, and other dogs, the universal Man existing in Socrates, Plato, and other people, and so on. Like Aristotle, the Ming dynasty Confucian philosopher Wang Yangming similarly agreed with Zhu Xi, that individual things were controlled by li, but disagreed with Zhu, that the li could exist apart from particulars.

Like Aristotle (see chapter 2), the Vaisesika tradition in India also held that "generality" was a "category" or predictable quality of individual substances. Statements, they said, predicate one of six "categories" of an object—substance, quality, action, generality, individuality, and inherence (*Padarthadharmasamgraha*, ch. 1). That is, if we ask what kinds of things we can know and say about an object, for example, Fido, both Aristotle and the Vaisesika philosophers answer that we can say and know that Fido is a dog (substance), that Fido is small, brown, and short haired (quality), that Fido is a guard dog (action), and that Fido is a canine, a pet, a mammal, an animal, and a living entity (generality). And like both Aristotle and Xunzi, Vaisesika philosophers recognized higher and lower levels of generality (Fido is a dog, dogs are mammals, mammals are vertebrates, and so on).

> Of generality, or universality, there are two kinds, the higher and the lower; and it serves as the basis of inclusive or comprehensive cognition. The higher (or highest) generality is that of 'being'; as it is this that extends over the largest number of things; and also because it is this alone that is a generality pure and simple, always serving, as it does, as the basis of comprehensive cognitions. The lower generalities are 'substance' and the rest, which extend over a limited number of things. These latter, being the basis of inclusive as well as exclusive cognitions, are sometimes regarded as individualities also.
>
> *(ibid.)*

The last sentence in the aforementioned passage sounds much like Aristotle. When we say Fido is a dog, the word "dog" refers to a larger category of things, including many individual entities like Fido, although "dog" is a smaller category than "mammal," "animal" or, the largest of all, "thing." But in a different sense, "dog" (what Aristotle called species) can also be used to refer to an *individual* entity, that (particular) dog (e.g., Fido), because that is how we identify what that individual is. If we ask, "What is that particular thing?" the answer is "a dog." A dog is what it basically or essentially is; that is, "dog" defines the individual and makes it what it is, makes it the particular thing that it is (a dog and not a cat or bird). As Aristotle put it, "dog" is its nature or essence. Since things cannot exist, at least as we know them, as bare particulars, but only as things of a definite and determinate kind, it follows that below the level of "dog" we can no longer talk about an individual thing. If it is a thing at all, then it must be a thing belonging to the lowest level of generality—a dog, a cat, and so on.

This indicates, once more, how absolutely fundamental to human cognition our classificatory kind of understanding is. Perhaps the Buddhists and Vedantists are right when they say that in reality there are no individual things in the world (either because reality is "empty," as the Buddhists say, or because there is only one thing, Brahman, as the Vedantists say). But that is not how the world appears or can ever appear to a human being. As long as we are looking at the world with this human body and human nervous system (brain, sense organs, and so on), the world will always appear to us as a plurality of causally connected, semipermanent entities of this or that kind—an interconnected world of dogs and cats, trees and snakes. This is what makes the world of our experience seem, for the most part, meaningful and comprehensible—because we normally see objects in terms of our own conceptual and linguistic meanings. As we saw in our discussion of logical paradoxes in chapter 2, and as "Absurdist" fiction writers like Sartre, Ionesco, Beckett, and Camus are fond of pointing out, when we do, on rare occasions, catch a glimpse of things separated from any meaningful classification, these things appear disturbingly alien and absurd. In his autobiographical novel, *Nausea*, Sartre describes how such ordinary objects as a street car seat and park bench suddenly become alien and repugnant when they have been separated from the conceptual meanings we usually attach to them.

> I murmur: "It's a seat," a little like an exorcism, but the word stays on my lips: it refuses to go and put itself on the thing. It stays what it is. . . . Things are divorced from their names. They are there, grotesque, headstrong, gigantic and it seems ridiculous to call them seats or say anything at all about them; I am in the midst of things, nameless things. Alone without words, defenseless, they surround me. . . . I sank down on the bench, stupefied, stunned by this profusion of beings without origin: everywhere blossoming, hatching out. . . . It was repugnant.

(Sartre 1959)

Like their Western counterparts, Chinese philosophers, such as Zhu Xi, have also been concerned with the relation of universals or essences to individual things. Individual things are what they are because of a common nature, essence, or principle (li) that they share with others of their kind. The Taoists similarly spoke of the "de" of each kind of thing—the de of the tomato plant, the de of the ox, the de of the bamboo, and so on. Thus the world is made up of individuals belonging to natural kinds, each of which is defined and controlled by its universal principle or essence (all the dogs being formed alike by the Form or li or de of dogness, which differentiates dogs from cats, which share a different Form or li or de of catness and so on).

A tomato seed will grow into a tomato plant, and not a bamboo plant, because of its inner tomato li or de. Similarly, Aristotle said the "form" of each entity was the "formal cause" of that thing becoming what it is rather than some other thing. What causes the tomato seed to become a tomato plant is the "form" of tomato within the seed. Today we would probably speak of the genetic code within the DNA of the seed which determines what the plant will develop into.

These then are some of the attempts by realist philosophers to recover some limited reality for ordinary physical objects, while admitting the basic truth of the antirealist argument that nothing that changes can be fully real. Notice that the antirealist argument does not actually remove or destroy ordinary physical objects or our everyday experience of them. All it does is change their characterization (description, classification) from "real" to "not real." When the argument has done its worst, these objects are still there in front of us, just as before. What has changed is that we no longer say of these things that they are "real." We simply reclassify them as "appearance" instead of "reality." But they are still there in some sense or another.

What difference does it make whether we say that ordinary physical and mental objects (like myself) are to be classified as "real" or "unreal"? In one sense, as A. J. Ayer (British, twentieth century) and other antimetaphysical positivists have asserted, it makes no difference whatsoever. Because the question of their "reality" or "unreality" is a metaphysical one, the positivists argue, it is empirically unverifiable and therefore cannot make the slightest difference in the actual world of our everyday experience. And, in a sense, this is perfectly true. Whether I say that the weeds in my vegetable garden are real or unreal, whether I hold them to be material or mental, they are there and I must either weed them out or lose part of my garden.

But from another point of view, it does make a difference what metaphysical view one holds. The world may visually look much the same to a materialist (who holds that only matter exists) and a dualist (who holds that both mind and matter exist), but they may well feel differently about death, the dualist seeing the possibility of life after death (the mind or soul, being separate, could exist apart from the body) and the materialist seeing none (since they do not recognize any separate mind or soul).

Whether it is *desirable* for the soul to outlive the body is, of course, another question! From the Buddhist point of view, the belief in a permanent soul is the source of all of our *problems*! All of our human anxiety about life, the Buddhists say, stems from the mistaken belief that our selves are real and substantially unchanging entities and that we live in the midst of similarly real and unchanging physical objects. Thus, the Buddhist metaphysical theory of the unreality of the individual self, mind, or soul would lead to supreme happiness, and would therefore make a big difference in one's experience of the world. The Greek and Roman atomists similarly argued, but for very different reasons, that the fear of death was due to the mistaken belief in the immortality of the mind, self, or soul—which they feared could be eternally tortured in the flames of Hell. Epicurus and Lucretius say the good news is that there is no mind or soul, so when one dies one literally will not feel a thing!

So it does seem to make a difference which metaphysical view one holds, though more specifically *what* difference it makes depends on one's general cultural outlook. For the Hindu, salvation depends on the existence of an eternal, unchanging self (atman). But for the Hindu, this "self" is not the conscious mind (jiva) we are ordinarily aware of in everyday life (which most of us in Western culture see as being immaterial and hope will be immortal but which the Hindu sees as being part of the body), but rather the unseen "real Self," the atman, which is identical with the whole of reality (known as Brahman). For the ancient Hebrews, life after death did not depend on the existence of a mind or soul separate from the body. They believed in the "resurrection of the body," that one's body lay in the grave until the "Day of Judgment" at the end of the world when one's long-dead body would rise up and live on for eternity, whether in Heaven or Hell. Although the idea may have originated with Pythagoras (sixth century B.C.E.), Socrates was the first Western thinker we know of to develop the idea that a person is composed of both a soul and a body and that the soul is our real self and is eternal, being born again and again into different bodies. This idea gradually became part of the Christian belief system, though in a modified form (since God created everything, God created the soul, and therefore the soul is not, as Socrates thought, older than the body, but the same age as the body, though, from this point on, the soul will certainly last much longer than the body—indeed forever). But whatever one's general cultural outlook, it does seem to make a difference whether we think of minds or souls as "real" or "unreal."

So, while metaphysics is not a science describing the world, much less a supersensible "real" world, it does function as a general guide, or orientation, laying down a kind of map, or an overview, providing an overall sense of direction. As such, metaphysics is useful and maybe even necessary, but only if we drop the pretense that it is some sort of super science—the science of the supersensible—a kind of religion.

5

Ethics

*L*ET us now turn to another branch of philosophy—ethics, also known as moral philosophy. The main question of ethics is whether there are any universal, crosscultural, normative standards for good and bad and right and wrong, and if so, what they are. In all branches of philosophy, there are skeptics, as we have seen, and ethics is no exception. To the above question, the moral philosophy skeptic says, no, there are no universal, crosscultural, ethical standards—it is all culturally relative.

Of course, we find different practices observed in different societies, but that does not always mean that these different societies hold different moral principles or standards. The ancient Eskimos used to send their elderly grandparents off to freeze to death when they could no longer contribute to the work of the community, but why did they do this? Was it because they had different moral standards from our own? That is, was it because, while we value human life, they did not? Or was it simply because of the harsh living conditions they had to face and the necessity that everyone who took food and other resources had to be able to contribute? Or we learn that some ancient societies would kill their senior citizens while they were still healthy and active, not because they hated them or did not respect human life, but actually as a favor to these older family members and friends! How so? Because they believed that human beings enter the afterlife in the same physical condition they were in at the moment they died; so waiting until your grandparents are bedridden and senile would condemn them to an eternity of such poor quality of (after)life. Sometimes societies observe distinct practices, then, not because they hold different moral principles, but because they find themselves in unique circumstances or because they hold different beliefs about the world.

159

Even where we do find different moral standards upheld in various societies, does that make all of them right? Slavery and human sacrifice used to be universally practiced in all cultures around the world, and are still practiced in remote corners of the world today. But do we want to say that these practices are morally justifiable in those societies where they are or were practiced? On the other hand, perhaps we feel that it is wrong to be intolerant of other people, that we should not impose our moral principles on other people, but should allow them to follow their own guidelines as autonomous human beings. But in that case, are we not championing at least one universal moral standard, the principle that everyone should practice tolerance and support human autonomy? But if so, is that not a rejection of relativism, which denies any universal moral standard?

And even if we do support the moral principles of tolerance and autonomy, are these the *only* moral principles, and if there are others, do tolerance and autonomy always take precedence over the others? Suppose you see that your neighbor is constantly undermining the self-confidence of her children. Would you try to intervene? Probably not. Why? Because in this case you probably think that one has a right to lead one's own life as one sees fit and to raise one's children according to one's own guidelines, and that it is wrong for others to interfere. But what if you began to notice signs of severe physical abuse? Burns appear on the children's hands, arms are broken, bruises regularly appear, unmistakable sounds of beatings are heard from inside the house. Would you now intervene? Probably. But why? Have you forgotten the value of tolerance and autonomy? No, but these are now outweighed by other factors, so you would do something—you might suggest counselling, you might call the police, or you might get in touch with children's services agencies.

Another approach which, like ethical relativism, is more of a challenge to moral philosophy than a contribution to it is egoism, which does offer a kind of guide to life ("always look out for number one") but which is not really a moral theory. Why? Because ethics aims at a doctrine that could be recommended to everyone, one, that is, that is universal, and it is hard to see how egoism can be openly universal. If you were an egoist, would you want everyone else to be an egoist too? You might think that you will get ahead if you always act selfishly, out of your own self-interest, but is that how you want everyone else to behave? Most egoists do not advocate egoism as a general rule, but prefer to live in a world where everyone *but themselves* acts altruistically, out of consideration and concern for the well-being of others. It is like a robber or con man; they do not want to live among other robbers or con men, but in a community of law-abiding, trusting, caring individuals. So if ethics is a standard of conduct that could be advocated for everyone, then egoism is not an ethical theory.

But philosophers who think there *are* universal, crosscultural, normative standards for what is right and wrong and good and bad, cannot agree among themselves and offer very different answers as to what those standards are. As we will see, some philosophers judge the moral worth of an action by its results or consequences. The utilitarians, for example, maintain that everyone should always to do that which will produce the greatest happiness or pleasure for the greatest number of people. Other moral philosophers hold that an action must be judged by the intention of the agent, regardless of the consequences. The woman who rushed into the burning building to save her neighbor's three children actually died in the blaze, along with all three children. But we do not condemn her, because her intentions were good—she did not intend to cause the death of four people, but to save the lives of three children.

But the oldest moral theory is one based on human nature. This theory says that we should follow our human nature (if that human nature is basically good) or control and socialize our human nature (if it is bad). Let us start with this theory, since it follows from our previous discussion (chapter 4) of universals and particulars (in the sense that you and I are particular individuals who share the same universal human essence, or nature). Is there a human nature, and if so, what is it? Like Western philosophers, Eastern philosophers, especially the Chinese, have been interested in the problem of human nature. Although Chinese, Western, and Indian philosophers approached this question from very different sets of cultural assumptions, their analyses turn out to be quite similar. Chinese philosophers approach this question against the backdrop of a whole set of ancient (prephilosophical) assumptions about the dual contributions to human nature of "Heaven" (tian) and "Earth" (di) and/or the dual contributions of assertive forces (yang) and submissive forces (yin); Western philosophers look at the issue from the Platonic background of "universals" shaping the structure and function of individual things; and Indian philosophers develop their theories having inherited an ancient religious belief in the distinction of an ordinary, empirical ego (jiva) and a hidden, but more real transcendent Self, atman, which is our real nature. Nonetheless, what these philosophers actually say about human nature is similar, as are the problems they confront in constructing their theories.

Of course, people are different from one another—each individual is different from all other individuals, and the people of one part of the world often seem very different from the people of other parts of the world. But philosophers wonder how much of this difference is due to conditioning, socialization, environment, and education, and how much, if any, we are born with. Are there any respects in which all human beings are fundamentally alike at birth? How much of the way we are is due to "nature" and how much to "nurture"? How much of a person's success or failure in life is due to inherited, genetic factors and how much to the influence of family, education, and socialization? This is the central question of human nature.

We have been saying that philosophy starts out as a criticism of traditional culture; philosophy calls all conventional, traditional ways of thinking and behaving into question. Every society will have its conventional forms of behavior—customs, rituals, manners, morals, and so on. But these conventional forms of behavior (precisely because they *are* conventional) differ from society to society. What makes us think *our* way of doing things is better than someone else's? How can we *justify* one particular set of conventions as opposed to others? Is there some basis in reality, that is, some nonconventional foundation, built into the very nature of reality, at least the reality of human beings, in terms of which we could justify *some* social conventions and condemn *others*? If so, what is this realistic, natural basis?

This is what led philosophers everywhere (in India, China, and Greece) to distinguish what is "natural" from what is "conventional" (in India, "nama" and "rupa"; in Greece, "nomos" and "physis"; and in China, we can think, for example, of Zhuangzi's statement that the four legs of the horse are "of nature" while the halter is "of man"). This is what led to the search for "human nature," that is, the natural, realistic foundation for any legitimate social conventions. If a long-standing traditional convention is in conformity with, in accordance with, or is an expression, fulfillment, or development of this innate "human nature," then it is "good." If not, it is "bad," or at least morally neutral.

This was particularly a problem for philosophers like Kongzi (Confucius) and Plato, who were trying to provide a philosophical justification for the traditional virtues of their own societies of that time (the traditional Greek virtues of wisdom, courage, temperance, and justice, and the Chinese traditional virtues of ren (human heartedness), li (propriety), yi (righteousness), and zhi (knowledge)). Their critics were quick to point out that they were merely defending existing customs and conventional traditions, attempting to prescribe for everyone the virtues traditionally appropriate to one particular class within that specific society, and that this carried no rational (universal) weight outside of their distinct societies and classes within those societies.

The Taoists particularly favored the "natural" over the "artificial" and mercilessly criticized the Confucianists for their emphasis on the humanly created, and therefore "artificial," civilized culture of art and literature, ritual and custom—all those things one is not born with but which must be learned and imposed on children through an elaborate process of socialization and acculturation. The Taoists were especially critical of the Confucianists' attempt to actively foster and promote morality. Sometimes the Taoists expressed themselves by saying that one should practice wu wei, which literally means "nonaction." But the context makes it clear that they did not mean simply doing nothing, which is impossible, but rather not acting in a too deliberate, purposeful, or self-conscious way—that is, not trying so hard, but just letting things take their natural course. As the fourth-century neo-Taoist, Kuo Xiang, says in his Commentary on Zhuangzi, "'Non-activity' does not mean folding one's arms and remaining silent. It means allowing everything to follow what is natural to it, and then its nature will be satisfied." We should therefore be like nature, or the Tao, in which everything is done without ever consciously trying to do anything—the seed sprouts and grows into a mature plant, without planning or consciously trying or thinking about how to do this.

> Tao invariably does not do, yet there is nothing that is not done.
>
> (Laozi, *Tao De Jing*, V. H. Mair, trans.)

This is part of the universal Taoist principle of "reversal" by which the Taoists believe all of nature operates, in which the strong will get weaker and the weak will get stronger, the poor will get richer and the rich will get poorer.

> The crooked shall be straight; the empty filled; the worn out new; one having little will obtain more; one having plenty will be without. The high is lowered. The low is brought up. From those having abundance it will be taken away. Those who have little will be replenished. The weakest in the world will overcome the strongest. What is expected to shrink, must first be stretched. What is expected to weaken, must first be strengthened. What is expected to be destroyed, must first be built up.
>
> (*Tao de Jing*)

The moral of this Taoist principle is that the way to be strong and famous is to be weak and unknown (since such a person can only become stronger and better known, while the strong and famous can only be "heading for a fall"), as when we say, in Western culture, "the first shall be last, and the last shall be first."

> The Sage, putting himself in the background, is always to the fore. Remaining outside, he is always there. Is it not just because he does not strive for any personal end that all his personal ends are fulfilled?
>
> He does not show himself; therefore he is seen everywhere. He does not define himself; therefore he is distinct. He does not assert himself; therefore he succeeds.
>
> (*Tao de Jing*)

Trying too hard to do anything, the Taoists thought, only proves how *lacking* one is in that regard. Trying too hard to be funny, for example, only shows how little natural sense of humor one actually has. Also, the Taoists argued that, generally speaking, the harder we try, the less we succeed! Suppose someone advises me to lighten up, to be more relaxed, or more graceful. But clearly, in these cases at least, the Taoists are right—the harder I try, the more I fail! By *trying* to be relaxed and graceful, for example, I become even more uptight and awkward. Morality, like humor and lightheartedness, cannot be learned by rote, mechanically following some set of rules, the Taoists insisted, but must spring from the heart spontaneously. A mother does not protect her infant because of having read some philosophy book, but naturally and spontaneously. But since morality is generally pitted against natural impulses, training us to do what we do not want to do and not to do what we want to do, the Taoists were firmly opposed to morality as it is generally understood, that is, as a set of socially approved guidelines or rules to which we are all expected to conform.

Of course, one could argue that it is possible to assimilate and internalize the social rules that we have learned so that eventually they become habitual and "second nature" to us. Kongzi (Confucius) remarks that when he turned seventy he could do whatever he felt like without fear of doing anything wrong. By age seventy, he had so well trained himself (so well internalized the virtues) that he actually preferred (liked and enjoyed) being virtuous. (Of course, at age seventy he may have been less able to do some of the naughty things he was tempted to do in his youth!) The skillful pianist or tennis player seems to perform naturally, effortlessly, and spontaneously, though we know that in fact this is the result of many years of practice and training. Still, to become a truly righteous person, as the Confucian moralists want us to, is extremely difficult and can never become habitual or second nature for any but a handful of individuals. And, on the other hand, insisting that people merely follow traditional and polite forms of behavior, as they thought the Confucianists were also doing, only leads to decadence and a deterioration of the childlike goodness of the natural person, and can never be more than a culturally relative customary morality for a particular society—or a particular class within a particular society.

In a traditional, feudal society (before philosophy), there are no moral standards applicable to everyone, only customary standards of behavior defining each class of persons within the society. So, for example, farmers should be hard working and obedient, warriors should be brave and strong, the priestly class should be wise and holy, and so on. Philosophical ethics begins when an attempt is made (following the breakdown of this traditional feudal morality) to find a universal foundation for one set of standards (generally those of the nobility) and to extend those standards to everyone in the society, and indeed to everyone in the world. But from the very beginning of philosophy, the critics have challenged whether this move is legitimate.

Friedrich Nietzsche was a late nineteenth-century German scholar of Greek language and culture who defended the criticism made by Greek Sophists like Thrasymachus, that what Plato claims are universal virtues obligatory for everyone are in fact nothing more than the traditional (prephilosophical) Greek virtues of the warrior class of aristocrats. Nobles were taught to be strong, brave, honest, and proud, for example, but not the ordinary farmers or fishermen. And if that is true, Nietzsche argues, then is Thrasymachus not right after all when he says that "good" people are the strong and noble ones, and if so, then do they not have the *right* to rule and be obeyed by the ordinary people?

In China, the Taoists argued similarly that Confucianism was trivial because it had no foundation in reality (or "nature," the Tao) but was merely conventional. Like Plato, Kongzi and his followers tried to extend the traditional (prephilosophical) virtues of the ruling, warrior-class nobility to include everyone (or at least everyone in China). To this the followers of Kongzi, beginning with his grandson Tzu Ssu and later Mengzi, replied that Kongzi's defense of the traditional Chinese virtues could be reconstructed on a natural, realist basis (though Kongzi himself did not do this). And so they proceeded to argue that the traditional Chinese virtues were the natural fulfillment and development of the innate human nature with which every human being is born.

Of course, all human nature theorists acknowledge that the way a person actually turns out as an adult depends on *both* their inborn nature and also on their socialization (through education, early family training, and so on)—human nature, they said, is only a *tendency* that can be either developed or frustrated by socialization. But, as we will see, different Confucian philosophers laid different emphases on the relative strength of innate human nature versus the need for socialization—Mengzi laying the greatest stress on the role of human nature, Dong Zhongshu and Xunzi laying far more stress on the role of social conventional reinforcement and training, and Gaozi explaining everything on the basis of socialization and denying any role for human nature.

Among Western philosophers, Sophists like Protagoras argued that "man is the measure of all things," that is, that moral standards are created by human beings and therefore differ from society to society. The Sophists, in other words, were "cultural relativists," denying the existence of any universal, crosscultural "natural" basis for morality, and insisting instead that morality is relative to the particular country, culture, or society—"when in Rome, do as the Romans do." And it was precisely to counteract this Sophistic cultural relativism that Plato introduced his theory of Forms, especially the Forms of Justice, Temperance, Courage, and Goodness. If these are Forms, then they are eternal and universal, and *not* culturally relative social constructions. Furthermore, Plato argued, much like the Confucianists did, that the nature of all human beings is such that in order for anyone to be a healthy, happy, and successful human being, they must be just, temperate, courageous, and good.

Is there a human nature common to all human beings or not? At first we might think this question could be settled empirically—just look and see whether human beings from different countries, social backgrounds, and historical periods are all alike in some ways, and if so, in what ways exactly. But a little reflection will reveal that this is not nearly as easy as it first appears. As a matter of fact, people are quite *dis*similar, but it is hard to tell whether these differences are due to the fact that there *is* no human nature or simply to the effects of different kinds of education and socialization on a fundamentally similar human nature.

Aristotle, for example, said that human beings were by nature rational. But if we look to see for ourselves, we see that most people behave irrationally much of the time. Does this mean Aristotle was wrong? Or does it simply mean that although human beings are born with the capacity to think and behave rationally, this disposition is frequently offset by other factors—their emotions, their "animal instincts," or lack of training and discipline of their rational capacity? How can we tell which of these hypotheses is true?

Perhaps we could examine young children who are two or three years old. But probably even they have been influenced in some ways by their culture. Some tests indicate that very young boys respond to identical situations quite differently than young girls, boys being more aggressive, girls more submissive. But does this prove that boys are "by nature" more aggressive and that girls are more submissive? Many feminists would say not; all this shows they would say, is that even by the age of two or three boys have already been acculturated to behave more aggressively and girls to behave more passively.

Similarly, when Freudians claim that human beings are by nature selfish and aggressive and followers of Eric Fromm, that they are by nature more loving and social, there is clear counterevidence against *both* theories—against Freud, we find many loving, social people; against Fromm, we find many selfish, aggressive individuals. And of course, it would be morally and politically impossible to entirely remove infants from their parents in order to conduct more scientific tests.

Theories of human nature are therefore *normative*, and not entirely empirical. When Aristotle says human beings are rational by nature, he means that people are more truly human when they display their rationality and that they abandon their human nature when they behave irrationally. This normative claim implies that human beings *should* behave rationally, not that they actually do. Part of this normative claim is that in general it is good to follow one's nature. If you are a mouse, you ought to follow your mouse nature—be the best you can be as a mouse. But if you happen to be a human being, you should follow your human nature—be the most you can be as a human being, fulfill your human potential.

But that will only make sense if our human nature is something good and positive—being rational, loving, and so on, and not evil and negative— being aggressive, selfish, greedy, and so on. We certainly would not want to advise a potentially violent young person to "live up to his full potential"! These human nature theorists therefore attribute some *positive* capacity to human nature—that people are inherently rational, loving, and so on. And these are theories that interpret human nature to mean some characteristic that is *unique* to human beings, something that no other creatures possess. The theory holds that we normatively ought to live up to our unique human capacity.

But other human nature theories stress not what is unique to human beings but what human beings share with the other animals (desire for food, comfort, sex, personal survival, etc.), and therefore argue that human nature is evil and should be controlled and modified by society. These theories often are used to support intrusive and repressive governmental measures to control our inherently wicked tendencies. Theories that argue that human nature is evil generally mean by human nature *all* of the instincts with which we are born, most of which we share with the lower animals, whereas those theories that argue that human nature is good generally mean by human nature only the distinctively human characteristics, those we do *not* share with the lower animals.

Those human nature theorists who hold that human nature is good would naturally like to encourage all of us to follow our basic nature. In general, they say, it is good to follow one's nature, and if that nature is said to be something positive, like being rational or loving, then it is socially constructive and educationally sound to encourage young people to follow their basic human nature. When Aristotle says human nature is rational, he means that this is what human beings are capable of, in ways that other life forms are not, that thinking and behaving rationally is a uniquely human potential.

By the same token, those human nature theorists who hold that human nature is evil would like to encourage society to *modify* and *alter* our *wicked* human nature. In either case, human nature theorists are talking about the good or wicked *capacities* or *potentialities* of people, not what they always or necessarily are. Both those who say human nature is good and those who say it is bad agree that people as we actually find them are neither all good nor all bad. Those who say human nature is evil think that people are likely to become evil (if left to themselves) but that they can also become good (if properly socialized). Those who say human nature is good agree that people can become evil (if they are abused or mistreated) but that they can also become good (if allowed to follow their own inherent nature).

So claims about human nature are also claims about capacities and potentialities, not simply empirical generalizations about actual behavior. But human beings have many capacities, the potential to be and do many different things. If human nature theorists are claiming no more than the fact that people are *capable* of this or that, the claim is far too weak—people are capable of anything—murder, altruism, hard work, laziness, creativity, conformism, and so on. If that is all that is being claimed, it is tantamount to *denying* that there is a human nature. As we will see shortly, this is basically Gaozi's argument that there is no human nature—human beings are equally capable of being molded into any form or shape society chooses; therefore, there is no single tendency we could call human nature.

Claims about human nature must assert more than a mere capacity or potentiality; they must claim that there is a *tendency* for people to be or act a certain way—along with the normative injunction that, since it is generally good to follow one's nature, this is therefore how people *should* behave (or for those who think it is generally bad to follow one's nature, that society should curb our inherently wicked nature).

This is the point of Mengzi's (Mencius's) story of the bare hill that has been cleared of trees. Originally, Mengzi says, the hill was heavily forested, but woodsmen came and cut down all of the trees. At first, the trees grew back each spring, and for many years the farmers had to cut them back again and again. Only after many years did the trees finally die out completely and the hill become bald and bare. Mengzi's point is that even though the trees were cut down, their *tendency* was to keep growing, which is why it took so long to finally clear the hillsides permanently of trees.

> There was a time when the trees were luxuriant on the Ox Mountain, but as it is on the outskirts of a great metropolis, the trees are constantly lopped by axes. Is it any wonder that they are no longer fine? With the respite they get in the day and in the night, and the moistening by the rain and dew, there is certainly no lack of new shoots coming out, but then the cattle and sheep come to graze upon the mountain. This is why it is as bald as it is. People, seeing only its baldness, tend to think that it never had any trees. But can this possibly be the nature of a mountain? Can what is in man be completely lacking in moral inclinations? A man's letting go of his true heart is like the case of the trees and the axes. . . . If [a man's] dissipation happens repeatedly, then [finally] the man is not far removed from an animal. Others, seeing his resemblance to an animal, will be led to think that he never had any native endowment. But can that be what a man is genuinely like? Hence, given the right nourishment, there is nothing that will not grow, while deprived of it there is nothing that will not wither away.
>
> (Mengzi, *Mengzi*, in Chan, *Sourcebook Chinese*)

There is a force *inside* of the trees, and it is a force that moves in only one direction (directing the trees to keep growing as trees of that particular species). There also are forces *outside* of the trees, some of which support the force within the trees (rainfall, sunlight, good soil, and so on) and others that are diametrically opposed to the inner force of the trees (woodcutters cutting down the trees to be used as firewood and building materials). But if the force within the trees is encouraged and allowed to continue, then there can be only one outcome—the continued growth of that particular species of tree. The same applies to human nature theorists. All other things being equal, and in the absence of defeating conditions, people generally will tend to be rational, selfish, loving, aggressive, or whatever it is claimed is our human nature.

So claiming that all people do in fact actually exhibit all the time what is claimed to be their "human nature" is much too strong a claim (since it is too easily falsified); but, on the other hand, merely claiming that all people have this capacity or potentiality is far too weak a claim (since this is too easy to prove; i.e., it is not falsifiable). What needs to be shown is that there is a tendency, disposition, and proclivity (an innate force within the thing) to behave one way over another, and that that is how people will in fact behave in the absence of defeating conditions.

It is these defeating conditions that explain why things do not develop their nature. All theories of human nature must therefore have an "escape clause" by which to explain counter examples. If people are by nature rational, why do they so often behave so irrationally? If people are by nature selfish, why do they so often act out of love and concern for others? Human nature theorists claim that this is how people would behave were it not for certain defeating conditions, for example, perhaps their emotions overwhelm their fundamentally rational nature; or it could be that their physical, animal instincts (of aggression, sex, fear, food, power) clash with an underlying, loving human nature; or, finally, that a basically aggressive and selfish human nature is offset and curbed by socialization and education and a system of rewards and punishments. Any theory of human nature must therefore have a plausible way of explaining away evidence contrary to its particular claims. If a philosopher claims that human nature is rational, he or she must have some way of explaining the fact that people often are *not* rational.

Let us now turn to some philosophical theories of human nature, starting with the Confucian tradition, beginning with Kongzi. Kongzi (Confucius) himself did not have a theory of human nature, but said only that at birth all people are "close" (jin) to one another but that through education they became "far" (yuan) apart. This suggests that Kongzi thought that there *was* a human nature, but he never said what it was—all people are born alike, he said, but he never said *how* they were alike at birth.

Two followers of Kongzi, Mencius (Mengzi, fourth century B.C.E.) and Xunzi (third century B.C.E.) did speculate on what human nature was, but each came up with opposite conclusions. Mengzi (like Plato and Aristotle) held that human nature was basically good, while Xunzi (like Hobbes) said that human nature was basically evil. Later, another Confucianist, Dong Zhongshu, developed a more sophisticated theory of the conflict within each person between his human nature and his instinctual feelings as a kind of compromise between Mengzi and Xunzi.

According to Mengzi, all human beings have the "beginnings" or "sprouting" of goodness within them. That is, all people are born with the potential and tendency to be kindhearted and virtuous, though Mengzi also said that this potential can be nourished and developed, thus the individual becoming a good person, or else neglected, thwarted, and perverted, thus becoming a bad person. Mengzi is not saying, then, that children are moral beings from birth. He realizes that they must be trained and taught, and that they learn by practice and experience. He also realized that children who are neglected or mistreated will usually turn out badly. Nonetheless, his theory holds that in either case, there is an innate tendency or disposition to be good. In the right environment, an acorn will grow into an oak tree, as that is its nature to do so; though robbed of water, sunlight, and proper soil, the seedling's growth will be stunted, and it will shrivel and finally die.

In Mengzi's most famous example, he asks what the immediate and spontaneous response is of any person upon seeing a child about to fall into a well. Mengzi does not want us to think this over for five or ten minutes, but to react instinctively. What do we feel like doing? Mengzi says everyone naturally and spontaneously wants to rush to help the child, but this does not mean that everyone is a morally good person, it only means that everyone is born with the "beginnings" (the "sprouting") of the Confucian virtue of "ren," or "human heartedness," along with the "beginnings" or "sprouting" of the other traditional Chinese virtues of righteousness, propriety, and wisdom.

No man is devoid of a heart sensitive to the suffering of others. My reason . . . is this. Suppose a man were, all of a sudden, to see a young child on the verge of falling into a well. He would certainly be moved to compassion, not because he wanted to get in the good graces of the parents, nor because he wished to win the praise of his fellow villagers or friends, nor yet because he disliked the cry of the child. From this it can be seen that whoever is devoid of the heart of compassion is not human, whoever is devoid of the heart of shame is not human, whoever is devoid of the heart of courtesy and modesty is not human, and whoever is devoid of the heart of right and wrong is not human. The heart of compassion is the germ (or beginning) of benevolence [ren]; the heart of shame, of dutifulness [yi]; the heart of courtesy and modesty, of observance of the rites [li]; the heart of right and wrong, of wisdom [zhi]. Man has these four germs [beginnings] just as he has four limbs. For a man possessing these four germs [beginnings] to deny his own potentialities is for him to cripple himself. . . . If a man is able to develop all these four germs [beginnings] that he possesses, it will be like a fire starting up or a spring coming through.

(ibid.)

In Mengzi's debate with Gaozi, Gaozi (like Sartre, the French philosopher, 2,000 years later) argues in effect that there *is* no human nature, that there is no greater tendency for people to be good than to be evil or indifferent. In other words, Gaozi argued that human beings are infinitely pliable or malleable—they can be made to become anything whatever, and there is no greater disposition or proclivity to become one thing rather than another. Gaozi's analogy is with the flow of water. Water, Gaozi argues, can be made to flow east, west, south, or north. All one has to do is dig a channel from a lake in an eastward direction to get the water to flow east. But if someone blocks that channel and digs another southward, then the water will just as easily flow toward the south. The water itself, Gaozi insists, has no built-in tendency to flow in any given direction, and in that sense, by analogy, human beings have no inherent nature.

> Gaozi said, "Human nature is like whirling water. Give it an outlet in the east and it will flow east; give it an outlet in the west and it will flow west. Human nature does not show any preference for either good or bad just as water does not show any preference for either east or west."
>
> *(ibid.)*

Like Gaozi, the twentieth-century French philosopher Jean-Paul Sartre also holds that there is no innate human nature with which everyone is born, but whereas Gaozi emphasizes the role of society in shaping each person differently, Sartre stresses the freedom of each person to become whomever he or she wants to be. According to Sartre, each person is completely free to create his or her own individual nature, simply by acting on how he or she chooses to be. If you drop out of school and join the army, you have chosen the kind of life and the kind of person you want to be. Our so-called human nature, Sartre says, is simply a humanly constructed idea that we are free to accept or reject.

> [We existentialists] think that existence proceeds essence. . . . Just what does that mean? Let us consider some object that is manufactured, for example, a book or a paper-cutter: here is an object which has been made by an artisan whose inspiration came from a concept. . . . Therefore, let us say that, for the paper-cutter, essence [concept] precedes existence. . . . When we conceive God as the Creator, He is generally thought of as a superior sort of artisan. . . . When God creates He knows exactly what He is creating. Thus, the concept of man in the mind of God is comparable to the concept of paper-cutter in the mind of the manufacturer. . . . Thus, the individual man is the realization of a certain concept in the divine intelligence. In the eighteenth century, the atheism of the [French] philosophes discarded the idea of God, but not the notion that essence precedes existence. . . . [According to

this view,] man has a human nature; this human nature, which is the concept of the human, is found in all men, which means that each man is a particular example of a universal concept, man. . . . [We existentialists say, on the contrary] that existence precedes essence. This means that man exists, turns up, appears on the scene, and only afterwards defines himself. If man, as the existentialist conceives him, is indefinable, it is because at first he is nothing. Only afterwards will he be something, and he himself will have made what he will be. Thus, there is no human nature.

(Sartre, *Studies in Philosophy*)

Gaozi's view, on the contrary, is that each person is molded and shaped by the society in which they happen to have been born. In today's "nature-nurture" debate, it is all nurture, according to Gaozi.

Mengzi's reply is that although water can be made to flow with equal ease north, south, east or west, it nonetheless does tend to flow downward, and that indeed the only reason it can be made to flow westward, for example, is that it naturally flows down. In other words, to make the water flow to the west, one must dig the westward channel deeper than the surface of the lake. The water will always flow down; if the lowest level is the westward channel, then and only then will the water flow westward. Of course, one can also force the water to flow upward, Mengzi points out, as when splashing water, but this can only happen when constantly worked at—as soon as one relaxes, even for a moment, and leaves matters alone, the water naturally flows downward once more.

"It certainly is the case," said Mencius, "that water does not show any preference for either east or west, but does it show the same indifference to high and low? Human nature is good just as water seeks low ground. There is no man who is not good; there is no water that does not flow downwards.

"Now in the case of water, by splashing it one can make it shoot up higher than one's forehead, and by forcing it one can make it stay on a hill. How can that be the nature of water? It is the circumstances being what they are. That man can be made bad shows that his nature is no different from that of water in this respect."

(Mengzi, *Mengzi*, in Chan, *Sourcebook Chinese*)

In another debate with Mengzi, Gaozi argues that just as willow tree wood can be carved into any desired utensil, from a cup to a basket, and therefore, like the water, has no built-in tendency or nature of its own, so human beings can be molded into whatever kind of person the society wants or needs, and therefore human beings have no innate nature of their own. To which Mengzi replies that the willow tree does have its own nature, which is to continue growing as a willow tree. By cutting the willow tree down and carving it up into different sorts of utensils, Mengzi says, we are violating and destroying its nature, and so, through analogy, by following Gaozi's theory we would be violating the nature of human beings by forcing them to conform to some standard at odds with their own nature.

> Gaozi said, "Human nature is like the willow. Dutifulness is like cups and bowls. To make morality out of human nature is like making cups and bowls out of the willow."
> "Can you," said Mencius, "make cups and bowls by following the nature of the willow? Or must you mutilate the willow before you can make it into cups and bowls? If you have to mutilate the willow to make it into cups and bowls, must you, then, also mutilate a man to make him moral? Surely it will be these words of yours men in the world will follow in bringing disaster upon morality."
>
> (ibid.)

It is interesting to note that more than 100 years before this debate between Mengzi and Gaozi, Mozi held a position similar to Gaozi's (that there is no human nature). Mozi argued that the cause of the world's ills was the fact that people loved each other "partially," that you love your mother and your countrymen more than you love my mother and my countrymen, for example, and that the cure for the world's ills is therefore embracing universal, "impartial" love, in which everyone loves everyone else equally (so that you love my mother as much as you love your own mother).

> It is the business of the benevolent man to try to promote what is beneficial to the world and to eliminate what is harmful. Now at the present time [the Warring States period], what brings the greatest harm to the world? Great states attacking small ones, great families overthrowing small ones, the strong oppressing the weak, the many harrying the few, the cunning deceiving the stupid, the eminent lording it over the humble—these are harmful to the world. . . .
> When we inquire into the cause of these various harms, what do we find has produced them? Do they come about from loving others and trying to benefit them? Surely not! They come rather from hating others and trying to injure them. And when we set out to classify and describe those men who hate and injure others, shall we say that their actions are motivated by universality [impartiality] or partiality? Surely we must answer, by partiality, and it is this partiality in their dealings with one another that gives rise to all the great harms in the world. Therefore we know that partiality is wrong. . . .
> Whoever criticizes others must have some alternative to offer them. To criticize and yet offer no alternative is like trying to stop flood with flood or put out fire with fire. It will surely have no effect. Therefore: . . . Partiality should be replaced by universality [impartiality].
>
> (Mozi, Mozi, in Burton Watson, ed. and trans., Basic Writing of Mo Tzu)

Today we can think of many examples of Mozi's "partial love." The Serbs love only or mainly the Serbs, and therefore want to have a country (a nation-state) that is made up entirely of Serbs, and so they feel they must "ethnically cleanse" their country of all non-Serbs (i.e., Croatians and Bosnians). By the same token the Croatians love only or mainly the Croatians; the Tutsi's the Tutsi's; the Protestants of Northern Ireland the Protestants; the whites in Los Angeles the whites; and so on. Where there is competition between "us" and "them," then partial love leads "us" to hate and want to destroy "them." And so we have discrimination, ethnic cleansing, genocide, and warfare. How to stop this? According to Mozi, "Partial love should be replaced by universal, impartial love."

Of course Mozi realized (with the help of his Confucian critics) that this is contrary to our ordinary feelings; you will tend to favor your mother over mine. The Confucianists were naturally appalled at Mozi's rejection of the traditional virtue of "filial piety" (which they supported), that one's primary responsibility in life is toward one's own children and parents. The Confucianists therefore vigorously argued against Mozi's views on "impartial love," saying that since this was contrary to nature, no one would or could follow Mozi's advice (even if Mo were right). Nonetheless, Mozi argued, somewhat like Gaozi, that through a system of rewards and punishments people can be induced and socially conditioned to practice universal love (if not actually *feeling* equally loving toward everyone, at least *treating* everyone equally).

Specifically, he argued that if the ruler urges people to love one another impartially, they would strive to do so, and that since God created human beings and loves them all impartially, God wants us to love one other impartially and will reward us if and when we do and punish us if and when we do not, and that this, too, is a way to encourage people to embrace impartial love. But Mozi does not think or argue that we are born with a sense of universal love of humanity in our hearts—only that we can be trained to adopt such an attitude. In this regard, Mozi argues, like Gaozi, that human beings are infinitely pliable and can be molded into any form desired by the government (either to love partially or impartially). Mozi's analogy is to dyeing cloth.

> Watching a dyer of silk at work, Mozi sighed, saying, "What is dyed in blue becomes blue; what is dyed in yellow becomes yellow. When the silk is put in a different dye its color becomes also different. Having been dipped five times, it has changed its color five times. Therefore dyeing must be attended to with care!"
>
> (*ibid.*)

It is interesting to compare Mozi to Plato on this point. Plato also wanted to discourage the partial love of parents for their children because he felt that this inhibited a natural meritocracy. For example, if you want only the most qualified people to fill various jobs and responsibilities in the country, then you do not want parents giving their own children an unfair advantage—pushing their mediocre children to top positions through extra classes, coaching, friends in high places, family money and power, and so on. As long as children are raised by their own parents in the nuclear family, Plato argued, there is no way to combat this negative influence of "partial love."

We can see the same problem today. In our public educational system, we try to equalize educational opportunities. In the 1980s, various states (of the United States) experimented with "Robin Hood laws" in which, instead of funding public schools from the unequal property tax base of local communities (some rich, some poor), all property tax money would be pooled by the state and more equally distributed to all of the schools in the state. The problem is, will this really give the children of poor families an equal chance? Of course not. Even if they continue to send their children to the public school, wealthy parents will still be able to give their children a head start by buying them books, computers, musical instruments (with private lessons), private tutors, summer music or computer camps, and travel abroad—plus pushing them to do their homework, providing better role models of successful, educated adults, and so on.

Plato realized therefore that the only solution was a drastic one—to disband the nuclear family, which is precisely what he recommends in his book *The Republic.* In order to get the best people to rule in the ideal state, Plato argues that women will have to be given the same educational and career opportunities as men. Those highly intelligent and skilled women will be selected and trained as future rulers. Plato recognized that this would be an unpopular notion at the time (and it may still be, 2,500 years later). Added to this problem, he says, "there is one more difficulty in our law about women. . . . 'that the wives of our rulers are to be held in common, and their children are to held in common, and no parent is to know his own child, nor any child his parent.' " Children were therefore to be raised from birth in public nurseries so that no one would know who their children or parents were.

Plato, in other words, seems to agree with the Confucianists, that it will be difficult to overcome the natural love of parents for their own children and that only a powerful counterforce from "outside" disbanding the nuclear family in favor of state nurseries could overcome this natural tendency of all parents to give their own children a head start. Mozi does not think that this will be so difficult since, like Gaozi, he does not think there is any innate tendency toward partial love to overcome in the first place. Parents privilege their own children because that is what they were taught to do; if in the future they are taught to love everyone's children equally, then they will do *that*, and just as easily.

What Mengzi is saying, on the contrary, by analogy, is that while it is certainly true and important that we can shape and mold human behavior through education, we can only do this successfully when we work *with* an existing tendency of human nature. Only by modifying an already existing human nature can we modify human behavior. Every human society has rules for regulating human sexuality, for example, but how easily could we enforce upon everyone in the society total lifelong abstinence? Or imagine trying to institute sexual codes among creatures who had absolutely no sexual drives. Only if there is already a sex drive can we hope to regulate, modify, shape, channel it, and thereby alter human behavior.

Just as we can splash water upward, so we can attempt to stifle human nature. But the point is, how easy is it? Which is easier, restricting a teenager's food intake to one cup of watery soup a day or to two meals a day of low-fat, balanced nutrition? Both are difficult, but if the first is *more* difficult, does this not show that it is going against the grain of our inherent nature? Another way to put this is to distinguish the "inner" force within a thing and an "outer" force that operates on it from the outside. The "inner" force of the water is to flow down; the "outer" force operating on it is the action of splashing the water upward. The "inner" force of the willow tree is to continue growing as a willow tree, while the "outer" force acting on it is the insects or animals eating it, the drought stunting it, or the woodsman cutting it down.

> "As far as what is genuinely in him is concerned, a man is capable of becoming good," said Mencius. "That is what I mean by good. As for his becoming bad, that is not the fault of his native endowment. The heart of compassion is possessed by all men alike; likewise the heart of shame, the heart of respect, and the heart of right and wrong. . . . Benevolence, dutifulness, observance of the rites, and wisdom do not give me a lustre from the outside, they are in me originally. . . . There are cases where one man is twice, five times . . . better than another man, but this is only because there are people who fail to make the best of their native endowment. . . .
>
> "In good years the young men are mostly lazy, while in bad years they are mostly violent. Heaven has not sent down men whose endowment differs so greatly. The difference is due to what ensnares their hearts. Take the barley for example. Sow the seeds and cover them with soil. The place is the same and the time of sowing is also the same. The plants shoot up and by the summer solstice they all ripen. If there is any unevenness, it is because the soil varies in richness and there is no uniformity in the benefit of rain and dew and the amount of human effort devoted to tending it. Now things of the same kind are all alike. Why should we have doubts when it comes to man? . . . All palates have the same preferences in taste; all ears in sound; all eyes in beauty. Should hearts prove to be an exception by possessing nothing in common? What is it, then, that is common to all hearts (xin)? Reason and rightness. The sage is simply the man first to discover this common element in my heart. Thus reason and rightness please my heart in the same way as meat pleases my palate."

(Mengzi, *Mengzi*, in Chan, *Sourcebook Chinese*)

Xunzi argues, against Mengzi, that human nature is essentially evil, by which he means selfish and aggressively antisocial. It is only through education, training, discipline, and the threat of punishment, Xunzi argues, that people become socially cooperative.

> A warped piece of wood must wait until it has been laid against the straightening board, steamed, and forced into shape before it can become straight; a piece of blunt metal must wait until it has been whetted on a grindstone before it can become sharp. Similarly, since man's nature is evil, it must wait for the instructions of a teacher before it can become upright, and for the guidance of ritual principles before it can become orderly. If men have no teachers to instruct them, they will be inclined towards evil and not upright; and if they have no ritual principles to guide them, they will be perverse and violent and lack order.
>
> (Xunzi, in Burton Watson, ed. and trans., *Basic Writings*)

Somewhat like Hobbes's social contract theory (which we will examine in the next chapter), Xunzi speculates that originally men were free to follow their own selfish bent, without fear of recrimination or punishment. But when they realized that they were as often the victims of aggressive abuse as its perpetrators, that they were getting robbed as often as they were taking what they liked from others, they willingly accepted the authority of a ruler capable of maintaining order and punishing transgressions.

Like Hobbes, Xunzi argues from the essentially evil nature of men to the need for a strong central government authority to control human behavior by education and a system of reward and punishment. What do you suppose would happen, Xunzi asks, if this governmental authority were removed? Can anyone doubt that chaos would result as the strong rode roughshod over the weak with no law enforcement to prevent and punish them?

> Man's nature is evil; goodness is the result of conscious activity. The nature of man is such that he is born with a fondness for profit. If he indulges this fondness, it will lead him into wrangling and strife, and all sense of courtesy and humility will disappear. He is born with feelings of envy and hate, and if he indulges these, they will lead him into violence and crime, and all sense of loyalty and good faith will disappear. Man is born with the desires of the eyes and ears, with a fondness for beautiful sights and sounds. If he indulges these, they will lead him into license and wantonness, and all ritual principles and correct forms will be lost. Hence, any man who follows his nature and indulges his emotions will inevitably become involved in wrangling and strife, will violate the forms and rules of society, and will end as a criminal. Therefore, man must first be transformed by the instructions of a teacher and guided by ritual principles, and only then will he be able to observe the dictates of courtesy and humility, obey the forms and rules of society, and achieve order. It

is obvious from this, then, that man's nature is evil, and that his goodness is the result of conscious activity.

(ibid.)

Another group of philosophers argued that while human nature is fundamentally egoistic and pleasure loving, that there is nothing wrong with this, that it should not be curbed or restrained but that it is basically good and should therefore be encouraged. The Indian philosophical position known as Carvaca, the early Chinese Taoist Yang Zhu, and Western "hedonists" (meaning lovers of pleasure as the only good) such as Epicurus all held that seeking one's own pleasure is the only good thing in life and that that is therefore precisely what we should pursue. Since the general thrust of any social morality is to curb individual impulses, it is not hard to understand why this sort of "amoral morality" was never widely accepted.

One major difference between Mengzi's and Xunzi's theories of human nature is that Mengzi, like Aristotle, defines human nature as that which is *uniquely* and *distinctively* human, whereas Xunzi defines it as that which *all* people are *born* with, even if that is also shared by the lower animals. Relating his theory to ancient (prephilosophical) Chinese traditions, Xunzi says that human nature is the product of two factors—one is the contribution of Heaven (tian), which gives human beings the rational and intelligent capacity to be civilized, cultured, and virtuous, and the other is the contribution of Earth (di), which is our animal nature that we are conscious of as feeling and emotion. But whereas Mengzi says that we receive from Heaven the "beginnings" of moral virtue, Xunzi maintains that we receive from Heaven only the capacity or potentiality for virtue and civilized life. Thus, for Xunzi, at birth a person is just like one of the lower animals, except with the capacity which no other creature has of becoming civilized and virtuous. For Mengzi a newborn baby is already good, though on a small, rudimentary scale; for Xunzi a newborn baby is not good but, unlike a rabbit or a willow tree, it is capable of becoming so.

Mencius states that man is capable of learning because his nature is good, but I say that this is wrong. It indicates that he has not really understood man's nature nor distinguished properly between the basic nature and conscious activity. The nature is that which is given by Heaven; you cannot learn it, you cannot acquire it by effort. Ritual principles, on the other hand, are created by sages; you can learn to apply them, you can work to bring them to completion. That part of man which cannot be learned or acquired by effort is called the nature; that part of him which can be acquired by learning and brought to completion by effort is called conscious activity. . . . It is the nature of man that when he is hungry he will desire satisfaction, when he is cold he will desire warmth, and when he is weary he will desire rest. This is his emotional nature. And yet a man, although he is hungry, will not dare to be the first to eat if he is in the presence of his elders, because he knows that he should yield to them, and although he is weary, he will not dare to demand rest because he knows that he should relieve others of the burden of labor.

(*ibid.*)

If we define human nature as Xunzi does (as what all people are born with), then we will point to the tendencies people do actually have to be greedy, selfish, and aggressive, but if we define human nature as Mengzi does (as what is unique to people) then we tend to discount greedy behavior, since that is shared by the lower animals, and to emphasize instead the capacity of human beings to develop virtuous behavior, to become moral creatures, loving and caring for one another, concerned with the other's welfare. As Mengzi says, "Slight is the difference between man and the brutes. The common man loses this distinguishing feature, while the gentleman retains it."

(Mengzi, *Mengzi*, in Chan, *Sourcebook Chinese*)

Therefore, like Socrates, Mengzi treasures this distinctively human part above all the other parts of a person and urges us to honor, preserve, and develop that part of ourselves above all else.

Mencius said, "Life is what I want; dutifulness is also what I want. If I cannot have both, I would rather take dutifulness than life. On the one hand, though life is what I want, there is something I want more than life. That is why I do not cling to life at all costs. On the other hand, though death is what I loathe, there is something I loathe more than death. This is why there are troubles I do not avoid. . . .

"Benevolence is the heart of man, and rightness his road. Sad it is indeed when a man gives up the right road instead of following it and allows his heart to stray without enough sense to go after it. When his chickens and dogs stray, he has sense enough to go after them, but not when his heart strays. The sole concern of learning is to go after this strayed heart. . . .

"A man loves all parts of his person without discrimination. . . . There is not one foot or one inch of his skin that he does not love . . . [and] nurture. Is there any other way of telling whether what a man does is good or bad than by the choice he makes? The parts of the person differ in value and importance. Never harm the parts of greater importance for the sake of those of smaller importance, or the more valuable for the sake of the less valuable. He who nurtures the parts of smaller importance is a small man; he who nurtures the parts of greater importance is a great man."

(*ibid.*)

Socrates also held that we should value the distinctively human part of ourselves and, like Mengzi, he believed that it is better to die than to sacrifice this uniquely human part. When Socrates was on trial for his life on charges of corrupting the youth and offending the state religion, Socrates argued (in

Plato's *Apology*) that he would prefer death to stopping his philosophical activities (which his accusers interpreted as corrupting the youth and offending the state religion), because he considered this his primary moral obligation in life (he was indeed found guilty and sentenced to death, which we can read about in Plato's *Phaedo* and *Crito*). Against the common thinking of his day, Socrates argued that it is worse to do evil to others than to have evil done to oneself. Why? Because doing evil injures the soul, while evil done to oneself only injures the body, and not the soul. (Do you agree with Mengzi and Socrates? Later in this chapter, we will question why it is so difficult to convince most people of the value of developing the most distinctively human part of ourselves.) But whereas Mengzi sees this human part of ourselves as another bodily part, the benevolent heart that cannot bear to see others suffer (though the highest part coming from "Heaven," "tian," as opposed to the rest of the human body which people share with the lower animals and which comes from "Earth," or "di"), Socrates is the first in the Western tradition to describe the distinctively human part of ourselves as an immaterial "soul," which is quite distinct from the material body.

Notice how Mengzi responds to Gaozi's objection that human nature is simply what we are born with. Like Xunzi, Gaozi says, "The inborn is what is meant by 'nature.'" As D. C. Lau remarks, in the Chinese language of the time, the words for "inborn" (sheng) and "nature" (xing) were probably written the same (and even today are written almost the same), so that Gaozi's statement would have seemed at the time like an obvious tautology, as Mengzi himself remarks, like saying "white is white." But Gaozi uses this seemingly harmless tautology to infer that therefore since the inborn instincts of various animals are the same at birth, the nature of human beings is the same as the nature of lower animals. If we look at what we are born with, then Gaozi (like Xunzi) argues that dogs and people and horses are all born with the same instincts for hunger, sex, and self-preservation (as Gaozi says, "appetite for food and sex is nature"). Therefore, there is nothing unique about human nature, and the only reason people are in fact different from dogs and horses is that after they were born they were educated and acculturated—not because they have a different nature.

But Mengzi turns the argument around on Gaozi. If all animals are born with the same set of instincts, and if this is their nature, as Gaozi claims, then it follows that the nature of a dog is the same as the nature of a cow, which is absurd. The actual instincts of the dog and the cow may be the same, and indeed they may be much the same as those of a person, but the nature of the dog and the cow and the person are obviously different because they are capable of doing different things. A person has capacities that the dog and cow do not; therefore, the nature of a person is different from that of a dog or cow.

Gaozi said, "The inborn is what is meant by 'nature.'"

"Is that," said Mencius, "the same as 'white is what is meant by "white"'?"

"Yes."

"Is the whiteness of white feathers the same as the whiteness of white snow and the whiteness of white snow the same as the whiteness of white jade?"

"Yes."

"In that case, is the nature of a hound the same as the nature of an ox and the nature of an ox the same as the nature of a man?"

(ibid.)

Aristotle would agree with Mengzi that the important consideration regarding human nature is what human beings alone are capable of doing. According to Aristotle, all people have a vegetative nature (e.g., growth and nutrition) that they share with all living organisms, both plants and animals. In addition, Aristotle argues, all people also have an animal nature that they share with all of the other animals (desire for food and sex, self-protective instincts, sensation, and so on). But these do not make human beings human, because the vegetative and animal natures are not unique to human beings but are shared by other creatures. What properties, if any, do human beings have that no other creatures have?

In addition to the vegetative and the animal natures, Aristotle argues that human beings also have the capacity for reason, that is, for rational control, and that this capacity is not shared by any other creature in the universe. This is therefore our human nature, he says, our ability to use reason to control our desires, modify our behavior, improve our environment, create our culture, and so on. Again, as we noted earlier, each society will create a different cultural way to control human instincts, but they will all use reason to create *some* cultural way. Cultures differ from society to society, but *every* human society has a culture. The odd thing about human beings is that their nature is to artificially create a culture—language, religion, architecture, philosophy, art, and so on. It is natural for us to be artificial! And, according to Aristotle, we need reason to do this.

Although Mengzi does not stress rationality, as do Plato and Aristotle, as that which is distinctively human, he does stress the capacity of the heart-mind to think. Sometimes Chinese philosophers talk about xin as the center of emotion (the heart) and sometimes they refer to xin as the center of intellectual thinking (the mind). The reason for this is that the Chinese word, xin, means both mind and heart and is therefore best translated as "heart-mind."

Kung-tuzi asked, "Though equally human, why are some men greater than others?"

"He who is guided by the interests of the parts of his person that are of greater importance is a great man; he who is guided by the interests of the parts of his person that are of smaller importance is a small man."

> "[But] why are some men guided one way and others guided another way?"
>
> "The organs of hearing and sight are unable to think and can be misled by external things. When one thing acts on another, all it does is to attract it. The organ of the heart can think. But it will find the answer only if it does think; otherwise it will not find the answer. This is what Heaven has given me."
>
> *(ibid.)*

This passage from *The Mencius* contains the idea we came across earlier in our discussion of theories of knowledge, where we pointed out that the perception that that thing is a snake is a combination of the sensation of something long and thin and also the cognitive judgment that that thing is a snake (a judgment which may, of course, be mistaken, if, for example, it turns out to be a piece of rope and not a snake). Here Mengzi extends this insight to moral knowledge. If a man sees a woman, he may feel like having sex with her, but he will not necessarily immediately proceed to do so—he will have to think that the woman may not be willing; that he is married; that this is his boss's wife or his student; that they are in a public place; that he has to attend an important meeting in a few minutes; and so on.

In a sense, the difference between Mengzi, Plato, and Aristotle, on the one hand, and Xunzi and Hobbes, on the other, is very small. Both sides admit that people have natural desires for food and sex, and both sides admit that people have the capacity to resist those desires when it is dangerous or inappropriate to indulge them. It really comes down to the difference between saying we are all born with the "tendency" to do good and saying that we are all only born with the "potentiality" to become good. What is the difference? It is largely a matter of the relative weight we place on "nature" and "nurture." The question is, what is natural and what is learned? Both Xunzi and Hobbes admit that human beings are intelligent, and therefore, when they realize the difficulties that uncontrolled indulgence in the desire for food and sex can lead to, they seek to set limits on those desires.

But if *all* people do this, if this is *typical* of human behavior, Mengzi, Plato, and Aristotle ask, then is this not part of human nature? If it is so widespread, then is it not more of a *tendency* than a mere *potentiality*? Certainly the particular form of the restraint (let the elders eat first, do not have sex with your first cousin) is culturally relative and therefore learned, but every society we know of has and must have *some* restraints. Even among some of the lower animals, a hungry bird will restrain its desire to eat the cat's dried cat food if the cat is eating or is nearby.

Dong Zhongshu (second century B.C.) finds a middle ground between the views of Mengzi and Xunzi (though probably closer to Xunzi). He agrees with Mengzi, that in a sense human nature contains the "seeds" of goodness, but he disagrees with Mengzi that this is enough to say that human beings are by nature good. The "seed" of goodness is not actually good anymore than a tomato seed is a tomato, or an egg is a chicken. In order to become good, that "seed" must be nurtured and cultivated, thus agreeing more with Xunzi's emphasis on the necessary role of government to educate and train people to become good citizens.

> Goodness is like a kernel of grain; the nature is like the growing stalk of that grain. Though the stalk produces the kernel, it cannot itself be called a kernel, and though the nature produces goodness, it cannot itself be called good. The kernel and goodness are both brought to completion through man's continuation of Heaven's work, and are external to it; they do not lie within what Heaven does itself. What Heaven does extends to a certain point and then stops. What lies within this stopping point pertains to Heaven; what lies outside pertains to the teachings of the sage-kings. The teachings of the sage-kings lie outside the nature. Yet, when they are applied, the nature cannot but conform to them. Therefore I say that the nature possesses the stuff of goodness, but that it cannot by itself act for goodness.
>
> (Dong Zhongshu, in Chan, *Sourcebook Chinese*)

Another analogy Dong uses is the capacity of the eye to see. The ability of the eye to see is obviously a dispositional property. Dong asks an interesting question—can a person see when she is asleep? Well, in one sense, we would have to say no. If we put something in front of her, she is unable to see it while asleep. But in another sense, she *can* see it. All we have to do is wake her up! Even when she is asleep, she is not blind. Can you speak Swedish? Again, the answer is yes (in a sense) and no (in a different sense). Most of you cannot here and now carry on a conversation in Swedish; and in that sense you cannot speak Swedish. But if you were offered a billion dollars to learn Swedish in the next five years, you could—and in that sense you can (learn to) speak Swedish.

In terms of our earlier discussion, we can say that while Mengzi says that goodness is a natural "tendency" of people, Dong claims it is a mere "potential." That is why for Mengzi children are born with an innate goodness within them (though in a small and undeveloped manner), while Dong insists that children are *not* good until they have been socially trained to behave correctly (though, unlike a salamander, children are *capable* of moral training).

Dong Zhongshu also develops a theory, somewhat like Plato's, that human nature must compete with man's innate tendencies to greed and selfishness. Like Plato, Dong has a model of human psychology in which opposing forces are in constant conflict with one another. Unlike Xunzi, Dong does not include both factors within "human nature," and unlike Xunzi, Dong says both factors come from Heaven, not Heaven and Earth, as Xunzi held. By the beginning of the Han dynasty, roughly 200 B.C.E.–200 C.E., Confucianism had incorporated the rival Yin/Yang school of thought. Yin and Yang are univer-sally complementary forces, Yin being the submissive, yielding aspect of things and Yang its aggressive, active aspect. So, for Dong, the two competing forces that make up and determine every human being are both part of ourselves; the yang force we receive from Heaven, and "emotion and feeling" (the yin force), which also comes from Heaven. Everything in the world (including you and I) is made up of a mixture of these two yin and yang aspects. Just as Heaven (tian) is made up of both positive (yang) forces and negative (yin) forces, so there is an innate (yang) part of us that wants to be socially coop-erative, giving, and caring; but there is another innate (yin) part of us that wants it all for ourselves.

> The human body has within the nature and the feelings, just as Heaven has the yin and the yang. To speak of man's "basic stuff" and exclude from this his feelings is like speaking of Heaven's yang while excluding its yin.
>
> Human nature (the yang part) is responsible for the virtue of ren or love, while human feelings (the yin part) are responsible for the negative quality of covetousness.
>
> Truly, there exist in man both love and covetousness, each of which lies within his body. What is thus called the body is received from Heaven. Heaven has its dual manifestations of yin and yang, and the body likewise has the dual qualities of cov-etousness and love.
>
> *(ibid.)*

Of course, one could ask, if both of these tendencies are innate, then are they not both parts of human nature? Here the answer probably has to do with what we said earlier about human nature being a "normative" con-cept. Like Mengzi, Dong would like to say that human nature is the higher and better part of human beings, that morally good part (derived from the positive, "yang" aspect of Heaven) that human beings alone are capable of. The instinctive, emotional, physical part (derived from the negative, "yin" aspect of Heaven) that we all have but also share with the lower animals is just as innate, but it does not have the "normative" quality of the morally good potential of human nature.

Dong Zhongshu says that when Mengzi claims that people are good, he is comparing them to the lower animals. Compared to animals, people at least have the capacity for moral goodness. But that is not what we *should* be com-paring people to, Dong Zhongshu continues; we should be comparing peo-ple to the high moral ideal we demand of people. More like Xunzi, Dong Zhongshu argues that we should hold people up to a higher standard (of the zi, or sage), and in terms of *that* standard we cannot say that people are good, but rather that they are *not* good.

It is said by some [Mengzi] that since the nature contains the beginnings of good-ness, and the mind contains the basic stuff of goodness, how can the nature itself not be good? But I reply that this is not so. For the silk cocoon contains silk fibers and yet is not itself silk, and the egg contains the chicken, yet is not itself a chicken. . . . Nevertheless there are some [Mengzi] who say that the nature is good, and some [Xunzi] who say it is not good. That is because when they thus speak of goodness, they each mean something different by it. Inasmuch as the nature contains within it the beginnings of goodness, the fact that a child's love for its parents is superior to that of the birds and beasts may be called goodness. Such is what Mencius means by goodness. But goodness may also be defined [by Xunzi] as conformity to . . . the practice of loyalty, good faith, widespread love, generosity, and love or propriety. Such is what the sages meant by goodness. . . . Regarded in this way, what the sages called goodness is not easy to match. It is not the sort of goodness that is called such merely because it consists in being better than the birds and beasts. . . . Indeed, to be better than the birds and beasts is no more to be considered goodness than is being wiser than the plants and trees to be called wisdom. . . . Evaluated in com-parison with the nature of birds and beasts, the natures of all men are indeed good. But evaluated in comparison with the goodness of the sages, men's natures fall short.

(ibid.)

We can see how Dong's theory is more complex than either Mengzi's or Xunzi's. Dong's theory also is probably better able to solve the main problem afflicting any human nature theory—namely, explaining why people are not in fact the way the theory says they are supposed to be. Mengzi says people are inherently good, but in fact many people are wicked. Xunzi says that peo-ple are inherently wicked, but in fact many people are kind and loving. In either case, does this contrary evidence not undermine the theory? What any human nature theory needs, as pointed out earlier, is some way of reconcil-ing the truth of the theory with the apparently contradictory evidence. Of course, both Mengzi and Xunzi can say that it is social conditioning that alters one's basic human nature—for Mengzi, social conditioning may unfortunately thwart or pervert a person's basically good human nature, and for Xunzi, social conditioning will hopefully thwart and rechannel a person's basically egoistic human nature.

Dong's solution is more complex and ingenious. By combining Xunzi's and Mengzi's notions of what is meant by "human nature," Dong can say that people are born with conflicting tendencies within them. Every person is born with instincts for survival and self-protection, that is, with egoistic drives to get ahead of others, to take what one wants, and so on (the kind of charm-ingly selfish nature one often sees in young children before they have been socialized). But every person also is born with the capacity ("seeds") for becoming virtuous persons (ren or human-heartedness, yi or righteousness, li or propriety, zhi or wisdom, and so on). These two tendencies will always be in conflict with one another (excluding a few sages, like Confucius—at age seventy), and only with socialization provided by the state can the "seeds" of virtue be made to overcome our selfish instincts.

The Greek philosopher Plato (fourth century B.C.) worked out a similar solution. According to Plato, every person is born with three natures—two in conflict with one another (as in Dong's theory) and a third that can cooperate with either of the other two. The two in conflict are reason and desire. We can all remember occasions when we very much wanted to do something that reason told us would be a mistake—"I want to go the party tonight but I have a philosophy test tomorrow at 8 A.M.!" Like Dong, Plato argues that reason is the higher, normative nature that we should follow. The proper role of reason is to rule, Plato argues, but desire often tries to usurp that role. But the proper role of desire is to obey the dictates of reason, so normatively reason ought to rule and desire ought to obey reason.

But whichever wins, neither can actually carry out their actions without the third nature, will, the executive, active part of our nature—the part that actually carries out our desires and intentions. The person who quit smoking in the morning but is having a cigarette after lunch made the right decision in the morning but lacks willpower. (Later, at the party, I say, "I know I should be home studying for the philosophy test, but . . . ") Will can assist either reason or desire, but in the well-ordered person, will carries out the dictates of reason, and desire agrees to obey. Sometimes, as Plato observes, we notice this willpower in ourselves and in others as a kind of angry, defiant, indignant rejection of the temptations of the flesh.

> The soul of a thirsty man, just insofar as he is thirsty, has no other wish than to drink. . . . Now if there is ever something which at the same time pulls the soul the opposite way, that something must be an element in the soul other than the one which is thirsting and driving it like a beast to drink; in accordance with our principle that the same thing cannot behave in two opposite ways at the same time and towards the same object with the same part of itself. It is like an archer drawing the bow: it is not accurate to say that each hand is at the same time both pushing and pulling it. One hand does the pushing, the other the pulling. . . . Now, is it sometimes true that people are thirsty and yet unwilling to drink? . . . What, then, can one say of them, if not that their soul contains something which urges them to drink and something which holds them back, and that this latter is a distinct thing and overpowers the other? . . . And is it not true that the intervention of this inhibiting principle in such cases always has its origin in reflection; whereas the impulses driving and dragging the soul are engendered by external influences. . . . We shall have good reason, then, to assert that they are two distinct principles. We may call that part of the soul whereby it reflects, rational; and the other, with which it feels hunger and thirst and is distracted by sexual passion and all the other desires, we will call irrational appetite, associated with pleasure in the replenishment of certain wants. . . . Let us

take it, then, that we have now distinguished two elements in the soul. What of that passionate element [will] which makes us feel angry and indignant? Isn't that a third element? . . . Anger is sometimes in conflict with appetite, as if they were two distinct principles. Do we not often find a man whose desires would force him to go against his reason, reviling himself and indignant with this part of his nature which is trying to put constraint on him? It is like a struggle between two factions, in which indignation [will] takes the side of reason.

(Plato 1945)

Like the Chinese philosophers, Plato has provided a universal basis in nature (reality) for the traditional Greek virtues. Plato does not defend or justify these virtues simply because they are traditional within Greek culture. He argues that all human beings have this tripartite soul and that all human beings are happy and successful only when the three function as nature intended them to—that is, when Will assists Reason in ruling Desire (Appetite). Finally, Plato defines the virtues in terms of this theory of human nature. In *The Republic*, Plato defines temperance as the willingness of Desire (Appetite) to follow the dictates of Reason, and justice he defines as each part of the soul performing its proper function and not trying to take over the functions of the other parts of the soul, that is, where Reason rules Desire, Desire follows the dictates of Reason, and Will assists Reason in its control of Desire. Justice and temperance are not, therefore, culturally relative, but universal, crosscultural values for all human beings.

In several of Plato's Dialogues, Socrates describes the soul figuratively as a horse-drawn chariot in which the charioteer represents reason and of the two horses, an unruly horse represents appetite and an obedient, well-behaved horse represents will.

Of the nature of the soul, let me speak figuratively. And let the figure be composite—a pair of winged horses [appetite and will] and a charioteer [reason]. Now the winged horses and the charioteers of the gods are all of them noble and of noble descent, but those of other races are mixed; the human charioteer drives his in a pair; and one of them is noble and of noble breed [will], and the other is ignoble and of ignoble breed [appetite]; and the driving of them of necessity gives a great deal of trouble to him. I will endeavor to explain to you in what way the mortal differs from the immortal creature. The soul in her totality traverses the whole heaven appearing in different forms—when perfect and fully winged she soars upward, and orders the whole world; whereas the imperfect soul, losing her wings and drooping in her flight, at last settles on the solid ground—there, finding a home, she receives an earthly frame [a human body] which appears to be self-moved, but is really moved by her power; and this composition of soul and body is called a living and mortal creature.

(Plato, *Phaedrus*, Indianapolis, 1956)

Interestingly, there is a similar analogy of the soul, or self, to the charioteer in the Indian (Hindu) Katha Upanishad.

> Know the Self to be sitting in the chariot, the body to be the chariot, the intellect (buddhi) the charioteer, and the mind the reins. The senses they call the horses, the objects of the senses their roads. When the highest Self is in union with the body, the senses, and the mind, then wise people call him the enjoyer. He who has no understanding and whose mind (the reins) is never firmly held, his senses (horses) are unmanageable, like vicious horses of a charioteer. But he who has understanding and whose mind is always firmly held, his senses are under control, like good horses of a charioteer. He who has no understanding, who is unmindful and always impure, never reaches that place, but enters into the round of births. But he who has understanding, who is mindful and always pure, reaches indeed that place, from whence he is not born again.
>
> (Katha Upanishad, in R and M, Sourcebook Indian)

As in Plato, the point of the Indian analogy is the division of the person into potentially warring factions and the need for control by the central self, or soul, harmonizing all of the different aspects of the person. Unlike Plato, however, the divisions among charioteer, horses, and so on are not divisions within the self, or soul, but divisions within the overall person, including the body. Thus the horses are referred to as the senses, the reins are said to be the mind, and so on. And here we see broad cultural differences (Greek and Indian) intruding on a philosophical discussion. As we saw in chapter 4, much of the mental, conscious phenomena that Western philosophers associate with the self, Indian thinkers identify with the body and *separate* from the self, which they see as the "transcendent self" (the atman) behind the conscious mind we are aware of in everyday life. As the *Katha Upanishad* goes on to say (in a way we will recognize from chapter 4 as deeply influenced by Samkhya-Yoga),

> Beyond the senses there are the objects, beyond the objects there is the mind, beyond the mind there is the intellect [buddhi], and the Great Self is beyond the intellect. Beyond the Great Self there is the Undeveloped, beyond the Undeveloped there is the Purusha [or Person, or ultimate Self]. Beyond the Perusha [or Person] there is nothing—that is the highest goal, the highest road. That Self [the Purusha, or Person] is hidden in all beings and does not shine forth, but is seen by subtle seers through their sharp and subtle intellect.
>
> (ibid.)

And, of course, the "goal" of the chariot ride is also different in Plato and in the *Katha Upanishad*. For Plato (and Socrates), the goal of the charioteer who is firmly in command is a good life for the self or ego, both here and now and in the next life, whereas the goal of the Indian charioteer is to escape from samsara, "where he is not born again" (at least not as a conscious individual self or ego—not as the "I" that I know in daily life as myself).

For Dong Zhongshu, there are two, not three, parts to the self, and the better part he likens to a "seed" and not, as Mengzi says, a "sprout." In one way the difference between Dong Zhongshu and Mengzi is a matter of degree. Mengzi does not say that people are born as morally good individuals. He insists that this requires cultivation and training. He calls the innate goodness the "beginnings" ("sprouting") of goodness. Nonetheless, he differs from Dong Zhongshu in seeing more good in people than does Dong Zhongshu. For Mengzi, the "beginnings" of goodness are actually good, though on a small scale, which must be further encouraged and developed; for Dong Zhongshu, the "seeds" of goodness are not themselves good at all but only have the potential to become so.

The main difference between Mengzi and Dong Zhongshu is in their view of the role of government in fostering moral goodness. Mengzi would have government take a far less intrusive role, merely encouraging, cultivating the beginnings of moral goodness that already exist. Dong Zhongshu, like Xunzi, on the contrary, believes that government must mold and shape human beings who have the capacity for goodness but cannot become good without the intervention of the state.

A similar "nature/nurture" debate goes on today concerning the capacity of human beings to learn language. Of course, people are capable of learning a language, but how much of this is innate and how much is taught? Do parents teach children to speak, or do children just pick it up? Mengzi's theory is like those who say that children are not taught to speak a language but just pick it up in a favorable environment. Dong's view emerges if we ask whether American students will learn Swedish by just picking it up or only by hard study and rigorous practice. For Dong, becoming a morally good person is like someone from North America learning Swedish—it can be done, but only with a great deal of training, practice, and discipline.

Going back now to the beginning of this long discussion of ethics based on theories human nature, remember that it was the Taoist criticism of Confucius that motivated the Confucianists to base their ethics on theories of a universal human nature. Taoists criticized the Confucianists, saying that they were merely reinforcing the traditional customary Chinese virtues while they, the Taoists, based their theories on reality, that is, on what is natural. Thus the debate began between what is natural and what is conventional. If morality is entirely conventional, then we are left with cultural relativism. Confucianists, as we have seen, tried to answer this charge by finding a foundation for human morality in nature (that is, in a universal human nature).

But all of these Confucian theories are still too conventional to suit the Taoists; they are still quite "humanistic," or human centered in an important sense. They still see morality as something peculiar to and specially created by human beings. Of course, they want to ground ethics in human nature, but what they locate in nature (human nature) is not morality itself but only the *foundation*, the *basis*, for the *possibility* of morality. They look for something within human nature that provides a foundation for the possibility of moral training—sometimes very optimistically, as with Mengzi, arguing that human beings are actually born (with a "gift from Heaven") of the actual "beginnings" of moral virtue (which only needs nourishing) and sometimes less optimistically, as with Xunzi and Dong Zhongshu, that people are born with (given by Heaven) only the potentiality to become morally virtuous with a great deal of socialization and training. In either case (even with Mengzi), moral training in a human-centered society is extremely important.

The Taoists nonetheless reject even this degree of humanly created cultural imposition on nature—they do not see the need of imposing *anything* on human beings. They oppose the "humanistic" emphasis on the special place of human beings in the world. Human beings are just one more kind of thing in the world—there are lizards with their lizard nature (lizard de), and there are bamboo plants with their own peculiar bamboo nature (bamboo de), and there are human beings with the nature (human de) peculiar to them, and so on. Just as the bamboo unconsciously strives to live up to its nature, so human beings should also just "be natural"—rather than trying to modify, mold, and shape that nature by a humanly created artificial culture and civilization. Humanly created "culture" does not make people *better*, say the Taoists; it actually makes them *worse*. Like European "romantics" (e.g., Jean-Jacques Rousseau), they think the more natural (and uncultured) the person is, the better. Even today, many of us tend to sympathize with Rousseau's idea that Native Americans are somehow more noble and better human beings than the more technologically and scientifically advanced Europeans.

The main ethical principle of the Taoists is therefore "just be natural." But of course it is very hard for a human being to "be natural." Even to think of this as an alternative (to being conventional) is something only human beings can do (or not do). To tell someone to "be natural" implies that it is possible for them to *not* be natural, that is, to be conventional and unnatural. A chipmunk is not faced with this choice (so far as we know)—which is better, to be natural or unnatural? Suppose a chipmunk can safely grab some dried cat food; do you suppose it worries whether this is unnatural and therefore wrong? Or a mouse contemplating whether it is natural and therefore good to spend the winter months in a hole in the ground or to come inside my nice, warm house where there is plenty of bread crumbs and old pizza to pig out on all winter? Only human beings can ask this question because only we are capable of constructing many different lifestyles for ourselves—how to eat, dress, talk, house ourselves, govern ourselves, and so on.

To be sure, these alternative lifestyles are partially provided for us by the particular society into which we happen to have been born, but within any given society there is still a wide range of choices open to individual members of that society. In your own case, growing up in America at the end of the twentieth and the beginning of the twenty-first century, think of all the choices open to you—you can chose to be married and have children or not, to go for a highly paid career or a quieter, less stressful, but lower paid one, to be active in politics or not, to be conservative or avant garde, to give back to society or keep it all for yourself, to be deeply religious or not at all (or somewhere in between), and so on. Strictly speaking, it is probably impossible for any human being to be completely natural, if by natural we mean eliminating all human culture and civilization (socialization, acculturation). To literally be like a newborn baby would mean not talking, dressing, playing, or listening to any sort of music, with no games, religion, and on and on. What is more often meant is something less radical than that—simply to reduce, to be less culturally sophisticated and complicated, to live life more simply.

Some "postmodern" writers today, for example, Richard Rorty, argue in a similar way, that we do not need to (that it is unnecessary to) talk so much about, worry so much about, or try so hard and work so hard to change people into moral beings—if we did not say or do anything about morality, what real difference would it make? Would we all turn into psychopathic killers or abandon our family responsibilities, or go ballistic, wild, and crazy? Probably not; more likely we would just continue as we have, in our ordinary naive, unthinking way, helping our friends, paying our taxes, and being relatively good citizens. On the other hand, by continually harping on morality, we bring about some very bad results, the postmodernists argue—guilt trips, intolerance of others, feelings of righteous indignation and moral superiority to others, and a general moral rigidity and moral uptightness. To such people, we may feel like saying, "loosen up, be more natural—like the Taoists." Nonetheless, most moral philosophers, in both the East and West, have been unwilling to leave things to chance but have felt the need to reinforce and justify morality.

For Plato, as for Mengzi, justice is simply following our human nature, and therefore only the just person can be a happy, healthy, successful, fully developed human being. Only when Will assists Reason in ruling Desire (Plato's definition of justice) is a person truly happy and well adjusted. And this is Plato's longer answer to Thrasymachus's claim that we examined earlier (in chapter 1), that justice is nothing but what is in the interest of the stronger. You remember that Thrasymachus's point there was that it is better to be unjust than to be just! The only reason a person acts justly, Thrasymachus argued, is to avoid getting caught, and anyone strong enough or smart enough to avoid getting caught will naturally prefer to do the self-seeking but unjust thing. According to Thrasymachus, there is no intrinsic reason to be a just person; that is only for the stupid who do not know any better or the weak who cannot do any better for themselves by being unjust and getting away with it.

But has Socrates really answered Thrasymachus's challenge? Plato's rather long-winded answer—several hundred pages later—is that once we realize the true nature of justice, we can see that the unjust person is contradicting his inmost human nature, he is failing to be the most he can be as a human being, he is not allowing his reason to control his desire as nature intends, and he is therefore unsuccessful as a fully developed human being. But, even if we accept Plato's theory of justice and human nature, how bad do you think this would be for someone like Thrasymachus? The strong man Thrasymachus talks about who takes advantage of the weak in order to gain wealth, power, and position would probably reply to Socrates and Plato, "So, I'm not a fully developed human being—so what? I'm rich and powerful and having a ball. The fact that I could be more of a person by allowing my reason to rule over my desires doesn't bother me at all! Sorry."

This leads us to a terribly important question in ethics and one that is very hard to answer: Why should I be moral? We are taught from childhood to do the right thing, to be moral persons. But philosophers want to know *why*; they demand a justification; they want to know if there are any good reasons why a person should be moral rather than immoral. Why is it better to be moral than immoral? Of course, there are often *practical* or *prudential* reasons why we should be moral and avoid being immoral. That is, if we behave immorally, we may get caught and suffer the consequences. So, in our own self-interest, we should do the right thing. But, of course, that is not a *moral* reason to do the morally right thing. It is just saying that if society rewards those who follow certain moral rules (do not cheat, lie, steal, etc.) and punishes those who break such rules, then the smart, selfish person, the person who wants to get ahead, will naturally want to obey the moral rules—not because they are right but in order to better himself or herself. Naturally, it follows from this prudential, self-interested perspective that if one can help oneself by breaking the moral rules without getting caught, then by all means one should do so. But what this comes down to is that there is apparently no good (intrinsic) reason to be a moral person. Philosophers wondered if there was not some good reason why one should do the morally right thing, regardless of the consequences to one's self.

Chinese philosophers also raised this question. Kongzi (Confucius, sixth century B.C.E.) and Mengzi (Mencius, fourth century B.C.E.) said that we should do the right thing simply because it is right, or, more precisely, in order to be true to our basic human nature of ren, or humanity (and that *this* was intrinsically obligatory). Of the Confucian virtues, Kongzi said yi (righteousness) is doing the right thing because it is right, not because of "profit" (li). Ren is a higher virtue of sympathetic understanding of and concern for others. The criterion for ren (later called the "measuring square" of right action) is the negative Golden Rule ("Don't do anything to others that you wouldn't like done to you"). Generalize from your own self-regard to a similar regard and concern for others.

The superior person, Kongzi held, does the right thing, even though he or she knows it will not succeed (called "doing for nothing," *Analects*). Success depends on "ming" (fate or good fortune), and to "know ming" means to know the limits of your own ability to accomplish anything, the boundary beyond which things are "not in your power." This does not mean adopting a fatalistic attitude ("what will be will be"); it means that after we have tried as hard as we possibly can to do what we honestly think is right, we still may or may not succeed. We are not all powerful, and despite our best efforts, we may in the end fail—perhaps because of other more powerful people opposed to us; perhaps because of external circumstances, such as car trouble, a traffic accident, sudden illness—that is, forces genuinely outside of our control. Kongzi's theory of "ming" is to do what is in one's power and not to worry about what is not within one's power.

Nonetheless, Kongzi was constantly criticized for wasting his time on righteous projects that were bound to fail. Kongzi (Confucius) spent much of his life travelling from one kingdom to another trying to persuade the rulers to become just rulers, and, although he was generally given a polite audience by the king, no one ever followed his advice. Kongzi's critics told him it was foolish to pursue a goal, however honorable, that he knew was doomed to failure. In this respect, Kongzi is much like the eighteenth-century German philosopher Immanuel Kant, who argued that a morally good act is defined entirely in terms of the good intentions of the agent (acting strictly out of a sense of duty or moral obligation), and not at all in terms of the consequences or results of the action. But Kongzi's critics raise an important question, one we have been asking for some time now: Why be moral? If you know that your action is going to fail, and moreover is going to cost you in terms of time and energy and money, why do it? Kongzi and Kant say, because it is the right thing to do. But how convincing an answer is that?

Mozi (fifth century B.C.E.) argued, on the other hand, that we should do the right thing because of the rewards (li) we will receive by doing so and the punishment we will suffer in this life and the next if we do the wrong thing. By emphasizing the possibility of rewards and punishments in the afterlife, Mozi does provide a kind of answer to the question, why be moral? Because you cannot avoid punishment entirely, you will always get caught in the end, either by people in this life or by God in the life to come.

Sometimes, however, Mozi argues that we ought to do what will produce the best results for *everyone*, not just for ourselves, and here he sounds like the nineteenth-century British utilitarians (Jeremy Bentham, James and John Stuart Mill), who argued that we should always do what will produce the greatest happiness for the greatest number of people. But once the motive of reward is generalized to include people other than ourselves, then the same question arises once again, why *should* I do something to benefit other people? I might agree with Mozi and the utilitarians that the world would be a better place if everyone would do what would benefit everyone generally. But I may still wonder why *I* should act to promote the general good, as opposed to my own personal good. The ideal world might seem to be one in which everyone is kind and loving except me! (For Mozi, there also was the reward for obeying God's command that we love everyone equally and God's punishment if we disobeyed his command.)

Western philosophers also are concerned with this question. In *The Republic*, Plato uses a traditional Greek folktale of Gyges to dramatize the question Glaucon and Adeimantus put to Socrates in their request for a more complete answer to Thrasymachus, whether there is any *intrinsic* reason for doing the morally right thing. That is, apart from being rewarded for doing right and punished for doing wrong, is there any good reason for us to do the right thing and avoid doing what is wrong? In the story, a shepherd, Gyges, finds a ring one day, which he discovers makes him invisible whenever he turns the ring around and visible again by turning the ring back again. What do you suppose Gyges did with this ring? (What would *you* do?) He used this magical ring to seduce the queen, kill the king, and become king himself—all without getting caught.

The question Plato asks is, is there any good reason for behaving differently from Gyges? If we could talk with Gyges when he first discovers the ring and is wondering what to do with it, what would we tell him? We might want to tell him that he should not use the ring to do anything wrong, but suppose he asks us "why not?" What could we say to him? As Plato acknowledges, most people behave morally because society rewards them for being honest, truth telling, and so on, and punishes them for dishonesty and lying. If that is true, then the only thing bad about behaving immorally is getting caught. If you do not get caught, there is no problem! If there were rewards for doing the wrong thing but none for doing the right thing, and no punishments for doing the wrong thing (as with Gyges and his ring), why *should* we behave ourselves?

Plato's answer is that acting immorally inevitably makes us mentally sick and unhappy, and therefore no one would knowingly do the wrong thing. For Plato, as we saw earlier, the human personality is an interactive relationship among three parts—reason, emotion, and will. A healthy and happy personality, Plato argues, is one in which each part performs its proper role and does not usurp the role of the other parts. The proper role of reason is to rule over emotion and will. Emotion should obey reason, and will should carry out the orders of reason. When this occurs, a person not only behaves morally, but is mentally healthy and happy.

But is the unjust tyrant Thrasymachus describes "unhappy"? By "happy," Plato does not mean "feels good," but something like "successful," and "successful" only in the sense that, according to Plato's theory, all of one's mental faculties are functioning as they were designed to do by nature. We can still imagine Thrasymachus replying (if only he had written the book instead of Socrates's student, Plato) that the unjust tyrant is "happy" in the sense that he feels good because he has everything he ever wanted (and he never wanted to be a fully developed human being). How do you answer the person who says, "If by being unjust I can get all the things in life I want at the expense of failing to be a fully developed human being, well, that's just the price I am willing to pay"? (Of course, this presupposes that we accept Socrates's theory of human nature.) A slightly more philosophical immoralist could also argue, as Thrasymachus does in the earlier part of his argument, that Socrates is *wrong* about human nature; that human nature is to selfishly go for the gusto, get all you can, and that the so-called "unjust" strong men are simply those who are able to do what everyone naturally wants to do and would if they could. Perhaps, as Nietzsche argues at the end of the nineteenth century, it is the morally good person who is unnaturally repressing and rationalizing out of weakness her real aggressive nature and, vice versa, that it is the strong, aggressive person who is most naturally fulling her human nature. And this leads naturally to the position held by the nineteenth-century social Darwinians, who argued that, as the survival of the fittest, the rich and powerful *deserve* to be rich and powerful, and the poor and weak *deserve* to be poor and weak.

The German philosopher Immanuel Kant (eighteenth century) also tries to answer this question, why be moral? According to Kant, the moral person is one who is motivated to act, not out of inclination or self-improvement, but out of a sense of duty. For Kant, there are three motivations to act—first, simply because one feels like it ("inclination," as when you get a drink of water after class just because you feel thirsty), second, to get ahead in life (self-improvement, as when you study hard for an exam because you want a good grade to get a good degree to get a good job, and so on), and third, because it is the right thing to do (even if you do not feel like doing it and it will not advance your career). Only the last, acting out of duty, is a morally good action, according to Kant.

And how do we know what our duty is? We should follow what Kant calls the "categorical imperative"—like Confucius's "measuring rod," do not do anything that you would not want other people to do. So, whenever you are in any doubt about what you should do, ask yourself if you would be willing for everyone else to do what you are thinking of doing. If so, then do it; if not, then do not do it. Suppose I am tempted to break a promise I have made. Would I want everyone else to break their promises whenever they wanted to? No, because if everyone broke their promises at will, no one would trust anyone, and the whole institution of promising would cease to exist— and I certainly would not want that. Similarly in the case of lying—if everyone lied whenever it suited them, no one would trust anyone to tell the truth.

Notice that, in these cases at least, the reason we cannot will that everyone lie or break their promises whenever they feel like it is that it is *impossible* for everyone to lie and break promises whenever they feel like it. It is not just that this would result in a messy, awful world. Of course it would, but Kant cannot use this argument, since he thinks morality must not consider consequences—what would happen if everyone lied and broke promises? For Kant, this is not just a matter of bad consequences, but it is logically impossible and therefore contradictory to reason. Why? To successfully lie to someone, you must not only tell them something you know to be false, but you must also get them to believe it. But if everyone is allowed to tell lies whenever it suits them, then no one will believe anyone, so one cannot tell a lie. If everyone tells lies, then no one can. The same is true with promise keeping; if everyone is free to break their promise whenever it suits them, then there is no longer any difference between promising and merely saying one will do it, and in that case no one can either make or break a promise. If everyone is free to break their promises, then no one can break his or her promise.

In a curious way, therefore, to be an immoral person is to contradict reason, to be logically inconsistent. None of us particularly enjoys paying income tax, but we do not mind paying our share as long as everyone else pays theirs. This is like the "negative" Golden Rule of Kongzi—do not do something you would not want other people to do. If I am a thief, I do not want other people stealing; I want to be the only one. That is, ideally, I would like to be the only thief in a community of completely honest people. They never lock their doors, and they never steal from me. But the heart of Kant's position is the intuition we all share, that it is unfair of the thief to exclude himself or herself from the general rule not to steal—why does the thief think it is all right to steal but the rest of us cannot? What makes the thief so special? For Kant, then, to be a moral person is to follow those rules that can be universalized— whether one really wants to or not; whether it helps one or not.

And why, according to Kant, should one want to be a moral person? Because, otherwise, one is not living in accordance with the demands of reason. And what is so bad about that? Because it is this ability to self-regulate our behavior according to reason that gives us our unique worth as human beings. (Recall how both Plato and Aristotle also defined the uniqueness of human beings in terms of reason and rationality, though not in the same way as Kant.) But, again, how crushing is this to the immoral person—"Okay, by being immoral I am rejecting the basis for what makes human beings valuable and noble, but that's not what I'm interested in—I'm interested in making lots of money, having power and influence, and a good time, and it seems to me the best way to achieve those goals is to be thoroughly immoral."

Utilitarians, on the other hand, like John Stuart Mill (nineteenth century), side with Mozi. There is no way to determine whether anything is right or wrong, except to measure its profit/loss ratio, that is, its balance of benefit over harm. If the king whom Gyges killed was a wicked tyrant, and Gyges turned out to be a benevolent ruler, then what he did was good. Of course, as Mozi is quick to point out, there also is God to worry about. Perhaps Gyges can fool the people, but can he fool God? Mozi argues that God will punish evildoers. So Gyges, if he is a utilitarian (and a theist), will have to consider carefully not only the rewards and punishments in this life but those in the life to come.

Since morality exists in every society as a limitation on selfish behavior, egoism (the view, for example, of the Chinese Taoist Yang Zhu, that one should always do what is in one's own best interests) is seldom considered a moral theory, as we saw at the beginning of this chapter. The opposite of egoism is altruism, the view that we should do whatever will help other people, and altruism is therefore an important part of the moral code of most societies. But who, exactly, are these "other people" we are supposed to help? Do they include everyone in the world, or just our family members, friends, and close associates? When Jesus said "love your neighbor as yourself," he was asked, "but who is my neighbor?" How far beyond oneself does altruism extend? What exactly are our obligations toward other people?

Kongzi (Confucius) held that we hold primary responsibilities to our parents and children, that is, to members of our own families, and that that takes precedence over and must be fulfilled before our obligations to others. Mozi disagreed, arguing that we have an equal obligation to all human beings alike, and that it is precisely the partial love and concern for members of our own families and ethnic and regional groups that lead to strife and warfare. Peter Singer and other contemporary Western utilitarians agree with Mozi, that we have as strong an obligation to help people we do not know who are starving halfway around the world as we do our next-door neighbor. If good is to be measured, on the utilitarian calculus, by the total increase of happiness in the world over unhappiness, then there is no reason why making my daughter happy is any more important or better than making a Cambodian farmer's daughter happy.

More generally, in Western philosophy, the question is raised about the distinction between strict obligations, which we may have toward our own children, for example, and supererogatory love or mercy ("beyond the call of duty"), which we should feel toward everyone. This distinction appears, for example, in the difference between the Christian virtue of loving everyone as much as we love ourselves and members of our own families and Kant's categorical imperative, which suggests that feelings of universal love (being "inclinations") are morally irrelevant. In short, the interesting and important question raised by both Chinese and Western philosophers is whether "love is all you need."

Is it *possible* to love everyone equally? And even if it is possible, *should* we love everyone equally? Can you love my mother as much as you love your own mother? Will you help my mother as much as you are prepared to help your own mother? And even if you could, should you? Suppose on payday I give all of my monthly salary to various needy strangers I meet on my way home from work. What do you suppose my husband and children would say to me? Are they right? Do they have a stronger claim on my salary than the needy strangers I tried to help? Recall our earlier discussion of Mozi's challenge to the Confucian idea of "filial piety," Mozi arguing that we should love all people equally, "impartially." One question is whether we *can* do this (remember Plato's drastic strategy in *The Republic*, disbanding the nuclear family in favor of state nurseries as the only way of overcoming the natural tendency of parent's partial love for their own children).

The other question is whether we *should* love all people equally (impartially)? Kongzi's point is that you have a special obligation to your own children and parents. Because your parents raised you, you now owe them a special obligation that you do not owe anyone else in the world. Because parents knowingly chose to bring helpless infants into the world, they have a special responsibility to their own children.

Many people have criticized Kant's moral theory for denying the moral worth of helping others out of love. Remember that for Kant, of the three motivations to act, inclination, self-interest and duty, only duty is morally praiseworthy; so if love is a kind of inclination, then it has no moral worth. But what exactly do we mean by "love" in this context? You remember the story of the Good Samaritan. Why does the story mention Samaritans? Because they were the hated enemies of the Jews—the Jews and the Samaritans hated each other. So when the Samaritan sees the wounded Jew, we do not imagine that the Samaritan likes him or feels a desire to be close to him. On the contrary. Nonetheless, he helps him. Why? Because the Jew is a human being. If we mean by "love" a feeling (or inclination) of liking, wanting to be near, and so on, then it seems impossible to love everyone equally. But if we mean by "love" respect for a person simply as a human being, then in that sense we can and should love all people equally. And in *that* sense, both Kant and Kongzi would accept the idea that we should "love" everyone equally. That seems to be what Kongzi (Confucius) means by "ren," often translated as love, or human heartedness. The term is used in several different ways in Kongzi's writings, but the most consistent sense of the term is to treat people as you would want to be treated, to use your own experience as a kind of yardstick, as Kongzi says in one passage, to measure how you should treat others. (Of course, this yardstick is not infallible—if I love to be thrown into a cold shower at 4:30 A.M. every morning, is that how I should treat my roommate?) This does not mean you have to like someone, much less love someone, but simply to recognize that that person is just as much of a human being as you are, therefore equally deserving of respect and fair treatment.

But notice the shift in the meaning of the word "equally"—always a philosophically troubling term. Does it mean to love everyone the same amount or to the same degree—to love your mother as much as I love my mother? Or does it mean to love everyone *without exception*—even though in different amounts or in varying degrees? What seems possible and morally obligatory is to love everyone equally in the sense of respecting every human being in the same way, that is, simply as a human being. What seems impossible (for most of us) is to love everyone equally in the sense of liking, caring for, and wanting to help everyone in the same amount or to the same degree.

But again, returning to our question, why should I be moral, why *should* we love everyone in *any* of these senses? The world would certainly be a better place if everyone loved everyone else, but until they all do, or at least most of them do, why should I be the first to get the ball rolling? Why should I be moral? Again, it seems the best answer we can come up with, and the one Kant gives, has to do with not wanting to contradict reason—unless there is some good reason why I should be treated differently from other people, then reason dictates that all human beings should be treated the same, and since that includes me, it follows that I should treat other people as well as I would treat myself. So to be immoral is to be logically inconsistent.

But again, we have to ask how great a loss this is to the immoral person. "Yeah, you're right, I'm not being consistent, but you know, that's not really keeping me awake at night; I still prefer being rationally inconsistent—treating myself much better than anyone else and using other people to better my own position—that's what works for me!" What if we add to this, as Aristotle and Kant do, that it is this rational element within people that differentiates human beings from other creatures and gives us our unique value and worth? Will this convince the immoral person to change her ways? First, the immoralist might reject this theory of human nature, denying that rationality is what is distinctive or important about human beings. Second, even if the immoralist agrees that rationality is an important human trait, he or she may interpret rationality as a useful egoistic tool in getting ahead in life and taking advantage of the fools. And finally, even if the immoralist sees rationality as important and interprets it as Aristotle and Kant and other philosophers do, he or she might still not see what this has to do with him or her—"Yes, that's a great thing about human beings, but I've decided I'm personally better off not participating in that—just because I'm a human being doesn't mean I want to or have to strive to be a well-developed human being—in my own case, I'm trying to overcome this human capacity to be a wimp!" As we saw earlier, Mengzi and Socrates argue that most people refuse to follow the most precious part of themselves, which is their most distinctively human part. To Mengzi and to Socrates, this seems a great loss, but to most people it does not. What about you? What are some of the things which you think would make you a better human being? Do you really want to pursue those things?

Why should I be moral? Maybe the question can only be answered within a moral framework; maybe it is impossible to logically convince the immoral person. Philosophy, we have been saying, is a reflection of our ordinary intuitions. What this means in this case is that philosophical ethics cannot operate in a vacuum, but only within the context of certain widely accepted assumptions about the moral life of human beings. In the absence of all intuitions about the role of morality in social life, philosophical ethics makes no sense. Ethics therefore cannot start absolutely from scratch, from "ground zero," to prove that there are good reasons for being a moral rather than an immoral person. Only when we start from a set of commonly shared prephilosophical assumptions—that morality is important to the full development of the individual person, as well as to the smooth functioning of society—can we go on to meaningfully ask the philosophical questions—What are the best moral standards? Are those standards consistent with one another, and if they are in conflict, how can these different standards nonetheless be reconciled and harmonized (for example, which ones have priority over others and why), or if they cannot be reconciled, then which are better and why?

Philosophy can only do so much, and we should expect of it no more and no less than that. As we have seen before (throughout this book), philosophy criticizes our traditional, commonsense intuitions, in the sense that it demands reasons, justification, clarity, and consistency, not in the sense that it flatly contradicts or denies our most deeply held commonsense intuitions (that things do not change, that there is no plurality, that there are no distinctions among things, that no one knows anything—that there is no right or wrong).

6

Social and Political Philosophy

*T*HERE are two main questions of social and political philosophy—first, do we need a government (or state) at all, and
second, if we do, what is the best form of government? The
most common answer to the first of these two questions comes from what is
known as the "social contract" theory, which appears in both Eastern and
Western philosophy from ancient times to the present, and which also offers
important suggestions for answering the second question.

Plato is one of the first Western philosophers to discuss what later
became known as the "social contract." This appears in the discussion we
looked at in the last chapter (from Plato's *The Republic*) as to why we should
do the right thing, that is, whether there is any *intrinsic* reason, apart from its
practical benefit, in acting morally. As we saw in Plato's discussion of Gyges,
who discovered the magic ring, if we could be certain we would not get
caught, would there by any reason not to take advantage of the situation?

Earlier, in discussing the "rectification of names," we also mentioned
Thrasymachus's attempt (also in *The Republic*) to define justice as injustice and
injustice as justice, that is, to redefine justice as the strong taking advantage
of the weak (which had traditionally been called injustice). Since words tend
to retain their old meanings, it is always hard to change them (at least very
quickly). And so we saw Thrasymachus's difficulties in expressing himself
(and winning the argument against Socrates). Despite these difficulties, however, we can see what Thrasymachus is up to. There is at least a pragmatic and
an egotistic sense in which it is good to be bad. Why do people tell lies, or
cheat on an exam, or steal things? Obviously, in order to help themselves
(lying to get out of an awkward situation; cheating to pass a course; stealing

to get something one cannot afford). What Plato is asking is whether there is any *intrinsic* reason for doing the right thing, even if one could benefit from doing the wrong thing and (with the help of Gyges's ring) get away with it.

Following this discussion with Thrasymachus, Glaucon suggests that perhaps there is no such reason. Maybe, Glaucon proposes, we only do the right thing so others will not inflict injury on us. Maybe, if I had all the power in the world, the best thing for me would be to take advantage of everyone else and, like Gyges, become the richest and happiest person in the world ("I'd rather be a hammer than a nail"). But I cannot be sure I am that powerful, and it is going to be dangerous to find out, since I will surely run into some stiff competition. On the other hand, if I am weak, then everyone will take advantage of me, and I will be the most miserable person in the world. Basically, we are all in the same boat, and once we all realize this (with the use of reason, or rational reflection), then, Glaucon suggests, we agree with one another on a kind of second-best compromise (a version of social contract)—to give up the best but avoid the worst by agreeing not to take advantage of one another. I will not rob you if you will not rob me, and I agree in advance to support a police and legal system to prevent robbery and to punish robbers, including myself if need be.

> What people say is that to do wrong is, in itself, a desirable thing; on the other hand, it is not at all desirable to suffer wrong, and the harm to the sufferer outweighs the advantage to the doer. Consequently, when we have had a taste of both, those who have not the power to seize the advantage and escape the harm decide that they would be better off if they made a compact neither to do wrong nor to suffer it. Hence they began to make laws and covenants with one another; and whatever the law prescribed they called lawful and right. That is what right or justice is and how it came into existence; it stands half-way between the best thing of all—to do wrong with impunity—and the worst, which is to suffer wrong without the power to retaliate. So justice is accepted as a compromise.
>
> (Plato 1945)

The question Glaucon raises is not quite the full-blown question, why we need a government (or state) at all, but an important part of that larger question, namely, why do we think (where did we get the idea) that obeying and enforcing the law is just and right and disobeying and breaking the law is unjust and wrong? In the context of *The Republic*, the question is given an even more specific thrust—is there any *intrinsic* reason to think that doing the right thing and being a just person is good (that is, whether it is good in itself)? And, of course, Glaucon's tentative answer (which he hopes Socrates will refute) is, no, there is no intrinsic reason to be just and defend and enforce the law; there is only the extrinsic or prudential reason that without it we (or at least the weaker among us) would be much worse off than we are now (at the mercy of the bullies and tyrants of the world).

Despite its early anticipation in Plato's *The Republic*, however, the social contract does not become a major topic of philosophical debate within Western philosophy until the seventeenth and eighteenth centuries, when it formed the main theoretical basis for justifying the American and French revolutions at the end of the eighteenth century. As we pointed out in chapter 1, it is tempting to think of Western culture in general as being essentially democratic and individualistic (and Asian cultures, in contrast, as being essentially authoritarian and communitarian). But in fact individualism is a relatively new idea in the world, arising first in the West, that is, in Europe, not because of anything genetic or racially distinctive about Europeans, but as a response to a much larger context of social change involving many interconnected social phenomena—the rise of the middle class, the growth of large cities, the industrial revolution, and the emergence of the nation-state.

Democracy and individualism arise, in other words, everywhere in the world—today in Asia, Africa, the Mideast, and so on—as an adjustment to these modern developments. As Karl Marx pointed out (mid nineteenth century), the modern liberal philosophy of the rights and freedoms of the individual arose in the seventeenth century as a defense of the rising middle class. In the medieval period, a feudal hierarchy prevailed in which each person was born into a distinct class locked into a tight set of duties and obligations to classes above and below it. In such a society, no one has the right or freedom to venture out on their own, rejecting or moving beyond this preordained system of social relationships, and in such a society everyone is unequal, depending on their place in the social hierarchy. But as more individuals broke free from these rural feudal principalities to establish themselves as businesspersons in the rapidly growing cities of Europe (London, Paris), they began to express a new set of ideals designed to strengthen their position—their right to pursue their own individual (mainly business) interests, to educate their children as they saw fit, to move to wherever opportunities seemed to beckon, and, at least among their peers within the expanding middle class, to be more or less equal to everyone else, and, finally, the right to rule themselves through a one-person, one-vote democracy. Gradually the power and wealth of the middle class overwhelmed that of the older aristocracy, and the liberal democratic ideals of the newly dominant middle class came to dominate social thought and reality. The social contract is one of the main sources of justification for this new social arrangement.

The social contract is an attempt to answer the question, why do we need a government at all? That is to say, what right has the state to force me to do what I may not want to do? And on the other side of the coin, what moral obligation or duty, if any, do I have to obey laws I may not want to follow (such as paying income tax, driving with a seat belt)? Of course, the state has the power to compel me to obey, and I have good prudential (or selfish) reasons to obey laws I do not like. I hate seat belts, but I prefer wearing them to paying a fine and then seeing my car insurance costs go up. If I refuse to pay my income tax, to take another example, the state has the power to simply take it from my bank account or confiscate my property or put me in jail, and, knowing that, I probably will choose to obey the law rather than to face any of these alternatives. But the philosophical question is the normative question— what *right*, if any, has the state to force me, and what *moral obligation* or *duty*, if any, do I have to obey?

How can we answer such a question? We have said from the beginning (chapter 1) that philosophy is a reflection of our own commonsense intuitions. Well, what are those intuitions? Sometimes they are hard to focus on and harder still to articulate. We need a little help, some device to stimulate our reflective powers. Remember Descartes's use of "systematic doubt" as a way to quicken and focus his reflection on how to discover what he knows for sure? Or suppose we began thinking that the fairest way to decide anything among competing interest groups is the most impartial way, but then we wondered how to figure out what the most impartial way is. To help us sharpen our reflections on this question, we might try to imagine what an outside observer would say, or we might try "putting ourselves in the other person's shoes." (In dividing a pastry among two children, the parent lets the first child cut the pastry into two pieces with the understanding that the second child will get first choice of the two pieces. Do you think it will be divided fairly?) Or, again, the best way to remember why you need something you have always had and therefore take for granted is to imagine what it would be like to lose it. Suppose I begin thinking that friendships are a waste of time. Sometimes my friends forget about me or leave me or abandon me or "stab me in the back." Why do I need friends anyway, I wonder? By just "staring" at the question, I may come up empty, drawing a blank. But if I try to imagine what life would be like without any friends, then I may be able to answer my own question. Without friends, I would have no one to share my good and bad times with; I would be all alone—I would be miserable. And now I realize why I need friends—I have already answered my question. I need friends to share the good and bad times with, to enjoy some companionship, and to not be all alone.

So in the case of the social contract. We are not investigating some historical event that happened long ago before there was any government. As far as we know, human beings always lived in social groupings with some form of governing body. The social contract is an imaginary thought experiment designed to sharpen our intuitions and to enable us to answer the question of why we need a government (one that has the right, as well as the power, to compel us to do what we may not want to do and one we feel some duty to obey, even when we do not really feel like it). And so we try to imagine, as in our earlier friendship example, what it would be like to be without any form of government. If, as in our example, we imagine such a state of affairs to be bad, we can ask *why* it is bad, what is bad about it, and what makes it so bad, and that will tell us why we need a government (that is, to correct all of these bad things).

But since this is an imaginary thought experiment (and our intuitions vary somewhat from person to person), different philosophers are liable to imagine the situation differently. And of course, how we answer the question of why we need government will obviously depend on how we imagine what it would be like without any form of government (traditionally called "the state of nature"). Some philosophers performing the social contract thought experiment have come to the conclusion that there is nothing wrong with the state of nature and that there is therefore no good reason why we need or should have a government. This is the position known as "anarchism." Anarchism is the skeptical answer within social and political philosophy. As we have seen, every branch of philosophy has a skeptical answer to the central normative questions of that branch. When the epistemologist asks what the difference is between knowledge and belief, the epistemological skeptic says, none—so-called knowledge is just a conceited form of belief. When the metaphysician asks what the difference is between reality and appearance, the metaphysical skeptic says, none—so-called reality is just an overconfident trust in appearance. When the moral philosopher asks if there are any universal, crosscultural standards of right conduct, the moral skeptic says, no—all so-called moral standards are merely culturally relative, and anyone who claims the moral standards of her or his society are absolute is simply being ethnocentric.

So to the question, what justifies a government ordering citizens to do what they may not feel like doing, the anarchist (skeptic) says, nothing—governments have no such right. We need not think of the anarchist as a bomb-throwing fanatic. It may only be someone who argues that there is no moral duty or obligation to obey the laws of the state and that the state has no right to boss us around. Most anarchists obey the law most of the time, not because they feel a moral duty to do so, nor because they feel the state has that right, but simply to stay out of jail and avoid being hassled by the police. (There may be a lot more anarchists out there than you think!)

But in every branch of philosophy the skeptical answer ends the philosophical search. If you accept the skeptical solution, then that is the end of philosophy for you. There is nothing more to be said. (If you are looking for a very short philosophy course, take one from a skeptic!) Obviously, only those who think there could be an answer will spend the time and effort working on and so contributing to the ongoing history of philosophy. So the skeptics have not made a big impact on the history of philosophy, except to lay down a series of challenges for the nonskeptics. In the case of social and political philosophy, only those philosophers who come to the conclusion that life in the "state of nature" would be intolerable are led to continue the search for answers. *Why* is it bad, and what could be done to *improve* the situation, leading finally to theories justifying the need for the state.

Among Western philosophers who do not take the skeptical route, but imagine the "state of nature" to be intolerable, we still find very different accounts of just how bad it is and what it takes to improve the situation (and therefore what the best form of government is, assuming we need one to correct the evils in the state of nature). Two of the most famous social contractarians in the Western tradition that span this wide diversity of opinion are Thomas Hobbes and John Locke.

Hobbes imagines the state of nature to be, frankly, awful—"nasty, brutish, and short." In fact, he says, it is nothing less than a state of war of every person against every other, if not actually fighting all the time, at least being constantly prepared to fight. Since in the state of nature there is no law or law enforcement or criminal justice system, there is nothing to prevent a person from doing what he or she pleases and has the power to accomplish. In the state of nature, everyone has complete freedom, or an unlimited right to do as he or she pleases (and can get away with). But as Glaucon realized in *The Republic,* although I have the right and freedom to take from you, you also have the right and freedom to take from me. And since Hobbes argues that no one is that much stronger than the others (even the strongest can be overpowered in his or her sleep at night or by an organized gang), this leads to a state of constant civil unrest and anarchy.

But we also are rational creatures, able to evaluate our situation and consider our alternatives. As a result, Hobbes imagines we would do anything to end such a terrifying state of nature, and so are happy to agree with others to jointly give up all of our rights and powers forever to an absolute sovereign who will never be subject to censor, criticism, or being thrown out of office. For Hobbes there is simply no alternative—either a state of war or a permanent totalitarian dictatorship. Only the all-powerful dictator can end the war of each against every other. So the best form of government, for Hobbes, is an absolute dictatorship. Hobbes actually used this argument to support the threatened monarchy of his day against the rising tide of democratic forms of government.

Men have no pleasure, but on the contrary a great deal of grief, in keeping company, where there is no power able to overawe them all. For every man thinks that his companion should value him at the same rate he sets upon himself. . . . So that in the nature of man, we find three principal causes of quarrel. First, competition;

second, diffidence [insecurity]; thirdly, glory. The first makes men invade for gain; the second, for safety; and the third, for reputation. . . . Hereby it is manifest that during the time men live without a common power to keep them all in awe, they are in that condition which is called war; and such a war as is of every man against every man . . . [in which] the life of man [is] solitary, poor, nasty, brutish, and short. . . . [In] this war of every man against every man . . . nothing can be unjust. . . . It follows, that in such a condition every man has a right to everything. . . . [But from the] general rule of reason, that every man ought to endeavor peace, as far as he has hope of obtaining it . . . and that a man be willing, when others are so too, as far-forth, as for peace, and defence of himself he shall think it necessary, to lay down this right to all things; and be contented with so much liberty against other men, as he would allow other men against himself. . . . [Men are lead finally to the social contract], or covenant of every man with every man, in such a manner, as if every man should say to every man, "I authorize and give up my right of governing myself, to this man, or to this assembly of men, on this condition, that you give up your right to him, and authorize all his actions in like manner."

(Thomas Hobbes, *The Leviathan*, 1967)

Locke's account of the social contract is quite different. First of all, Locke does not imagine the state of nature as being nearly as bad as Hobbes's state. For Locke, while there are no civil laws yet in force, there is what he calls the "law of nature" governing human behavior, even in the state of nature. By the "law of nature," Locke means the practical reasonableness of human beings, as he imagines them, not to arbitrarily and unnecessarily go out of their way to attack their neighbors. If I rob your garden at night, you are likely to do the same to me. And if someone gets hurt, the "revenge" taken out on me may be even worse than I inflicted on you—leading to a constant no-win Hatfields-and-McCoys type of feud.

But since I am not without reason, even in the state of nature, I can anticipate this and so, Locke thinks, I will not attack you and hope that you will not attack me. So, things are not as bad as we find them in Hobbes's state. Nonetheless, our lives are far from perfect, because there will always be a few individuals who will try to take advantage of the situation (and there is always the possibility that we will let minor grievances get emotionally out of hand, like the Hatfields and McCoys), and in the state of nature, there will be no recourse or remedy, except to take the law into our own hands. Like Hobbes, Locke recognizes that everyone has unlimited rights and freedom in the state of nature, especially the right to personal property, along with the right to punish those who try to attack or rob us. And like Hobbes, Locke argues that rational people in the imagined state of nature would, in order to better secure themselves and their property, agree among themselves to jointly give up their *unlimited* personal rights and freedoms (but not *all* of their rights and freedoms) to a common government set up to protect those rights and freedoms.

But unlike Hobbes, this government would not be someone designated by the people, but the people themselves who "incorporate themselves," as Locke says, into a government, deciding everything jointly either by direct referendum or by periodically electing those to represent them. And unlike Hobbes, the government so constituted has the right to rule only as long as it keeps its end of the bargain (the social contract) to protect our rights and freedoms. Just as Hobbes's description of the state of nature and the resulting social contract reflected his political views supporting the monarchy, so Locke's account reflects the experience of his family suffering from religious persecution in England. People must be protected *from* governmental intervention into their private lives, Locke had come to believe, and not just protected *by* government. Since the only justification of government, by this argument, is the consent of the governed (consenting to "sign" the social contract), the government loses all right to rule if and when it loses the consent of the people, and the people, therefore, have a right and even an obligation to remove that government, by force if necessary, and to exchange it for another one that will defend its rights. One reason Thomas Jefferson used so much of Locke's theory in his *Declaration of Independence* was due to Locke's justification of the right of a people to rebel against their government.

> To understand political power aright, and derive it from its original, we must consider what state all men are naturally in, and that is a state of perfect freedom to order their actions and dispose of their possessions and persons as they think fit, within the bounds of the law of nature, without asking leave, or depending upon the will of any other man. A state also of equality, wherein all the power and jurisdiction is reciprocal, no one having more than another. . . .
>
> Men being . . . by nature all free, equal, and independent, no one can be put out of this estate, and subjected to the political power of another, without his own consent, which is done by agreeing with other men to join and unite into a community for their comfortable, safe, and peaceable living one amongst another, in a secure enjoyment of their properties, and a greater security against any that are not of it. . . .
>
> When any number of men have so consented to make one community or government, they are thereby presently incorporated, and make one body politic, wherein the majority have a right to act and conclude the rest. . . .
>
> Governments are dissolved when . . . the legislative acts against the trust reposed in them [as] when they endeavor to invade the property of their subjects, and to make themselves or any part of the community masters of arbitrary disposers of the lives, liberties, or fortunes of the people.
>
> Whenever the legislators endeavor to take away and destroy the property of the people, or to reduce them to slavery under arbitrary power, they put themselves into a state of war with the people, who are thereupon absolved from any further obedience. . . . Whensoever, therefore, the legislative shall transgress this fundamental rule . . . they forfeit the power the people had put into their hands . . . and it devolves to the people, who have a right to resume their original liberty, and by

the establishment of a new legislative . . . provide for their own safety and security, which is the end for which they are in society.

(Locke 1970)

In Chinese philosophy, we find several discussions of a social contract theory of the origin of the state, although they are not the same in all respects as those in Western philosophy. The Chinese versions are in general agreement with Western versions on the statement of the *problem*, that is, the description of the state of nature and the need arising from that to form a state, but they are less in agreement on the *solution* to that problem, tending on the whole to argue that the ancient wise rulers (and not the people themselves) saw the problem and inaugurated human government to correct the situation. Although Mozi says "there was a selection of the person" to rule, it is not clear who made the selection—whether the people or the ancient sage kings or even "Heaven." Nonetheless, it is clear that Mozi's idea of the kind of government issuing from the social contract is much closer to Hobbes's than to Locke's. The resulting government, Mozi holds, will be an unquestioned dictatorship calling all the shots.

> In the beginning of human life, when there was yet no law and government, the custom was, "Every man according to his own idea." . . . As a result, father and son and elder and younger brothers became enemies and estranged from each other, and were unable to reach any agreement. The people of the world worked against each other with water, fire, and poison. . . . The disorder in the [human] world was like that among birds and beasts. Yet it was evident that all this disorder was owing to the want of a ruler. Therefore there was a selection of the person in the world who was virtuous and able, and he was established as the Son of Heaven [who] issued a mandate to the people, saying, . . . "What the superior thinks to be right, all shall think to be right; what the superior thinks to be wrong, all shall think to be wrong."
>
> (Mozi, *Mozi*, in Watson, Burton, ed. and trans., *Basic Writings*)

In Xunzi, it is clear that it is the ancient kings and not the people who realized the gravity of the situation and stepped in to solve it. Nonetheless, in his description of the state of nature as the problem to be solved, Xunzi's version of the social contract is quite similar to that of Hobbes's, especially in his account of the wicked and selfish nature of human beings outside of an organized society.

> Man's nature is evil; goodness is the result of conscious activity. The nature of man is such that he is born with a fondness for profit. If he indulges this fondness, it will lead him into wrangling and strife, and all sense of courtesy and humility will disappear. He is born with feelings of envy and hate, and if he indulges these, they will

lead him into violence and crime, and all sense of loyalty and good faith will disappear. Man is born with the desires of the eyes and ears, with a fondness for beautiful sights and sounds. If he indulges these, they will lead him into license and wantonness, and all ritual principles and correct forms will be lost. . . . Therefore, man must first be transformed by the instructions of a teacher and guided by ritual principles, and only then will he be able to observe the dictates of courtesy and humility, obey the forms and rules of society and achieve order. . . . In ancient times the sage kings realized that man's nature is evil, and that therefore he inclines toward evil and violence and is not upright or orderly. Accordingly they created ritual principles and laid down certain regulations in order to reform man's emotional nature and make it upright, in order to train and transform it and guide it in the proper channels. . . . [They] set up laws and standards to correct it, and meted out strict punishments to restrain it. As a result, all the world achieved order and conformed to goodness. Such is the orderly government of the sage kings and the transforming power of ritual principles. . . . Now let someone try doing away with the authority of the ruler, . . . and then watch and see how the people of the world treat each other. He will find that the powerful impose upon the weak and rob them, the many terrorize the few and extort from them, and in no time the whole world will be given up to chaos and mutual destruction.

(Xunzi, in Burton Watson, ed. & trans., *Basic Writings*)

Unlike Locke, Xunzi does not imagine for a moment that everyone in society is politically "equal," in the sense that everyone in the society is equally capable of making good political decisions. For Xunzi, every one is naturally born superior to some and inferior to others, and the good society is one in which every person willingly recognizes his or her place in the society and remains content within it. Throughout, Xunzi stresses the importance of custom and tradition (li) in organizing society into a hierarchical system in which each person sticks to his or her particular "station" in life and performs all of the duties (yi) owed to those in stations above and below his or her own.

Fire and water possess energy but are without life. Grass and trees have life but no intelligence. Birds and beasts have intelligence but no sense of duty [yi]. Man possesses energy, life, intelligence, and, in addition, a sense of duty. Therefore he is the noblest being on earth. He is not as strong as the ox, nor as swift as the horse, and yet he makes the ox and the horse work for him. Why? Because he is able to organize himself in society and they are not. Why is he able to organize himself in society? Because he sets up hierarchical divisions. And how is he able to set up hierarchical divisions? Because he has a sense of duty. If he employs this sense of duty to set up hierarchical divisions, then there will be harmony. Where there is harmony there will be unity; where there is unity there will be strength; and where there is strength there will be the power to conquer all things. Thus men can dwell in security in their houses and halls.

(*ibid.*)

Following Kongzi and Mengzi (with whom Xunzi disagreed on many other issues), Xunzi argues that the successful ruler must be a morally good person who understands the principles of good government. Like Mengzi, Xunzi argues that there are definite limits to the power of government; without the support of the people, not even the most powerful tyrant can continue long in power.

> If [foreign invaders] carry out a military expedition against him [the ruler], it must be with the support of their own people. But if their own people favor the good ruler, look up to him as a father or mother, and rejoice in him as in the fragrance of iris or orchid, and on the contrary regard their own rulers as so many wielders of branding irons and tattooing knives [ancient Chinese forms of punishment] as their foes and enemies, then, human nature being what it is, even if the people should be as cruel and violent as the worst tyrants, how could they be willing to fight for the sake of men they hate and do harm to ones they love? For this reason such evil rulers will be overthrown.
>
> *(ibid.)*

Although Mengzi did not explicitly formulate what could be called a "social contract" theory, he did state quite clearly that the only legitimate function of government was to benefit the ordinary people and make their lives better. And this does imply a tacit agreement or consent between the ruler and the people—insofar as the government lives up to its normative function, then the people have a desire and an obligation to obey the ruler, but insofar as the ruler fails to fulfill his rightful role, the people have the desire and the right to overthrow the ruler and even kill him. A ruler who practiced benevolence toward his people (a true "king," if we use words correctly) would be loved and supported by the people, while one who practiced cruelty toward his people (not a true king but a tyrant) would be reviled and, if possible, thrown out of office, even killed. Mengzi indicates that he regards this as natural, inevitable, legitimate, and even sanctioned by the "will of Heaven."

It was an ancient idea in China, long before philosophy, that a king was selected "by the mandate of Heaven." This is not a philosophical theory but simply part of the general culture of that time and place. But the interesting philosophical question is, how can we *tell* when a *de facto* ruler actually has the mandate of Heaven and when he has lost it or is about to lose it? Of course, a *de facto* king can always say that the fact that he is still king is proof enough that he still enjoys the mandate of heaven. But if a usurper can topple the king, the usurper can then claim that the old king had lost the mandate of heaven and that he, the new king, now possesses that mandate.

But apart from sheer power to take control of government, what is the criterion for possessing or losing the mandate of Heaven? This is the normative, philosophical question whose answer leads to a theory of government. Mengzi says that the sign that the de facto king has the mandate of Heaven is that he is accepted not only by the gods but also by the ordinary people; and the clearest sign that he has lost the mandate is his loss of acceptance by the ordinary people.

> Wan Chang said, "Is it true that [Emperor] Yao gave the Empire to Shun [who was not his son]?"
>
> "No," said Mencius. "The Emperor cannot give the Empire to another."
>
> "In that case who gave the Empire to Shun?"
>
> "Heaven gave it him."
>
> ". . . Does this mean that Heaven gave him detailed and minute instructions?"
>
> "No. Heaven does not speak but reveals itself through its acts and deeds."
>
> "How does Heaven do this?"
>
> "The Emperor can recommend a man to Heaven but he cannot make Heaven give this man the Empire. . . . In antiquity, [Emperor] Yao recommended Shun [who was not his son] to Heaven and Heaven accepted him; he presented him to the people and the people accepted him. Hence I said, 'Heaven does not speak but reveals itself by its acts and deeds.' "
>
> "May I ask how he was accepted by Heaven when recommended to it and how he was accepted by the people when presented to them?"
>
> "When he was put in charge of sacrifices, the hundred gods enjoyed them. This showed that Heaven accepted him. When he was put in charge of affairs, they were kept in order and the people were content. This showed that the people accepted him. Heaven gave it to him, and the people gave it to him. Hence I said, 'The Emperor cannot give the Empire to another.' "
>
> (Menszi, *Mengzi*, in Chan, *Sourcebook Chinese*)

The main criterion for Mengzi is the selection of the best person for the job—and this will not always or necessarily mean that the job should go to the Emperor's son.

> If Heaven wished to give the Empire to a good and wise man [who is not the Emperor's son], then it should be given to [that] good and wise man. But if Heaven wished to give it to the [Emperor's] son, then it should be given to the son. In antiquity, Shun recommended Yu [who was not his son] to Heaven, and died seventeen years later. When the mourning period of three years was over, Yu withdrew, . . . leaving Shun's son in possession of the field, yet the people of the Empire followed him [Yu], just as, after [Emperor] Yao's death, the people followed Shun instead of Yao's son. [Emperor] Yu [in turn] recommended Yi [who was not his son] to Heaven, and died seven years later. When the mourning period of three years was over, Yi withdrew to the northern slope of Mount Ch'i, leaving [Emperor] Yu's son [Qi] in possession of the field. Those who came to pay homage and those who were engaged in litigation went to [Yu's son] Qi instead of Yi. . . .

[Yao's son] and Shun's son were depraved . . . [while Yu's son] Qi was good and capable. All this was due to Heaven and could not have been brought about by man. When a thing is done as though by no one, then it is the work of Heaven; when a thing comes about though no one brings it about, then it is decreed.

(*ibid.*)

Mengzi is often portrayed in the book *Mengzi,* or *The Mencius* (written by Mengzi's followers, recording his sayings) as bravely criticizing the king for failing to live up to his kingly duties to the people.

Mencius said to King Hsuan of Ch'i, "Suppose a subject of Your Majesty's, having entrusted his wife and children to the care of a friend, were to go on a trip to Ch'u, only to find, upon his return, that his friend had allowed his wife and children to suffer cold and hunger, then what should he do about it?"

"Break with his friend."

"If the Marshal of the Guards was unable to keep his guards in order, then what should be done about it?"

"Remove him from office."

"If the whole realm within the four borders was ill-governed, then what should be done about it?"

The King turned to his attendants and changed the subject.

(*ibid.*)

Several passages from *The Mengzi* make it plain that the main criterion of good government is satisfying the needs of the people.

The men of Ch'i attacked and defeated Yen. King Hsuan said, "Some advise me against annexing Yen while others urge me to do so. . . . If I do not annex Yen, I am afraid Heaven will send down disasters. What would you think if I decided on annexation?"

"If in annexing Yen," answered Mencius, "you please its people, then annex it. . . . If in annexing Yen you antagonize its people, then do not annex it."

(*ibid.*)

Mencius often argues that the king should fulfill his duty to the people out of a sense of righteous duty, simply because it is the right thing to do. But occasionally Mencius also offers consequentialist or utilitarian reasons.

There was a border clash between Tsou and Lu. Duke Mu of Tsou asked, "Thirty-three of my officials died, yet none of my people would sacrifice their lives for them. If I punish them, there are too many to be punished. If I do not punish them, then there they were, looking on with hostility at the death of their superiors without going to their aid. What do you think is the best thing for me to do?"

"In years of bad harvest and famine," answered Mencius, "close on a thousand of your people suffered, the old and the young being abandoned in the gutter, the able-bodied scattering in all directions, yet your granaries were full. . . . This shows how callous those in authority were and how cruelly they treated the people. Tseng Tzu said, 'Take heed! Take heed! What you mete out will be paid back to you.' It is only now that the people have had an opportunity of paying back what they received. You should not bear them any grudge. Practice benevolent government and the people will be sure to love their superiors and die for them."

(ibid.)

The king who serves the people will have a prosperous and happy kingdom; the king who fails to serve the people will receive little or no cooperation from the people; and the king who actually mistreats his people may very well be overthrown.

Mencius said, "The Three Dynasties won the Empire through benevolence and lost it through cruelty. This is true of the rise and fall, survival and collapse, of states as well. An Emperor cannot keep the Empire within the Four Seas unless he is benevolent; a feudal lord cannot preserve the altars to the gods of earth and grain unless he is benevolent. . . . To dislike death yet revel in cruelty is no different from drinking beyond your capacity despite your dislike of drunkenness."

(ibid.)

As Mencius makes clear, even in an autocratic monarchy, there are limits to the power of the king. Superficially it may seem that the king can do whatever he likes with impunity. But in the long run, if the mass of people is not behind him, then his rule will be unsuccessful and will probably be a short one.

Mencius said, "It was through losing the people that Chieh and Zhou lost the Empire, and through losing the people's hearts that they lost the people. . . . There is a way to win the people; win their hearts and you will win the people. There is a way to win their hearts; amass what they want for them; do not impose what they dislike on them. That is all. The people turn to the benevolent as water flows downwards or as animals head for the wilds."

(ibid.)

Mengzi, like other Confucianists, argues that the key to good government is moral leadership on the part of the rulers. The king has a duty, as the king, to serve the people faithfully and to work for their well-being. If he fails to fulfill his obligations to the people, he risks an uncooperative and a recalcitrant public in which nothing gets done, or worse, he risks being overthrown and possibly killed. But if, on the other hand, the king is himself a morally virtuous person and rules in a morally just way, then the people will love and follow him and in their own lives and in their own relations to others will try to live up to the moral standard set by the king. And so the whole country is better off. This is an example of what we might call the moral theory of good government. One of the differences between the social and political theory of Mengzi's and that of Xunzi's (both Confucianists) is that while Xunzi emphasizes the Confucian virtue of li, or custom, Mengzi stresses the Confucian virtue of ren, or human heartedness. For Xunzi, the key to an orderly society is the observance of traditional social custom (li), whereas for Mengzi, a good society is one in which the citizens, following the example of their king, are actually loving and benevolent and show respect for one another (ren)—surely a lofty but difficult goal to achieve!

At the opposite extreme from the Confucianist moral theory of government were the Taoists and legalists. The Taoists basically said, do not do anything; just let things take their natural course—"leave well enough alone" or, "if it ain't broke, don't fix it." The legalists, on the other hand, were "law and order" types who thought that the best way to rule a society was by a system of strict rewards and punishments. Let us look at each of these in turn.

According to the Taoists, everything happens naturally, spontaneously, of its own accord. The principle that directs the growth and development of everything in the world is not some cause or force from outside, but something that comes from within the individual. This is the natural and therefore preferred order of things; the worst thing one can do, especially a government leader, is to try and improve on this natural order by enacting and enforcing laws.

> The people are difficult to keep in order because those above them interfere. That is the only reason why they are difficult to keep in order.
>
> (Laozi, *Tao De Jing*, 1990)

Of course, one could argue that it is also natural for human beings to try to change and improve things. It seems perfectly natural for people, including government leaders, to feel that things are not going as well as they might and therefore try and figure out what would make them better, setting about finally to enact laws that will bring about those changes. But for the Taoists, it is better for governments to leave the people alone. Ordinary people have been managing their affairs from time immemorial, not by following formally enacted laws, but simply by following time-honored traditions and customs. Generally speaking, these work just fine. By trying to make things better, the ruler may be upsetting these established customs, thereby confusing people, making them angry, and in the end only making things worse.

Before governments found it necessary to introduce harsh laws to regulate behavior, and punishments to enforce those laws, people lived more simply without the need for laws. Thus, the ruler should therefore try to keep things at this simple, primitive level; better not to give the ordinary people fancy ideas or encourage them to improve their lot, but keep them ignorant and simple.

> In the days of old those who practiced Tao with success did not do so by enlightening the people, but by causing them to be ignorant.
>
> (*ibid.*)

The Confucianists are wrong, therefore, to encourage knowledge and virtue. By insisting on increasing knowledge and acquiring virtue, you make people feel that they are ignorant and immoral, that the people *need* to study and learn things that they *do not know* and that they *need to reform* their ordinary ways of behaving.

> The difficulty of ruling the people is commensurate to the amount of their knowledge. Therefore those who rule by giving knowledge are despoilers of the state. Those who rule without giving knowledge, are the state's good fortune.
>
> (*ibid.*)

Ironically, even moral education is bad according to the Taoists, because it tries to force on people something overly sophisticated and difficult that goes against their nature. In direct opposition to the Confucianists, Taoists even rejected the indoctrination of the traditional virtues of ren, yi, li, and so on.

> Banish wisdom, discard knowledge, and the people will be benefited a hundredfold. Banish human-heartedness (ren), discard righteousness (yi), and the people will be dutiful and compassionate. Banish skill, discard profit, and thieves and robbers will disappear.
>
> (*ibid.*)

If you have to *teach* morality, that is a sure sign that things have been allowed to seriously deteriorate. When things are running smoothly, the people know what to do and how to behave in a natural, spontaneous way—without thinking about it and without the need of books, and formal instruction. And just like children, people are happier this way, not feeling inadequate and unhappy because they are constantly being told how ignorant or sinful or uneducated or uncultivated they are.

It also is a mistake, the Taoists argue, to encourage the acquisition of expensive goods and, more generally, of acquiring a higher standard of living. This only makes people feel envious of their richer neighbors and thus they start plotting how to lie and steal and even kill to enrich themselves. The wise ruler will keep the people ignorant of fancy, expensive goods. If they never see such things, they will never want them and will never be tempted to stray from their simple, everyday lives to acquire things they cannot afford.

> If we cease to set store by products that are hard to get, there will be no more thieves. If the people never see such things as excite desire, their hearts will not be confused. Therefore the Sage rules the people by emptying their minds, filling their bellies, weakening their wills, and toughening their sinews, ever making the people without knowledge and without desire.
>
> He who is content suffers no humiliation; he who knows where to stop, cannot be harmed.
>
> There is no disaster greater than not knowing contentment with what one has: no greater sin than having desire for acquisition.
>
> (Laozi, *Tao De Jing*, 1990)

On the other hand, once the ruler has allowed these inflated desires and this unnecessary competition among the people, then the ruler must promulgate and enforce laws to prevent people from stealing and taking advantage of others. But the more laws are passed and enforced, the more people see the laws and the government as their enemy, and therefore the more they will try to break these laws and overthrow the government—requiring still more laws and even more severe punishments, always in a vicious downward spiral.

> The more restrictions and prohibitions there are in the world, the poorer the people will be. The more sharp weapons the people have, the more troubled will be the country. The more cunning craftsmen there are, the more pernicious contrivances will appear. The more laws are promulgated, the more thieves and bandits there will be.
>
> (Laozi, *Tao De Jing*, 1990)

In their social and political philosophy, the Taoists resemble Western anarchists, like the Russian Pierre Kropotkin (1842–1921), who argue that not only does the government have no right to enforce its laws on the people, but also that there is no need for governments to alter, redirect, or improve upon the well-established, time-honored customs of the ordinary people at the village level by the imposition of laws enforced by the military and the police. Anarchists do not long for a romantic return to the "state of nature" as described by the social contractarians, in which it is "every man for himself." Instead, like the Taoists, they are thinking of traditional social customs that have always regulated social activities at the local level—as opposed to governmental intervention by force of law at the national level.

In remote parts of Mexico, India, and Africa, even today, almost everything runs smoothly without any imposition from a national government passing laws in the capital hundreds of miles away—which simply makes very little difference in the daily lives of the people. Marriages are contracted, children are born, farms are maintained, festivals are held, funerals are performed, and local disputes settled—all without the assistance (or interference) of the national government. No one is needed to *enforce* the laws, since there *are* no laws—there is simply no need at this local level for formal law. Until recently, when communications have greatly improved, villagers in developing countries did not even know, much less care, when the national government had been ousted and a new one installed. Even in the United States, think about how much of the ordinary affairs of daily life are conducted without federal or state regulation. In many smaller U.S. towns there is not even a full-time police force, and yet the crime rate is far below that of the nearest large metropolitan area. As Kropotkin puts it, speaking of rural nineteenth-century Russia,

> As man does not live in a solitary state, habits and feelings develop within him which are useful for the preservation of society and the propagation of the race. Without social feelings and usages, life in common would have been absolutely impossible. It is not law which has established them; they are anterior to all law. . . . They are spontaneously developed by the very nature of things, like those habits in animals which men call instinct. They spring from a process of evolution, which is useful, and, indeed, necessary, to keep society together in the struggle it is forced to maintain for existence. . . .
>
> But side by side with these customs other desires, other passions, and therefore other habits and customs are evolved in human associations. The desire to dominate others and impose one's own will upon them; the desire to seize upon the products of the labor of a neighboring tribe; the desire to surround oneself with comforts, without producing anything, whilst slaves provide their master with the means of procuring every sort of pleasure and luxury—these selfish, personal desires give rise to another current of habits and customs. . . .
>
> But as society became more and more divided into two hostile classes, one seeking to establish domination, the other struggling to escape, the strife began. Now the conqueror was in a hurry to secure the results of his actions in a permanent form. . . . Law made its appearance under the sanction of the priest, and the

warrior's club was placed at its service. Its office was to render immutable such customs as were to the advantage of the dominant minority. Military authority undertook to ensure obedience. This new function was a fresh guarantee to the power of the warrior; now he had not only mere brute force at his service; he was the defender of law.

(Kropotkin, *Selected Writings on Anarchism and Revolution*, 1970)

As we saw earlier, in the feudal period there was no need for formally enacted laws and their enforcement by military and police branches of the government. People generally followed traditional practices simply out of habit and the force of long-standing custom. But as this feudal order began to break down, in India, China, and the West, a new system of social organization appeared, along with the need for a new way or ordering and controlling society. As military invaders conquer foreign states, they face the problem of how to impose their will on their hostile subjects. The new ruler certainly cannot expect the people to willingly, instinctively obey—and certainly not out of habit or custom. The new ruler has been their traditional enemy. Their ancient social unit, and all of its traditional customs, have been destroyed. Now the new rulers can only establish explicitly written laws and enforce them by the power of the military and the police.

With the rise of nation-states, which since the sixteenth century have absorbed many smaller feudal kingdoms, inevitably comes the rule of law enacted and enforced by national governments. This is even more true today than it was in Kropotkin's day. In the increasing globalization of the world, the anarchist picture of the traditional village operating on the basis of ancient custom, rather than law, appears more and more a romantic anachronism. In the modern world, events at the nation-state and international levels increasingly impact everyone at every tier, and it is difficult to see how villagers, however remote, can long remain aloof from and indifferent to events on the national and international scenes. And once they have begun to be affected, they naturally will have an interest in and therefore will want to have a say in how those national policies are decided and implemented. Full-blown anarchism is not taken seriously by anyone in the world today, although the call for *relatively less* government regulation of our lives is frequently heard (those who argue today, for example, that we do not need a legalized national education or health care program, since these issues are better decided by individuals at the local level).

The legalist (Fa Jia) theory was best expressed by Han Feizi at the end of the Warring States period (third century B.C.E.). The legalists did not think it was enough to just leave the people to their traditional customs, as the Taoists recommended, but they also thought transforming everyone into a moral agent, as the Confucianists proposed, was too much. Neither sort of advice really takes into account what the rulers themselves want. As Thrasymachus pointed out, actual rulers are generally not interested in being morally good, nor are they satisfied in just keeping the people quiet and docile. In fact, rulers usually have their own agendas—things that they want to accomplish—either to gain fame by conquering neighboring kingdoms or enriching themselves and their families (or both).

Since most of these early philosophers were trying to persuade the rulers of the time how best to govern, the legalists, or realists, as they are known in Western philosophy, thought it was better to advise these rulers about how to achieve what the rulers themselves wanted than it was to try to get them to accept the moralistic goals of the philosophers (who had no experience in ruling). The problem Plato and Confucius faced in training kings to be philosophers is that the kings did not *want* to be philosophers. (Imagine the sixteen- or seventeen-year-old Alexander sitting through Aristotle's lectures on moral and political philosophy, dreaming of the day when he would take over from his father, leading his armies on an adventurous conquest of what is now North Africa, Turkey, Iran, Afghanistan, and northern India.)

Legalists (political realists) therefore drop the more ambitious normative project of formulating the goals or ends that governments *ought* to strive for, opting instead for a more instrumental approach of how to achieve the goals or ends that the rulers already had (in most cases, as Thrasymachus saw, to increase, or at least maintain, their own power, wealth, and fame). Legalism, or political realism, therefore resembles ethical egoism, which we discussed briefly in chapter 5, which seeks to advise individuals about how to achieve the goals they already have, rather than normatively advising them about what goals they ought to seek—if you want to get ahead in your career, then you had better butter up the boss and do not help younger subordinants too much, and if you have to "cut a few corners" in the process, then by all means do so (but do not get caught). Think about political advisors today—are they advising the President about how to achieve normative goals, or on how to maintain and increase political power (and that of their party) without breaking the law (how often do we hear the excuse, whenever shady affairs have been exposed, that, strictly speaking, no laws were broken)?

To accomplish these political goals, the legalists advised the rulers to adopt a law and order administration supported by a strict system of rewards and punishments. Like their Western counterparts, the legalists were "realists," arguing that it was not necessary for the king to be a morally virtuous person or for the bulk of the population to practice moral behavior. All the king needed to do, the legalists maintained, was to decide what he wanted and then to ensure compliance by formulating very clear laws with absolutely certain rewards (for obeying these laws) and punishments (for disobeying them)—and the people would do whatever the king wanted. After all, he was the king, and did not have to follow someone else's moral principles—certainly not those of a philosophy teacher! Like Thrasymachus, the king could propose whatever he wanted and could call this "justice" and make others call it "justice" as well—however inherently unjust his proposals may in fact have been. And since he had the army to back him up, he could not be seriously challenged.

At first, this sort of political realism seems smart and sophisticated. But as we saw in examining Mengzi earlier, there do seem to be limits to the power of even the most absolute monarch. Without some measure of support from the common people, it may be difficult to get enough cooperation from the people to carry out whatever civic tasks the king desires. And with a great deal of civil unrest, his own position may be in jeopardy. Even the king may not have enough soldiers to police every action by the populace or to defend against a serious insurrection. And of course the soldiers themselves come from the populace and their loyalty is therefore always in doubt, especially when their wives, mothers, children, and friends are suffering at the hands of the ruler.

In the feudal period (2000–500 B.C.E.), social harmony was maintained by li (custom) as practiced and maintained by the aristocrats and by xing (punishments) applied to the ordinary people. In those days, people did not do the right thing from "the moral point of view," because they felt it was the morally right thing to do, but simply because this was the prescribed mode of behavior for anyone born into a particular class. As the feudal order broke up during the Warring States period at the end of the Zhou dynasty (700–200 B.C.E.), Confucianists attempted to convert the customary li of hereditary status into an inwardly felt and inner directed moral imperative for *everyone* (though initially only for an educated middle class). The Taoists advocated a near-anarchist "back to nature" simplification in which government does little and simply lets the people do their own thing—as they have traditionally done for centuries. The legalists, on the other hand, tried to extend the role of *punishment* (and rewards) more broadly to everyone—aristocrat, educated elite, and peasant.

Why should one do the "right" thing? In a primitive society, because it is unthinkable to do otherwise (taboo)—the heavens would fall, one would be struck down by lightening. In a feudal society, because one's position in the class into which one was born dictates such behavior (otherwise one dishonors oneself and one's class). In Kongzi's and Mengzi's vision of society, because it is the morally right thing to do and one wants to be a fully developed moral human being. In Taoism, because one wants to be natural. In the legalists' society, because one will be rewarded if one does and punished if one does not. The developmental psychologist Lawrence Kohlberg would regard Kongzi and Mengzi as being the most morally developed, that is, most adult, and the legalists as being the most immature, that is, least adult (although, as we pondered in the previous chapter, it is not clear that the legalists would be terribly crushed by this judgment).

Whereas the Confucianists tried to base good government on a moral basis (let the ruler set the proper moral example for the people who will willingly follow his example), the legalists tried to construct a foolproof pragmatic method that would enable the military strong man to rule effectively without the need for special knowledge or moral ability. The king does not need to justify his dictates to anyone, but, with sufficient power, his laws are as absolute and unshakable and unavoidable as the laws of nature.

> The intelligent ruler carries out his regulations as would Heaven, and handles men as if he were a divine being. Being like Heaven, he commits no wrong, and being like a divine being, he falls into no difficulties. His power (shih) enforces his strict orders, and nothing that he encounters resists him. . . . Only when this is so can his laws be carried out in concert.
>
> (Han Feizi, in Burton Watson, ed. & trans., *Basic Writings of Mo Tzu . . .*)

Most Chinese philosophers were conservatives, revering the past and urging a return to the "good old days," as Kongzi thought the Zhou dynasty had been. Han Feizi, on the other hand, was a legal and historical realist. Unlike other philosophers of the time, he argued that different historical epochs face different problems requiring different solutions and that the solutions of the past are not necessarily appropriate for the present. (Note that in ancient China before the unification in the third century B.C.E., people from Sung were always the butt of jokes showing how stupid and naive people could be.)

> There was once a man of Sung who tilled his field. In the midst of the field stood a stem of a tree, and one day a hare in full course rushed against that stem, broke its neck, and died. Thereupon the man left his plough and stood waiting at that tree in the hope that he would catch another hare. But he never caught another hare and was ridiculed by the people of Sung. If, however, you wish to rule the people of today by the methods of government of the early kings, you do exactly the same thing as the man who waited by the tree. . . . Therefore affairs go according to their time, and preparations are made in accordance with affairs.
>
> (*ibid.*)

In the new expansionistic military dictatorships following the end of the feudal period, a strict system of rewards and punishments for clearly formulated and promulgated laws is a much surer way of ensuring compliance than moral education. Even if we enact a system of universal moral education, how many people are actually going to become moral agents, always doing the right thing simply because it is the morally right thing to do?

> In his rule of a state, the sage ruler does not depend upon men doing good themselves, but brings it about that they can do no wrong. Within the frontiers of a state, there are no more than ten people who will do good of themselves; nevertheless, if one brings it about that the people can do no wrong, the entire state can be kept peaceful. He who rules a country makes use of the majority and neglects the few, and so does not concern himself with virtues, but with law.
>
> *(ibid.)*

The ruler also needs shu, the art of personnel management. He need not do the work himself but simply hold people to their "job description" (rectification of names)—"holding the actualities responsible for their names." As a strict pragmatist, the ruler is not concerned with methods to achieve results but only with the results. If the minister lives up to his job description, he is rewarded, or otherwise, punished. After a while, incompetents do not bother to apply.

Under the legalist system, even the philosophers must prove their worth to the ruler and be punished or rewarded according to how well they are able to help the ruler. Both Han Feizi and Li Ssu had studied under the Confucianist, Xunzi. But while Han Feizi was a native of the small state of Han, Li Ssu was a native of Chin and became a high-ranking minister under Ying Cheng, the ruler of the Chin state. When Ying Cheng finally conquered all of China in 221 B.C.E., and established himself as Chin Shih Huang Di, the first Emperor of all of China, Li Ssu became a very powerful person. When the Emperor heard of Han Feizi's fame as a political theorist and invited him to court as an advisor, Li Ssu became jealous and had Han Feizi executed on charges of spying for the defeated state of Han. Later, in 213 B.C.E. Li Ssu convinced the Emperor to burn all of the philosophy books except those of the legalists, and to kill all of the philosophers, including the Confucianists, who resisted (hopefully Xunzi was no longer alive to witness the fate of his student, Han Feizi, and other philosophers at the hands of another of his students, Li Ssu). Until the end of the Chin dynasty and the beginning of the Han dynasty in 206 B.C.E., power politics became the sole determination of the success of the rulers, as well as the philosophers who advised them.

In a sense, the legalist ruler follows the Taoist wu wei injunction, "doing nothing, yet there is nothing that is not done" (a good management principle). And all of this rests securely on the simple but basic foundation of human self-interest.

> In ruling the world, one must act in accordance with human nature. In human nature there are the feelings of liking and disliking, and hence rewards and punishments are effective. When rewards and punishments are effective, interdicts and commands can be established, and the way of government is complete.
>
> (*ibid.*)

Like his teacher Xunzi, Han Feizi thought human nature was evil; but unlike Xunzi, he did not want to change human nature through education and training but only to establish a workable system of government built on this evil human nature. Strangely like the Taoists, "don't fight the system; work with it."

> Just as the sun and moon shine forth, the four seasons progress, the clouds spread, and the wind blows, so does the ruler not encumber his mind with knowledge, or with overcoming selfishness. He relies for good government . . . on laws and methods (shu); leaves right and wrong to be dealt with through rewards and punishments; and refers lightness and heaviness to the balance of the scale.
>
> (*ibid.*)

That is, set up the system and then let the chips fall where they may. Even the Taoist, Zhuangzi, seems to agree with the legalist principles of management—"The superior must have no activity, so as thus to control events; but the subordinates must have activity, so as thus to be controlled by events. This is the invariable way" (Zhuangzi 1994). If someone applies for the position of tax collector, for example, he knows what his duties are. At the end of the year, the ruler sees what he has collected. If he is successful, the ruler rewards him; if not, the ruler punishes (and replaces) him. And of course it may not be his fault if he fails; there may be a period of drought and famine when it is simply impossible to collect the required tax revenue. Thus the tax collector is "controlled by events" (outside of his control), and, whether fair or unfair, like the good football coach of a losing team, he will lose his job—if not his head. Eventually, one way or another, the job gets done and yet the rulers have done nothing (except to employ the right management principles). If there are problems, the tax collector takes the heat—not the ruler who stands aloof, and even, like President Clinton, can take the side of the people against the Internal Revenue Service.

In another way, however, the legalists were the complete opposite of the Taoists. The Taoists held that human beings were completely innocent; the legalists that they were completely evil. The Taoists upheld individual freedom; the legalists absolute social control. The Taoists regarded the legalists as shallow pragmatists—they knew that certain methods worked, but they had no idea *why* they worked. As Zhuangzi said,

They do not know the fundamentals that underlie them. They speak about rewards and punishments, but do not know their beginning. . . . They know the implements of government, but not its principles. Such a one can be employed by the world, but is not sufficient to employ the world. He is a one-sided man and only knows how to talk.

(Zhuangzi 1994)

So, in a way, the Taoists agree with Kongzi and Mengzi (and Plato), that the ruler needs to have fundamental knowledge of the essentials of reality (especially of human nature).

Like the Confucianists, the legalists developed a social and moral philosophy in tune with the breakdown of feudal class distinctions. But the Confucianists were really much more revolutionary and idealistic—they thought they could transform human nature through moral education by developing throughout the population an inner sense of right and wrong, while the legalists were more realistic and pragmatic, developing methods for controlling people with the evil natures they have and are likely to continue to have. A similar contrast can be drawn between the realistic (perhaps even pessimistic) expectations of the capitalists, that human nature will always be selfish, greedy, and self-seeking, and the idealistic hope of the Marxists, that human nature can be transformed from selfish to altruistic, and self-seeking to socially cooperative. The collapse of communism in the former Soviet Union and eastern Europe would seem to signal a victory for the more pessimistic realists!

Western philosophers thought through the same dilemma as the Chinese, whether the ruler should be virtuous or merely strong. Like Han Feizi, Niccolò Machiavelli (Italian, 1469–1527) rejected the dominant thinking of his time, that, like the Confucianists, the ruler should be wise and virtuous and rule wisely and virtuously. Instead, Machiavelli held that the ruler should do whatever is necessary to preserve the state and to keep himself in power. Sometimes that would require him to be tolerant, liberal, and generous, but at other times it would require him to be harsh and unbending. Like Mengzi, he recognized the dangers of always being too harsh, for then the ruler ran the risk of being hated and thereby of being overthrown. But he also recognized the opposite risk, of appearing too soft and generous and therefore weak and thereby equally in danger of being overthrown by jealous rivals.

In general, then, we can say that Machiavelli was simply not concerned with the morality of political leaders, but only with what "works for them" pragmatically. Even where a ruler acts virtuously, he should not do this *because* it is virtuous but simply because, in that situation, that is what works. Where a ruler must lie or cheat or severely punish insurrection, he does not do so *because* he is wicked or immoral or enjoys playing the "bad guy," but, just as in the previous case, simply because this is what is called for in this particular situation. In certain situations, doing what will be perceived as "good" will rally the people around the ruler and give him and the state strength, but in other situations, the ruler must do what he can to make the people fear him and unquestioningly obey him. Think of how Machiavelli would advise American government leaders today: When should they stress environmental concerns, and when should they support big business against the "green" movement? When should they support and when should they bash gays and a gay lifestyle?

Machiavelli therefore encouraged neither virtue nor cruelty on the part of the ruler, but realism and pragmatism. His advice to the ruler was, "Do what you have to do to stay in power and keep your country from being overrun by a neighboring country—whether you are thereby perceived as a 'good' or a 'bad' ruler—just do whatever it takes." How much do you think things have changed since the days of Han Feizi (third century B.C.E.) and Machiavelli (fifteenth and sixteenth centuries)? On the one hand, we say it is wrong for our elected officials to lie or break the law (and they always run on the promise of a "squeaky clean administration"), but on the other hand, we do not seem terribly surprised or even disappointed when we learn that they routinely engage in these immoral and often illegal activities. Perhaps we have all become legalists and political realists.

Although Mengzi (Mencius) believed that the only legitimate role of government was to help the ordinary people, like Plato, he did not believe in democracy. Like Plato (in *The Republic*) Mengzi held that each person should specialize in the work for which he is particularly suited by nature; intelligent people should rule the country and those skilled in farming, pottery, and so on should engage in these activities and not take on the job of ruler.

Chen Xiang saw Mencius and cited the words of Xu Xing [i.e., Xuzi, who said] . . . to earn his keep a good and wise ruler shares the work of tilling the land with his people. He rules while cooking his own meals. . . .

"Does Xuzi wear a cap?"

"Yes." . . .

"Does he weave it himself?"

"No. He trades grain for it."

"Why? . . ."

"Because it interferes with his work in the fields."

"Does Xuzi make [his own iron and ceramic wares]?"

"No. He trades grain for them."

"To trade grain for implements is not to inflict hardship on the potter and the blacksmith. [They] also trade their wares for grain. In doing this, surely they are not inflicting hardship on the farmer either. Why does Xuzi not be a potter and a blacksmith as well so that he can get everything he needs from his own house? . . .

"It is naturally impossible to combine the work of tilling the land with that of a hundred different crafts."

"Now, is ruling the Empire such an exception that it can be combined with the work of tilling the land? There are affairs of great men, and there are affairs of small men. . . . Hence it is said, 'There are those who use their minds and there are those who use their muscles. The former rule; the latter are ruled. Those who rule are supported by those who are ruled.' "

(Mengzi, *Mengzi*, in Chan, *Sourcebook Chinese*)

As we can see from Mengzi and Hobbes, it is a great mistake to think that all Western philosophers support democratic forms of government and that all non-Western philosophers support totalitarian dictatorships. Plato is another example of a Western philosopher who was much opposed to democracy. The Greeks of Plato's day were familiar with many different forms of government, including both democracy and dictatorships, but also aristocracy, which Plato favored. An aristocracy is the rule by a select few people, selected either on the basis of a noble family background, which Plato rejected, or on the basis of natural superiority of qualifications, which Plato, like Mengzi in the earlier passage, approved.

Of course, this means that Plato, as well as his student Aristotle, completely rejected the modern notion of political equality. For Hobbes and Locke, people are more or less alike, or at least sufficiently similar as far as their ability to make political decisions is concerned. Not only did these modern social contractarians think that everyone ought to be "equal before the law" (that the law should treat each person like every other, with no favoritism), and not only that every human being was equally deserving of respect, as Kant held, but more controversially, that people were in fact sufficiently alike in intelligence and ability to make good political decisions—so that everyone is equally qualified to contribute their one-person, one-vote input in the democratic decision-making process. To this, ancient Greek and Chinese philosophers were adamantly opposed—people are different; some are qualified to make good political decisions because of superior intelligence, while others are not—the first should rule and the second should be ruled. (In the early decades of the United States who was considered fit to vote? Neither slaves, nor children, nor women, but neither were poor white adult male citizens eligible—only free white adult males of sufficient wealth were allowed to participate in the rights and privileges of government.)

Plato despised democracy because to him it indicated mob rule, the sort of ignorant irrationality that condemned Socrates to death. The rulers of the state should be those few people who really know how to govern, Plato thought, those who have studied and know what is really good and just (the Forms of Good and Justice) and how to apply that knowledge in constructing a good and just state. Indeed, according to Plato, like Mengzi, ideally only philosophers should rule—either the rulers should become philosophers, or the philosophers should become rulers. Like Kongzi (Confucius), Mengzi (Mencius), and Aristotle, Plato actually tried to train a young ruler, Dionysius of Syracuse. Needless to say, all four philosophers failed miserably!

For Plato, the ideal government is therefore rule by the best, those who know the most and care the most for ruling the state well, and that means rule by the most intelligent and rational and knowledgeable persons in the state. The ideal state is therefore one in which each class of persons does its own thing, that is, performing that role for which nature has best suited it. Earlier we discussed Plato's view of the three parts of the soul—reason, desire, and will. In Plato's outline of the ideal state in *The Republic*, Plato analyzes the functions of the state into three parallel parts: the legislative branch of government (parallel to reason in the soul), the executive branch of government (parallel to will in the soul), and everyone else, mainly the business class (parallel to desire in the soul). And just as the good individual and the good life is one in which will assists reason in the control of desire, so the good state is one in which the military assists the wise in ruling the ordinary people. This means that each part should do that for which it is best suited and not attempt to usurp the roles best suited to other parts, in particular, will should not assist desire in overturning reason, and the military should not assist the business community in overthrowing the philosopher-king.

And this leads to Plato's final definition of justice, the main task of *The Republic.* Plato's strategy in defining justice is first to describe an ideal state, that is, an imaginary state perfect in every conceivable way, on the assumption that such a state will display the traditional Greek virtues of wisdom, courage, temperance, and justice—that is, on the assumption that a perfect state will be wise, courageous, temperate, and just. Once we have described the ideal state, Plato argues, all we have to do is locate that part of the state where wisdom resides and we will have succeeded in correctly defining wisdom—and so for courage, temperance, and justice.

After locating wisdom (in the philosophers-rulers) and courage (in the military "guardians"), Plato argues that temperance and justice are to be found, not in any one part of the state, but in the relationship of the parts to one another. Temperance, then, is the willingness of the ordinary people to be ruled by the most intelligent and knowledgeable people in the state. And justice is the more general principle of "to each his own," that is, the principle of each thing performing its own proper function and not usurping the role best suited to others.

> I take it that our state, having been founded and built up on the right lines, is good in the complete sense of the word. . . . Obviously, then, it is wise, brave, temperate, and just. . . . Then if we find some of these qualities in it, the remainder will be the one we have not found. . . . To begin then: the first quality to come into view in our

state seems to be its wisdom, . . . and where does it reside? It is precisely that art of guardianship which resides in the rulers. . . . If a state is constituted on natural principles, the wisdom it possesses as a whole will be due to the knowledge residing in the smallest part, the one which takes the lead and governs the rest. . . . Next there is courage. It is not hard to discern that quality of the part of the community in which it resides so as to entitle the whole to be called brave. . . . Because anyone who speaks of a state as either brave or cowardly can only be thinking of that part of it which takes the field and fights in its defense. . . . Two qualities still remain to be made out in our state, temperance and the object of our whole inquiry, justice. . . . Take temperance first. . . . At first sight, temperance seems to be more like some sort of concord or harmony than the other qualities did. . . . Temperance surely means a kind of orderliness, a control of certain pleasures and appetites. . . . Temperance is not like courage and wisdom, which made the state wise and brave by residing each in one particular part. . . . Temperance works in a different way; it extends throughout the whole gamut of the state. . . . Temperance is the harmonious agreement between the naturally superior and inferior elements on the question which of the two should govern, whether in the state or in the individual. . . . The remaining one is justice. . . . We have been talking about [justice] all this while without ever understanding that we were giving some sort of account of it. . . . You remember how we have laid down, as a universal principle, that everyone ought to perform the one function in the community for which his nature best suited him. Well, that principle is justice. . . . When each class, tradespeople, military, guardians, keeps to its own proper business in the state and does its own work, that is justice and what makes a just society.

(Plato 1945)

The twentieth-century philosopher Karl Popper, in his book *The Open Society and Its Enemies,* rejected Plato's communitarian emphasis on what the individual can do to strengthen the state in favor of the modern liberal notion, which stresses the role of government in protecting the rights and freedoms of the individual. This liberal-communitarian debate continues into the twenty-first century, between those who champion the rights of the individual to be free from governmental restraint and those who stress the need for social cohesion and the obligations that the individual owes to the state—especially when it comes to the question of a fair and just distribution of the nation's wealth. Which is more important, the freedom of the individual to accumulate as much wealth as he or she can, even if this means that the poor get poorer, even as the rich get richer, or, on the other hand, a more equal distribution of the world's wealth, even if this means taking from the rich (through taxation, against their will) and giving to the poor, so that all have a more or less equal share of education, health, housing, food, clothing, and so on. And if both are important, how should the two be combined? That is the leading question of the twenty-first century. Think of the most difficult problems facing the United States today—universal health care, homelessness, inner-city slums, rotten public schools—how can these problems be solved without giving up the right of the better educated and more affluent to keep more of what they earn? Consider your own case—how much income tax (40 percent? 50 percent? 60 percent?) are you prepared to pay to support a more equitable distribution of the nation's wealth as you join (upon graduation) the relatively affluent upper middle class?

Fifteen years ago, this was the major "cold war" debate between the free market, capitalist Western democracies and the centralized, communist system of the Soviet Union, and its allies. But since the collapse of the Soviet Union this debate continues *within* every country of the world. The main problem today is how to more evenly divide up the nation's wealth among all of its citizens, without sacrificing the individual rights and liberties of those who have managed to legally acquire more of this wealth. Is it fair or just for some to have so much and others to have so little? But, on the other hand, is it fair to take away from those who have acquired more wealth honestly through superior intelligence, hard work, and talent, and, against their will, to give it to those who are inferior in these natural assets? Those on the libertarian Right argue for a distribution of the nation's wealth according to merit, talent, and aptitude; those on the liberal, egalitarian Left argue for a more equal distribution.

The most important work in social philosophy in the last fifty years is John Rawls's *A Theory of Justice*, published in 1971. Its importance lies precisely in Rawls's attempt to reconcile these libertarian and egalitarian ideals. In Rawls's theory, individual liberty is compatible with a more equitable distribution of wealth. How? Rawls's theory is based on a revival of the traditional idea of the social contract, although he uses the theoretical device of an imaginary contract, not to reconstruct the origin of the state, but as a way of deciding on the best system of social justice. In Rawls's renewed social contract, he asks us to imagine a group of individuals who are free, equal, and without bias, who must decide by unanimous consent which system of justice they and their families will henceforth live under. The system they choose, Rawls argues, will be the fairest. Why? Because they have made their decision in the most unbiased, impartial, and hence, fair, manner. (The child who cuts the pastry in two, knowing that his sister will get to choose the first piece, is forced to act in an unbiased, impartial manner—and so, greedy little punk that he is, cuts the pastry into two absolutely equal pieces.)

The parties in what Rawls calls the "original position" are by hypothesis rational, of average intelligence, and to ensure that they do not vote in a purely self-interested way, Rawls specifies that they must operate under a "veil of ignorance" that prevents them from knowing who or what they will be under the newly instituted system of justice. If you are confident you have "the right stuff," that is, the talents that your society needs and therefore rewards, you might be tempted to vote for a libertarian system of justice at the expense of egalitarianism. That is, you would probably vote for a system

of justice that specified that, given equal opportunity for training and education, without regard for race, gender, or national origin, each person would
be free to acquire as much wealth as they legally could and would have the
right to keep that wealth, even though others wound up with far less. If, on
the other hand, you know you are unemployable except for low-paying,
menial jobs, you will be tempted to vote for an egalitarian system of justice in
which everyone works as hard as they can at what they do best and yet all are
paid the same. But what would you choose, and how would you vote, Rawls
asks, if you did not know where you would wind up in the new society? If you
did not know, then you could not vote in a biased, self-interested way, and if
(like the first child in our earlier pastry-cutting example) you are thereby
forced to decide in an impartial manner, then, Rawls argues, would your decision not be the fairest and most just?

Rawls argues that the participants in the original position would choose
two principles of justice, the first supporting the traditional libertarian notion
of equal liberty for all, the second limiting inequalities of wealth to those
cases that actually benefit everyone, especially the least well off in the society.

1. Each person is to have an equal right to the most extensive total system of
    equal basic liberties compatible with a similar system of liberty for all.
2. Social and economic inequalities are to be arranged so that they are both:

    (a) to the greatest benefit of the least advantaged, consistent with the just
         savings principle, and
    (b) attached to offices and positions open to all under conditions of fair
         equality of opportunity.

(Rawls 1971)

Principles 1 and 2-b support the libertarian ideal of freedom and individual
rights, but principle 2-a sides with the liberal, egalitarian ideal, thus reconciling the frustrating and bitter dilemma that nations face in the libertarian-
egalitarian debate. Rawls agrees that we could legitimately pay medical
doctors more than most people because that is the best and maybe the only
way to ensure that we have a pool of qualified doctors—and that is certainly
to everyone's advantage. But, using Rawls's principles, would we have to pay
doctors as much as we do today? What about news broadcasters, or sports or
entertainment personalities? It is in everyone's interest to have good new
broadcasters, sports and entertainment stars, but how much more would we
have to pay them in order to have good quality sports, music, movies, and so
on? Probably not nearly as much as the average they are paid today. On the
other hand, we might have to pay school teachers and child care providers
more than we do today to get enough qualified people to do well what is obviously in the interests of the nation as whole.

Bibliography

ARISTOTLE. *Introduction to Aristotle*. Edited by Richard McKeon. New York: Modern Library, 1992.

CAMUS, ALBERT. *Myth of Sisyphus and Other Essays*. Translated by J. O'Brien. New York: Random House, 1991.

CANDRAKIRTI. *Reasoning into Reality,* trans. Christian Lindtner. Oakland: Dharma Publishing, 1987.

CHAN, WING-TSIT, ed. *A Source Book in Chinese Philosophy*. Princeton: Princeton University Press, 1963.

CHUANG TZU. (See Zhuangzi.)

DE BARY, WILLIAM THEODORE, ed. *The Buddhist Tradition in India, China, and Japan*. New York: Vintage Books, 1972.

DESCARTES, RENE. *Meditations on First Philosophy*. Translated by Donald A. Cress. Indianapolis: Hackett Publications, 1979.

EMBREE, AINSLIE T., ed. *Sources of Indian Tradition*. Vol. 1, 2d ed. New York: Columbia University Press, 1988.

EPICURUS. *Epicurus: The Extant Remains,* trans. Cyril Bailey. Oxford: Oxford University Press, 1926.

FIELD, GUY C. *Plato and His Contemporaries,* in *Studies in Philosophy*. New York: M. S. G. Haskell House, 1974.

FLOOD, GAVIN. *An Introduction to Hinduism*. Cambridge: Cambridge University Press, 1996.

FUNG, YULAN. *A History of Chinese Philosophy*. 2 volumes. Translated by Derk Bodde. Princeton: Princeton University Press, 1953.

———. *A Short History of Chinese Philosophy*. New York: Free Press, 1966.

GYEKYE, KWAME. *Tradition and Modernity: Philosophical Reflections on the African Experience.* Oxford: Oxford University Press, 1997.

JAMES, WILLIAM. *Pragmatism.* Cambridge, Mass.: Harvard University Press, 1975.

HOBBES, THOMAS. *The Leviathan.* Oxford: Clarendon Press, 1967.

HUME, DAVID. *An Enquiry Concerning Human Understanding.* Edited by Eric Steinberg. Indianapolis: Hackett Publications, 1977.

KANT, IMMANUEL. *Critique of Pure Reason,* trans. Norman Kemp Smith. New York: St. Martin's Press, 1933.

———. *Prolegomenon to Any Future Metaphysics.* Translated by Paul Carus. Edited by J. W. Ellington. Indianapolis: Hackett Publications, 1977.

KOLLER, JOHN M. *The Indian Way.* New York: Macmillan Publishing Company, 1982.

KOLLER, JOHN M., and PATRICIA KOLLER, eds. *A Sourcebook in Asian Philosophy.* New York: Macmillan Publishing Company, 1991.

KROPOTKIN, PIERRE. *Selected Writings on Anarchism and Revolution,* trans. Martin A. Miller. Cambridge, Mass.: M.I.T. Press, 1970.

LAOZI [LAO TZU]. *Tao Te Ching [Dao De Jing].* Translated by Victor H. Mair. New York: Bantam Books, 1990.

LOCKE, JOHN. *An Essay Concerning Human Understanding.* New York: NAL-Dutton, 1989.

———. *Two Treatises of Government.* Riverside, N.J.: Hafner Publications, 1970.

MASOLO, D. A. *African Philosophy in Search of Identity.* Bloomington: Indiana and Edinburgh University Presses, 1994.

NAGARJUNA. *Seventy Stanzas: A Buddhist Psychology of Emptiness.* Edited by David Ross Komito. Ithaca, N.Y.: Snow Lion Publications, 1987.

PERLEBERG, MAX. *The Works of Kung-Sun Lung-Tzu.* Westport, Conn.: Hyperion Press, 1990.

PLATO. *Phaedrus.* Indianapolis: The Library of Liberal Arts, 1956.

———. *The Republic of Plato.* Translated and edited by Francis M. Cornford. London: Oxford University Press, 1945.

RADHAKRISHNAN, SARVEPALLI. *Indian Philosophy.* 2 volumes. Oxford: Oxford University Press, 1923.

RADHAKRISHNAN, SARVEPALLI, and CHARLES A. MOORE, eds. *A Sourcebook of Indian Philosophy.* Princeton: Princeton University Press, 1957.

RAMANUJA. *Brahma Sutra with Bhasya of Ramanuja,* trans. and ed. Swamis Vireswarananda and Adidevananda. Calcutta: Advaita Ashrama, 1986.

RAWLS, JOHN. *A Theory of Justice.* Cambridge, Mass.: Belknap Press, 1971.

SARTRE, JEAN-PAUL. "Existentialism and Humanism," in *Studies in Philosophy.* New York: M. S. G. Haskell House, 1977.

———. *Nausea.* Translated by Lloyd Alexander. New York: New Directions, 1959.

STCHERBATSKY, F. T. *Buddhist Logic.* New York: Dover, 1962.

WATSON, BURTON, ed. and trans. *Basic Writings of Mo Tzu, Hsun Tzu, and Han Fei Tzu [Mozi, Xunzi, and Hanfeizi].* New York: Columbia University Press, 1963.

WINDEBAND, WILHELM. *History of Ancient Philosophy,* trans. Herbert E. Cushman. New York: Dover Publications, 1956.

WRIGHT, RICHARD A. (ed.), *African Philosophy.* Lanham, Maryland: University Press of America, 1984.

ZHUANGZI. *Wandering on the Way: Early Taoist Tales and Parables of Chuang Tzu [Zhuangzi].* Edited and translated by Victor H. Mair. New York: Bantam Books, 1994.

Glossary

Note: There is no recognized Romanized spelling for Chinese names; most scholars today prefer the Pinyin system used in Mainland China, though the older Wade-Giles is also widely used. Here we present first the Pinyin, which we also use in the body of the text, indicating the Wade-Giles spelling in parentheses. And for students' convenience, I have omitted special diacritical markings that are often used for Indian names spelled in the Roman alphabet.

advaita   Literally, nondual, the vedanta theory of Shankara that everything is a manifestation of the one reality, Brahman.

Analects (Lun Yu)   English translation of the sayings of Confucius (Kongzi), collected probably by the students of his students, and most likely the only writings actually from Confucius.

a posteriori   Knowledge gained through sense experience.

a priori   Knowledge gained independently of sense experience.

Aristotle (384–322 B.C.E.)   Greek philosopher, studied in Plato's Academy, later established his own school, the Lyceum. Accepted Plato's idea of universals, but denied Plato's theory of their independent existence apart from physical objects.

atman   Hindu term for the ultimate Self (distinct from the empirical self, the jiva, known to everyday experience), identified in the Vedanta tradition with Brahman, the ultimate reality.

Ayer, A. J. (1910–1989)   English logical positivist.

Berkeley, George (1685–1753)   Irish idealist philosopher who argued that only mind and its ideas are real.

Bhagavad Gita ("Song of the Lord")   Part of the long epic poem, the *Mahabharata*, combining Hindu theism with the Vedanta tradition (atman is Brahman, the ultimate, impersonal, underlying reality).

bhakti   A form of popular Hinduism in which religious experience is expressed as enthusiastic devotion to a particular deity.

Brahma   An Indian deity.

Brahman   Refers both to the ultimate reality (sometimes conceived personally, like a god, and sometimes impersonally, like a metaphysical principle) and also to the highest caste in India, originally a caste of priests.

Brahman Sutra   A late Upanishad attributed to Badarayana (second century B.C.E.), forming, through the commentaries of later scholars, such as Shankara and Ramanuja, the main classical text of Vedanta.

Buddha   Literally any enlightened being, but traditionally the honorific title for the founder of Buddhism, Shakyamuni Siddhartha Gautama (sixth century B.C.E.).

Buddhism   The world religion founded by Shakyamuni Siddhartha Gautama, spreading northeastward into Tibet, China, Korea, and Japan and southeastward into Sri Lanka, Burma, and Thailand. Philosophically important as the initial stimulus to a thorough philosophical critique of traditional Indian culture and thereby the origins of Indian philosophy.

Candrakirti   Buddhist philosopher.

Carvaca   Indian philosophical system of materialism, radical empiricism, atheism, and hedonism.

categorical imperative   Kant's highest ethical principle of moral universalizability, that one should not do what one would not want others to do.

Chan   Short for Chan-na, the Chinese transliteration (to sound like) the Indian term *dhyana*, meaning "meditation," known in the West by its Japanese pronunciation, Zen, a Chinese form of Mahayana Buddhism, borrowing from Madhyamika and Yogacara forms of late Indian Buddhism and Chinese Taoism.

Chi Tsang (sixth–seventh century C.E.)   Chinese San Lun (Madhyamika) Buddhist philosopher whose "double truth" doctrine (er ti) distinguished truth in the absolute sense from truth in the relative, everyday sense.

communitarianism   Social and political doctrine that a person's identity is tied to the group; the opposite of libertarianism.

Confucianism   Chinese philosophical and occasionally religious tradition based on the teachings of Confucius (Kongzi) and his followers, mainly Mencius (Mengzi), Zhu Xi, and Wang Yangming.

Confucius (551–479 B.C.E.)   The Latinized name given Kongzi, China's first and best-known philosopher, by Jesuit missionaries in 1687.

cultural relativism   The skeptical position concerning philosophical ethics, that there are no universal, objective moral standards, but that moral standards vary from culture to culture, such that what is morally right in one society may be morally wrong in another.

darshana   Indian term, usually translated "philosophy."

Da Xue (Great Learning)   One of the "Four Books" of Confucianism, though written long before Confucius (Kongzi), as determined by Zhu Xi and others in the Song dynasty (960–1279).

deconstruction   Late twentieth-century French literary theory (Jacques Derrida) rejecting or playing down the referential and representational function of language.

dependent origination   Indian doctrine, especially in Buddhism, denying any permanent substance, whether material or mental, and affirming instead that all existence is a state of constant process, flux, and change.

Derrida, Jacques (1930–)   French philosopher, founder of deconstruction.

dharma   Indian term meaning law, but also principle and truth.

Dharmakirti   Buddhist philosopher.

dharmas   Buddhist term for the ultimate things in the world.

dhyana   Indian term meaning meditation; later in Chinese (Chan-Na, or Chan) and Japanese (Zen) the word referred to a distinctive kind of Buddhism.

Dong Zhongshu (Tung Chung-shu, 179–104 B.C.E.)   Han dynasty Chinese Confucianist who synthesized the doctrines of Mengzi and Xunzi, arguing that human nature is a combination of good and bad elements. In 136 B.C.E., persuaded Han Emperor Wu Di to adopt Confucianism as the state ideology.

dualism   Metaphysical doctrine that there are two basic realities, mind and matter, in Indian Samkhya, prakriti and purusha.

egalitarianism   Social and political doctrine that everyone deserves an equal share of the social goods (which should therefore be divided equally among everyone).

empiricism   Epistemological doctrine that all reliable knowledge comes from the five senses (along with an internal intuitive sense).

Epicurus (341–270 B.C.E.)   Greek materialist, hedonist philosopher.

epistemology   Philosophical theory of knowledge; attempts to answer: What is knowledge and how does that differ from mere belief? What can we know, and what are the sources of reliable knowledge?

ethics   Moral philosophy, attempts to answer the question: Are there universal, objective standards of right and wrong, good and bad, and if so, what are they?

existentialism   Twentieth-century doctrine (Sartre) that the individual features of individual entities cannot be rationally reduced to universal essences and that the individual becomes whatever he or she is through his or her own actions (not through heredity or social conditioning).

Fung, Yulan (1895–199?)   Most important twentieth-century Chinese philosopher; introduced Chinese philosophy to a Western audience.

Gaozi (Kao Tzu)   Fourth-century B.C.E. Chinese philosopher whose writings are lost but who is extensively quoted in Mengzi as being an antagonist of Mengzi, arguing against Mengzi that there is any human nature.

Gong-Sun Lung   Early Chinese ming jia (school of names) philosopher who argued for the immutability of concepts such as hardness and whiteness ("The white horse is not a horse").

Gorgias (483–376 B.C.E.)   Greek skeptic who held that nothing could be known, and even if something were known, it could not be communicated.

gunas   Indian term, especially in Samkhya metaphysics, for the three strands of which everything (Prakriti) is composed, sattva, rajas, and tamas.

Gyges   Shepherd of ancient Greek folklore who found a magical ring and used it to seduce the queen, kill the king, and become king himself, discussed in Plato's *The Republic* to raise the question of why we should do the morally right thing if there is everything to gain by doing the morally wrong thing and no danger of getting caught.

Han dynasty (206 B.C.E.–220 C.E.)   The first great imperial Chinese dynasty, following the short-lived Qin dynasty (221–206 B.C.E.) that united all of China. During the Han dynasty, Confucianism was established (by Dong Zhongshu) as the leading, officially sanctioned state philosophy.

Han Feizi (Han Fei Tzu, 280–233 B.C.E.)   Student of Xunzi and founder of legalist philosophy (Fa Jia), killed by his student Li Ssu, who advised the king of Qin, later China's first imperial ruler, Shih Huang Di, to end disputes and to unify the country by burning all philosophy books (231 B.C.E.).

hedonism   Ethical doctrine that the only good is pleasure.

Heraclitus   Early Greek philosopher (sixth to fifth century B.C.E.) who denied anything permanent or substantial ("You can't step in the same river twice").

Hinduism   Considered today the religion of the majority of Indians, it is the name of a related group of religious traditions on the Indian subcontinent, evolving over 5,000 years into many different religious practices.

Hobbes, Thomas (1588–1679)   English materialist philosopher who held that human nature is selfish and aggressive, leading to social anarchy without the social contract.

Hu Shih   Early twentieth-century philosopher who studied with the American philosopher John Dewey, and who was the first (in 1919) to use the Chinese word for philosophy (zhe xue) to refer to Chinese writing.

Hui Shih   Early Chinese (fourth century B.C.E.) ming jia philosopher and friend of the Taoist Zhuangzi, who held that everything is constantly changing and relative.

human rights   Those entitlements that all human beings are said to be born with and have simply by virtue of being human beings; in the earlier eighteenth-century version, these included only individual rights and personal freedoms, but in the later nineteenth-century version was expanded to also include egalitarian rights to social goods and services.

Hume, David (1711–1776)   Eighteenth-century Scottish empiricist philosopher who denied any rational basis for the belief in causality or the belief in an underlying material or mental substance.

idealism   Metaphysical doctrine that only mind and its ideas are real, while matter is only an appearance.

Jain (pronounced "jine")   An Indian religion that began just before Buddhism in the sixth century B.C.E., like Buddhism in rejecting all theism, but unlike Buddhism in holding a pluralist conception of the universe consisting of many material and spiritual atoms, or jiva, in which salvation is the escape of the spiritual jiva from their entrapment in matter.

jiva   Indian term for self or soul or conscious mind; it is the "empirical self," the self each of us is aware of in everyday experience—not the ultimate, real Self, the atman, of which most of us are not aware.

Kant, Immanuel (1724–1804)   German philosopher who synthesized empiricism and rationalism and developed ethics of duty (categorical imperative).

karma   Indian doctrine that all action produces consequences for the agent in this life and the next (reincarnation).

Kongzi (Kung Tzu, Confucius, 551–479 B.C.E.)   Sixth century B.C.E., China's first philosopher and first teacher of classical learning.

Kropotkin, Pierre   Nineteenth-century Russian anarchist.

Laozi (Lao Tzu)   Fourth to third century B.C.E. legendary founder of Taoism (pinyin, Daoism), supposed author of *Dao De Jing* (*Tao Te Ching*), *Classic of the Way and Virtue.*

Legalism (fa jia, third century B.C.E.)   School of philosophy founded by Han Feizi that denied the Confucian idea that broad-based moral education was necessary to good government, in favor of a system of clear and certain legal rewards and punishments for whatever policies the government desires.

Leibniz, Gottfried Wilhelm (1646–1716)   German philosopher who developed substance philosophy to pluralist extreme, that the universe consists of many distinct individual substances (monads) which are nonetheless completely independent of one another.

li   Traditional Chinese virtue of propriety.

Li, Ssu   Third-century Chinese legalist student of Xunzi; advisor to Chin Shih Huang Di, China's first emperor, responsible for the death of Han Feizi and the famous book burning of 213 B.C.E..

libertarianism   The social and political doctrine of the personal rights and freedoms of the individual; the opposite of communitarianism, that social goods should be divided according to individual merit and contribution, that each person deserves what he or she earns.

Locke, John (1632–1704)   English philosopher, founder of British empiricism, liberal social political philosophy.

logic   Branch of philosophy concerned with standards for correct reasoning.

logical positivism (see **Ayer, A. J.**)   The view that a meaningful statement must be either verifiable (or falsifiable) by sense experience or logically true by definition (all bachelors are unmarried, tomorrow it will either rain or not rain).

Lucretius (96–55 B.C.E.)   Roman follower of the Greek hedonist and materialist philosopher Epicurus.

Madhva (1197–1276)   Theistic interpretation of Vedanta, in which God is distinct from individual selves and physical objects.

Madhyamika   Literally, the "middle way" between being and nonbeing, it is one of two important Mahayana schools of Buddhism (the other being Yogacara), founded by Nagarjuna and based on the doctrine that reality is empty (sunyata) of substantial (independent, permanent, self-subsistent) entities.

Mahayana   Literally, the "larger wheel," the name of one of two major groups of Buddhism (the other being Hinayana), which adopted the Boddhisatva ideal (one who delays entering Nirvana until all sentient creatures are enlightened), spreading northeastwardly into Tibet, China, Korea, Vietnam, and Japan.

materialism   Metaphysical doctrine that only matter is real, while mind is only an appearance.

Mencius   (see **Mengzi**)

Mengzi (Meng Tzu, Mencius, 371–289 B.C.E.)   Fourth century B.C.E., one of the leading interpreters of Kongzi (Confucius), arguing that there is a human nature and that it is basically good. All people are born with the "beginnings" or "sproutings" of the classical Chinese virtues (human heartedness, propriety, righteousness, and learning). In the Song dynasty (approximately 1000 C.E.), declared the major interpreter of Kongzi (Confucius) and his book (and that of his followers), *The Mengzi*, included as one of the "Four Books" of Confucian classics (along with the *Analects* (*Lun Yu*), *The Doctrine of the Mean* (*Zhong Yung*) and *The Great Learning* (*Da Xue*)).

metaphysics   Philosophical theory of reality; attempts to answer the question: What is reality, and how does it differ from mere appearance?

middle way   Buddhist ideal, originally of the balance between indulgence and asceticism and later (with Nagarjuna) between being and nonbeing.

Mill, John Stuart (1806–1873)   English utilitarian.

ming jia ("school of names," fifth to fourth centuries B.C.E.)   Early school of Chinese logic, including Hui Shih and Gong-Sun Lung.

Mohists   (see **Mozi**)

Mozi (Mo Tzu, Mo Ti, 479–381 B.C.E.)   China's second philosopher (after Kongzi, Confucius), founder of Mohism, a utilitarian who held that the world's problems are all caused by partial love and can only be corrected by impartial love.

Nagarjuna (second century C.E.)   Founder of the Madhyamika school of Mahayana Buddhism, in which reality is said to be fundamentally empty (sunyata). Author of *Mulamadhyamakakarika*.

natural law   Theory that Locke revived from Roman philosophers, that even in a state of nature, human beings are endowed with reason, which would prescribe certain obvious courses of action (e.g., not to attack others for fear of retaliation).

Nietzsche, Friedrich   Nineteenth-century German philogist who sought to reevaluate traditional values such as truth and kindness in terms of their evolutionary survival value to human existence.

Nyaya   Early Indian school of logic.

Parmenides   Early Greek philosopher (sixth to fifth century B.C.E.) who denied that reality could change in any way.

Plato (429–347 B.C.E.)   Early Greek philosopher who studied with Socrates, whom he later memorialized in his Dialogues (i.e., Plato's reconstructed conversations of Socrates with Sophists and others); founded the first Western institution of higher learning, the Academy, whose most famous student was Aristotle.

positivism   Form of empiricism, that we can only know what we can perceive through our five senses and any logical inferences derived from that.

qi (chi)   Ultimate matter-energy in neo-Taoist and neo-Confucianist metaphysics and cosmology.

Radhakrishnan, Sarvapalli (1888–1975)   First Indian philosopher to introduce Indian philosophy to a Western audience.

Ramanuja   Eleventh to twelfth-century Vedantist who modified Shankara's advaita (nondualism) in favor of a separate existence for the personal god (world soul), Brahman, the physical world, and individual souls.

rationalism   Epistemological doctrine that all reliable knowledge comes from reasoning.

Rawls, John   Contemporary American philosopher whose *A Theory of Justice* attempts to reconcile the libertarian Right and the egalitarian Left.

Reid, Thomas (1710–1796)   Scottish philosopher who defended common sense, rejecting the widely held empiricist theory (of Locke), that we do not perceive physical objects but merely sense impressions which we infer to have originated from physical objects.

ren (jen)   Traditional Chinese virtue of human heartedness.

Ricci, Matteo   Seventeenth-century Italian in charge of the early Jesuit missionaries to China; the first to refer to Chinese thinkers (Confucius, Mencius, and Zhu Xi) as "philosophers."

rishi   Indian word for reclusive, meditative hermits.

rupa (form)   Indian term for form, contrasted with nama, or name.

Samkhya   Hindu dualistic system based on the distinction of Purusha (consciousness) and Prakriti (matter).

Sartre, Jean-Paul (1905–1980)   French philosopher who founded existentialism.

Shankara (Sankara, 788–820 C.E.)   Best-known Advaita, Vedanta philosopher, holding a strict nondualist position in which individual souls and the physical world are really identical with the one reality known as Brahman.

Siddhartha (sixth century B.C.E.)   Name of the founder of Buddhism, Shakyamuni Siddhartha Gautama.

skepticism   Specifically in the case of epistemology, the denial of the possibility of knowledge, but more generally denying the possibility of any philosophical answers that are universal and objective, in ethics (cultural relativism), in social and political philosophy (anarchy), and so on.

social contract   The hypothetical agreement people would reach in order to overcome the dangers of living in a "state of nature" by forming a state with a governing body.

Socrates (470–399 B.C.E.)   Early Greek philosopher who wrote no philosophy but engaged fellow Athenians in discussions of mainly ethical issues; admired by Plato, most of whose writings are about these conversations, or "dialogues" of Socrates.

Spinoza, Baruch (1632–1677)   Jewish philosopher, developed substance metaphysics in monistic extreme, that there can be only one thing in the world, God, whose chief attributes are mind and matter.

state of nature   Hypothetical condition of life, that is, what it would be like, without any form of state or governing body, part of the social contract theory of the state.

sunyata (emptiness)   The Madhyamika Mahayana doctrine of Nagarjuna, that there is nothing permanent, independent, or self-subsistent in the world.

Tao De Jing   Literally, *The Classic of the Way and Its Power*, the earliest and most famous Taoist text, attributed to Laozi.

Taoism (Daoism)   An ancient folk tradition evolving into a religion (Tao Jiao) and a philosophy (Tao Jia), associated with Laozi and Zhuangzi.

tetsugaku   Japanese word used to translate "philosophy."

Thrasymachus   Early Greek Sophist (fifth century B.C.E.), appearing in Plato's *The Republic*, who argued that justice is nothing but the interest of the stronger.

Upanishads   The last of the sacred Hindu texts, beginning before the rise of philosophy in the sixth century B.C.E. and continuing thereafter for several hundred years; not critical, systematic philosophy proper, but a "precursor" of Indian philosophy about which leading Indian philosophers, such as Shankara and Ramanuja, wrote.

utilitarianism   Ethical doctrine (of John Stuart Mill and Mozi) that one should always do that which increases the greatest happiness (or pleasure) for the greatest number of people.

Vaisesika   Early Indian empiricist and atomist philosophy.

veda   Ancient sacred texts of India, including the *Rig Veda* and *Upanishads*.

vedanta   Literally, "the end of the vedas," a monistic synthesis of vedic literature in which only Brahman exists and the rest of the universe, including our deepest Self (atman), is said (by Shankara, for example) to be identical with Brahman—all is one.

Wang Chung (27–97 C.E.)   Taoist naturalist and materialist who rejected the tendency to anthropomorphically describe nature.

Wang Yangming (1472–1529)   Ming dynasty idealist neo-Confucian, often considered a "closet Buddhist."

Wittgenstein, Ludwig (1889–1951)   Austrian–British philosopher of language who argued that philosophers create problems when they abandon ordinary rules of linguistic usage.

Xunzi (Hsun Tzu, 298–212 B.C.E.)   Third century B.C.E., one of the leading interpreters of Kongzi (Confucius), who argued that there is a human nature and that it is basically evil and must be disciplined and civilized by social culture and education.

yang   positive force and/or ether in Chinese cosmological theories from the Han dynasty on.

Yang, Zhu (Yangzi)   Early Taoist egoist philosopher who refused to give up a single hair of his body to gain or save the whole world.

yi   Traditional Chinese virtue of righteousness.

yin   Negative force and/or ether in Chinese cosmological theories from the Han dynasty on.

Yogacara (fourth century C.E.)   Also known as Vijnanavada, idealist school of Mahayana Buddhism, founded by Asanga and Vasubandhu.

Zen   Japanese term for Chinese Chan Buddhist sect.

Zeno (fifth century B.C.E.)   Student of Parmenides who supported Parmenides's theory that change was impossible by showing the absurdity in his opponent's view that change was possible.

zhe xue   Chinese word used to translate "philosophy."

zhi   Traditional Chinese virtue of wisdom.

Zhou (Chou) dynasty (1100–700 B.C.E.)   The last of the feudal, Bronze Age dynasties, and the one greatly admired by Confucius (Kongzi).

Zhuangzi (Chuang Tzu)   Fourth century B.C.E., leading Taoist after Laozi, author of (most of) *The Zhuangzi*, important throughout Chinese history as an aesthetic and a literary model.

Zhu Xi (Chu Hsi, 1130–1200)   Most famous neo-Confucian scholar, revived Confucianism by blending Confucianism with Taoism and Buddhism.

Zi (Tzu)   Chinese word for master, or sage, meaning roughly "philosopher."

INDIAN

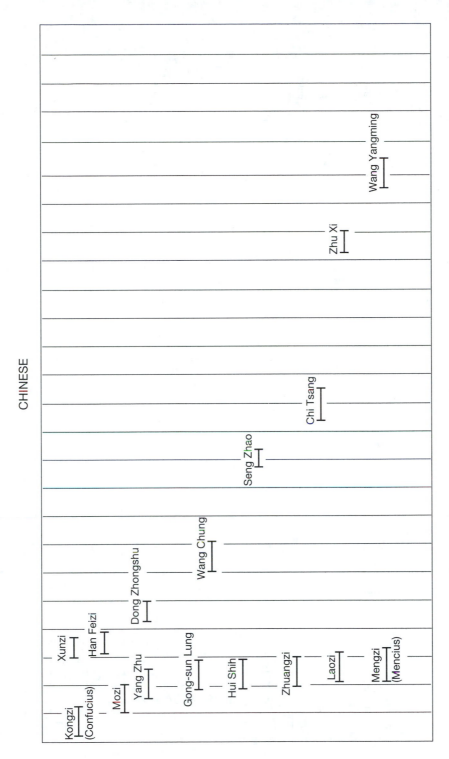

CHINESE

600 500 400 300 200 100 | 100 200 300 400 500 600 700 800 900 1000 1100 1200 1300 1400 1500 1600 1700 1800 1900

Kongzi (Confucius)
Xunzi
Mozi
Han Feizi
Yang Zhu
Dong Zhongshu
Gong-sun Lung
Wang Chung
Hui Shih
Zhuangzi
Laozi
Mengzi (Mencius)
Seng Zhao
Chi Tsang
Zhu Xi
Wang Yangming

245

WESTERN

600 500 400 300 200 100 | 100 200 300 400 500 600 700 800 900 1000 1100 1200 1300 1400 1500 1600 1700 1800 1900

Heraclitus
Parmenides
Epicurus
Zeno
Gorgias
Protagoras
Socrates
Cratylus
Democritus
Thrasymachus
Plato
Aristotle
Lucretius
Augustine
Aquinas
Hobbes
Descartes
Spinoza
Locke
Leibniz
Berkeley
Hume
Reid
Kant
Mill
Marx

600 500 400 300 200 100 | 100 200 300 400 500 600 700 800 900 1000 1100 1200 1300 1400 1500 1600 1700 1800 1900

Index

H

Han Feizi (Han Fei Tzu), 9, 219–21
Hedonism, 122, 124, 178
Hegel, Georg, 39, 137, 145
Heidegger, Martin, 8
Heraclitus, 8, 25, 45, 51, 55, 59, 113, 117
Hinduism, 11, 13, 14, 24, 26, 30–33
Hobbes, Thomas, 39, 169, 177, 182, 206–10
Hu Shi, 30
Hui Shi, 34, 50, 55, 58–60, 63, 74–76, 115–16, 120, 153
Human nature, 115, 161–62, 165–73, 176–85, 189–91, 195, 199, 209, 211
Human rights, 203–8, 229–30
Hume, David, 8, 81–86, 89–90, 126–27, 131–33, 148
Husserl, Edmund, 8, 138

I

Idealism, 106, 126–38
Illusion, 115–16
Immortality, 121–24, 141, 157–58, 193
Indeterminacy of translation, 48–49
Individualism, 39–41, 203
Infallibilism, 134
Inference, 80–83, 89–91, 95, 98, 102–3, 149
Infinite regress argument, 110
Islamic philosophy, 33–34

J

Jainism, 13, 16, 23, 24, 27–28, 30, 32
James, William, 1, 2, 12
Japanese philosophy (tetsugaku), 11, 12
Jefferson, Thomas, 208
Jia, 10, 12
Jiva, 28, 137, 140–42, 158
Justice, 69, 162, 187, 191–92, 195, 201–2, 207, 230–31

K

Kant, Immanuel, 8, 13, 88, 92, 103, 110–15, 193, 195–99
Karma, 26, 31, 34
Kierkegaard, Soren, 13, 33
Kohlberg, Lawrence, 221
Kongzi (Confucius), 9, 10, 22–26, 60–62, 66, 71, 80, 109, 162, 164–65, 169, 192–93, 196–99
Kropotkin, Pierre, 217
Kumarajiva, 116
Kuo Xiang, 163

L

Laozi (Lao Zi, Lao Tzu), 9, 96, 152, 215–17
Lau, D. C., 180
Law of nature, 207
Laws, 201–11
Legalism (Fa Jia), 215, 219–21
Leibniz, Gottfried, 8, 109
Li, 119, 130, 153–55, 162, 170, 176, 185, 193, 210, 215
Liberal, 203, 229, 230–31
Linguistic Philosophy, 123–24
Linguistic representation, 48–52, 79
Liu Xun, 57
Locke, John, 8, 72, 81–84, 126–28, 131–33, 139, 206–210
Logic, 13
Love, 173–75, 197–99, 214
Lucretius, 8, 121, 123, 157

M

Machiavelli, Niccolo, 225–26
Madhyamika, 7, 116, 131
Madva, 25, 33–37, 137, 144–45
Mahavira, 27
Mahayana, 128, 131
Mandate of Heaven, 211–13